Copyright,

M.P.Dawn Publi

Maps and Photographs By

Rigs and Other Drawings By D.A.Weaver.

Fish Recipes By Mrs P.M.Weaver.

First edition 1998

ISBN 1 902778 00 6

This edition published 2012

by

M. P. Dawn Publications

ISBN 1 902778 07 5

All rights reserved; no part of this publication may be reproduced or transmitted in any form or by any means electronic or mechanical including photocopy, recording, or in any information storage and retrieval system, without the prior written consent of the publishers.

FOREWORD

SEA ANGLING AROUND CORNWALL.

The beautiful and rugged Cornish coastline is home to a wide variety of saltwater species but they don't give themselves up easily. What you need to make the most of a sea angling session in our most westerly county is a little bit of inside information.

This of course can take time to accumulate, especially if you're only on a short summer holiday.

Inside the covers of "Sea Angling Around Cornwall" there is all the information needed to start off in the correct fashion ensuring you can successfully tackle the productive sea angling in the south west.

The marks, the tackle, the bait and which species you can expect to catch are all included in an easy to follow format.

A great deal of time can be wasted trying to fish an unfamiliar mark, using the wrong methods, tackle and bait. This little gem of a book eliminates all that, giving you the knowledge that will ensure you enjoy some pleasant trips in such a beautiful part of the country.

International Boat Angler, Editor of Total Sea Fishing,

Jim Whippy.

Local angler Tony Hale, fishing for garfish from the flat rock to the west of Black Head.

Sea Angling around Cornwall

Revised Edition

2012

By
M.P.Dawn Publications
D.A.Weaver

Dedicated to the memory of

Patricia Mary Weaver

Loving Wife, Mother, Grandmother

And

Great Grandmother

You are loved and missed so much

Rest in Peace

1938 — 2002

Contents

Introduction — Page 7

Be Safe, Be Comfortable . — Page 11

Fish Identification . — Page 17

Shore and Boat rigs . — Page 53

Bait and Presentation . — Page 87

Fishing Marks In Detail . — Page 119

Boat Angling. — Page 219

Cleaning and Filleting Fish . — Page 239

Fish Recipes . — Page 243

Introduction

This book has been written, in answer to many of the quires raised by visiting anglers to Cornwall, to give an answer to "where can I fish?" "what baits are best?" And "which method produces the fish?" These questions are commonly asked in most of the County's Sea Angling Centres and Tackle Shops.

One of the authors of this book, owned a tackle shop in Cornwall for a number of years, however the authors are enthusiastic anglers who have fished in the area for more than 50 combined years, from the shore and boat.

Throughout this book are a number of sketch maps covering the Cornish coastline from Plymouth on the south coast, around Cornwall and up the north coast to just past Bude, these are an aid to locating the fishing marks, however, we recommend the use of the relevant Ordnance Survey Maps in the Explorer series, for more detailed information, and also encourage the exploration of new areas to fish, all of the fishing marks listed in this book have the O.S. map reference at the top of the page.

One of Cornwall's main industries is tourism, so it is no accident that many of the named fishing marks can provide safe enjoyment for the non-fishing members of the family.

This is not a definitive guide to sea angling manual, but rather sets out to name areas, baits and methods of catching fish, all of which have stood the test of time and are tried and tested.

In writing this book, the areas and fishing marks visited, have produced many memorable fishing expeditions and moments, we hope that this book will enliven your angling in or around Cornwall and wish you all,

Tight Lines and Be Safe.

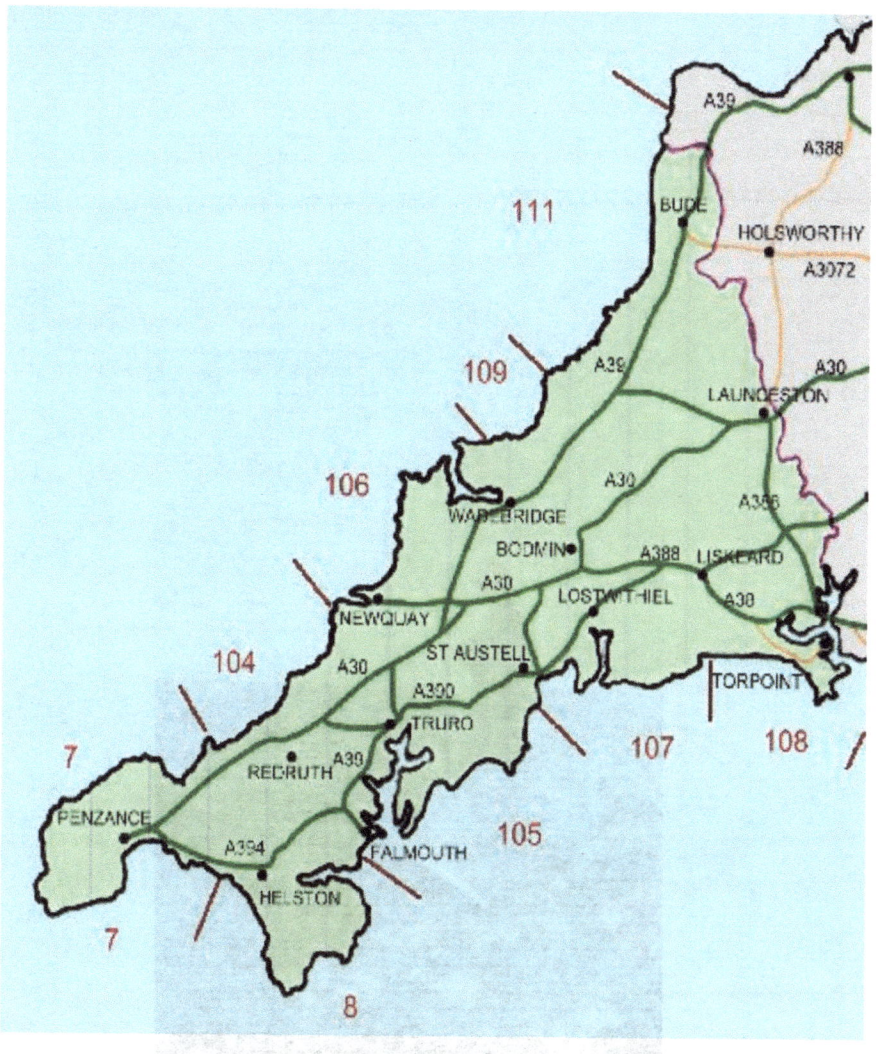

The areas in green on the above map, show the ground covered in this book, the numbers in red show the corresponding map numbers from the Ordnance Survey, Explorer Series, example, Penzance is covered by explorer series map 7.

It is recommended that the angler purchase the map that corresponds with the area to be fished, as these show the ground in greater detail.

Fishing off Blackhead

Be
Safe
Be
Comfortable

BE SAFE, BE COMFORTABLE

The Cornish coast is one of the most rugged in Britain. The County's weather can vary from idyllic sun baked days to gale lashed storms. The R.N.A.S Culdrose and R.A.F St Mawgan rescue helicopters are an ever-present part of the skies, along with the Cornish Air Ambulance, particularly during the summer months. During the year they are on constant call, rendering aid to seamen and anglers but also to people cut off by the tide or washed from the rocks. The R.N.L.I in Cornwall is one of the Britain's busiest, so a few words on elementary safety precautions must be included for the prospective angler to consider and hopefully act upon. You should remember that in risking your own safety, you may also be risking the safety, or life of the members of the rescue services. Never fish alone, even a sprained ankle on the rocks, will probably need assistance, even a minor problem can become an emergency if you are alone. Should you witness a serious problem, or be involved in an accident and can reach a telephone, you should dial 999 and ask for the Coast Guard. It is best when planning a fishing trip to let someone know where you are going and an approximate time that you expect to return. In an emergency a Mobile phone can be of assistance, but remember that at sea level, and below cliffs, a signal may be weak or even non existent. Know where you are, this sounds obvious, but you must be able to direct assistance to where it is needed, if a swift response is required to an emergency. Obtain a current Tide Table for the area, this will not only allow you to plan the times for your trip, but will also give you the approximate range of the tide so that you will not be cut off by rising water. Keep an eye on the state of the sea at all times.

A storm far out to sea can generate a swell which builds in height as it approaches land, this can quite easily flood over an apparently safe fishing platform. Some anglers use ropes to reach, and, or, secure themselves to a fishing platform, it is recommended that if a rope is needed for any of these, don't go!

Approach the fishing mark by land, if you can walk or scramble down to the mark, then you can also expect to get off this mark safely. When you approach a fishing mark from sea level at low tide you must either be certain of a dry route away, in the event of being cut off by the incoming tide, or you will have to be prepared to remain until the water level drops sufficiently, for you to return home safely, this can and often takes approximately 6 hours. There is a considerable link between being safe and the type of clothing we wear when fishing. Good strong footwear with soles that will resist slipping on wet rock, and with good ankle support, is the best type of footwear to use whilst fishing from the rocks. Ironically most of the best fishing marks require quite a lot of walking, often over rough terrain.

To partner the footwear, use a good pair of thick socks, in summer you will sweat less and in winter be warm. Even when beach fishing during the summer it is best not to go barefoot, a Weever fish sting or Razor shell cut can mar the trip and cause considerable pain.

During the summer months thin airy clothing is required, but you can still be cool and safe by wearing a floatation waistcoat, this modern floatation aid is light, comfortable, and does not impede your movement whilst fishing or casting. A word of caution however, most of these floatation jackets and suits will give you adequate buoyancy should you fall in to the water, but they will not turn you face up in the way that a self righting inflatable jacket will.

In winter a full flotation suit is ideal to give you an added safety advantage, in addition, coupled with several layers of thin clothing or a fleece one piece suit, will keep you warm on a frosty night. Keep your head warm with a thick woollen hat or balaclava, and wear a thick pair, of neoprene gloves to keep the cold from your hands, during the winter you can spend more time trying to keep your hands warm than actual fishing.

If buying new clothing for the purpose of fishing, get colours that are highly visible, military type combat clothing is designed for camouflage, these will keep you warm, however in the event of an accident, the visibility of clothing can play a major part in any rescue attempt.

When night fishing ensure that you have adequate lighting, either the liquid fuel anchor type lamp or a battery operated head lamp, to be sure that you have the correct light for the job at hand, you can always take both of these light sources with you.

Many accidents can, and have occurred during the process of landing a fish. A heavy fish off the rocks, can tempt your companion to climb down to the waters edge for the purpose of hand lining the fish back up the rocks. Use a landing net with a long handle or a long handled gaff (particularly for Conger eels).

A drop net is the best solution from harbour walls, and pier's. You must however, make sure that you are on firm ground, and never over stretch your self or lean over the edge of where ever you are fishing, many falls are caused by people over stretching themselves.

Above left: winter full floatation suit. Centre: Map, lights and phone etc. Right: summer floatation waist coat, boots etc.

Another method of landing fish, if you are a long way above the water, and a way down to the fish is either not possible, or very dangerous, is to use a flying gaff, this is made up from a length of rope and a grappling type treble hook, attached by a large snap link, the gaff hook is normally around 6 inches across,

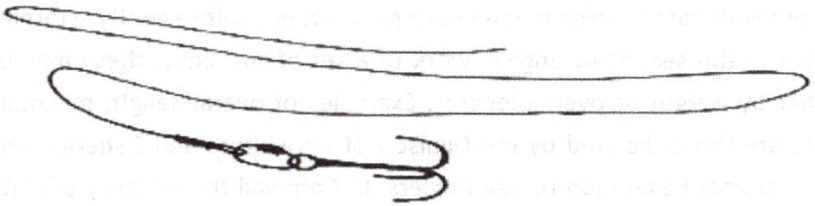

these must be handled with care as these are very sharp. The gaff is used by clipping the snap link over the shockleader and main line, now it is lowered down to the fish, where a sharp tug on the rope hooks the fish, it can now be pulled up the cliff, harbour or pier with comparative ease.

A further item of tackle which helps towards comfort more than safety are tip lights and star lights, these help to prevent eye strain, which can cause headaches and migraine. These also help to detect fish bites. Star lights can be used on the end of the rod or attached to a float, enables you to float fish in the evenings, when most fish are taken.

Tip lights can be purchased from local tackle dealers and come in a variety of colours, Red, Green and Yellow. The red ones are easier to see in the dark. A selection of these are shown below.

Finally take a flask of warm drink with you, Coffee, Tea or soup (not alcohol) and you will not only be safe, but also comfortable.

As anglers we have a self interest in maintaining the source of our sport and pleasure, in short we need to have a positive attitude towards conservation and other related environmental issues. Do not take fish unless it is necessary for either competition or for the table. Don't take it home for an ego trip, with its final resting place the dustbin. If you want to record your catch, weigh it and take a photograph, before gently returning it live to the sea. Most anglers work to a set of size limits these may be either by weight or overall length . Examples of overall length minimum sizes are those dictated by the Ministry of Agriculture and Fisheries, and the National Federation of Sea Anglers. In Cornwall the majority of clubs and anglers work to the minimum weight scale set by the Cornish Federation of Sea Anglers, and in most cases a fish taken from the above overall length systems fall well short of the CFSA weight minimum size. Fishing to a high minimum weight list helps in conservation of stock. Most Cornish fishing shops will be able to give information of these weights. Further as the policing of fish catches both commercial and sport is becoming more vigorous it is better to work to a conservative limit than to pick up a hefty fine.

Many anglers dig their own bait but this bait is also the food source for other marine creatures and birds, careless and excessive bait digging in some areas can have a detrimental effect on the ecology of the area. A few simple rules here can help to minimise the problem, take only what you need, refill trenches, replace rocks or other natural materials which have been moved, and lastly, do not dig for worms in boat mooring areas if you wish to retain friendly relations with the boating fraternity and the harbour master. Rubbish and litter left on beach and rock marks is at the least unsightly but it can also be dangerous to other animals and fishermen. It is unfortunately not uncommon to see sea birds with their legs tangled or amputated by discarded line. A discarded plastic bait bag on wet rocks can be lethal if trodden on, so at the end of your fishing trip please remove any rubbish of your own and if possible other peoples and bin it or take it home.

Fish
Identification

FISH IDENTIFICATION

The Species of fish shown in this book are the main fish caught from the boat and shores around Cornwall. Some species of fish are more plentiful than others, and many of these tend to look similar in size, shape and colour with many having the same fin arrangement. The habitat in which fish live, swim and feed can greatly affect the colour and markings on different species of fish.

On many fish there may be a size limit in force, depending on which area of the U.K. you happen to be fishing, an example of this is the N.F.S.A, which work on a minimum length of the fish, and the C.F.S.A. work on the minimum weight of the fish, if you are ever in doubt as to the limits on any species of fish, the best thing to do is to ask your tackle dealer as he or she should be very willing to help, and should be up to date on different limits in their area.

The M.A.F.F. can impose heavy fines if an angler is caught with under size fish, particularly Bass. If whilst fishing you happen to get stung, cut or bitten by any fish, it is wise to seek medical advice, some fish in the waters around Cornwall can be venomous or have sharp spines, which can cause infection.

Under sized fish that are to be returned must be handled carefully, it is best to handle them with wet hands or a damp towel, as this will prevent causing any damage to the fish scales, fins, eyes and rest of body. If returning a fish to the sea it is best to carry it down to the waters edge and not drop it from a great height.

The fish identification diagram is for the angler to examine so that he or she should be able to determine the correct name of fins e.t.c, and in doing so help towards the identification of various species of fish, however if in doubt, ask your local tackle dealer as he or she should be able to help with any identification marks that may have been missed by the angler.

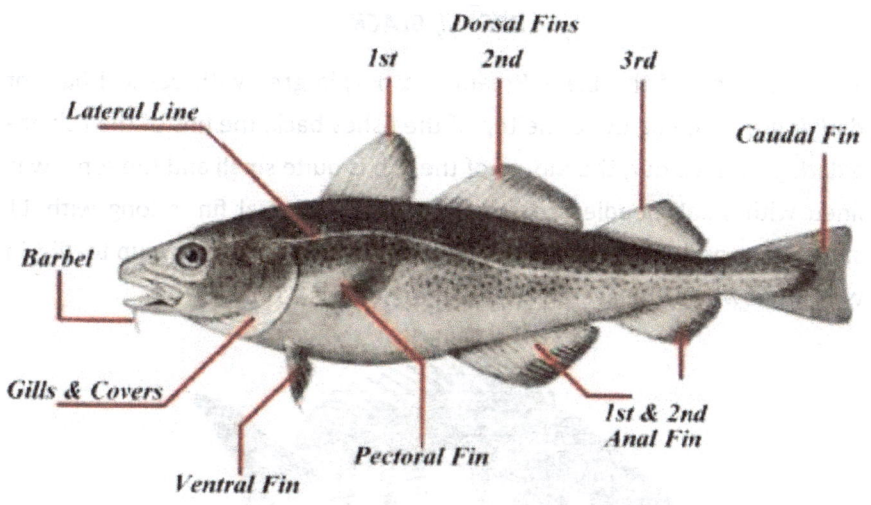

Please note there are 3 fish identification charts in this section

BASS.

This is one of the best known sea fish, renowned for feeding in rolling surf on storm beaches, however, having a tolerance for brackish water they are also caught in most estuaries throughout the U.K. The coloration of the Bass is a dark silver grey with a white under belly, it is sometimes possible to find a dark patch on the gill covers. the first dorsal fin is made up of very sharp spines,

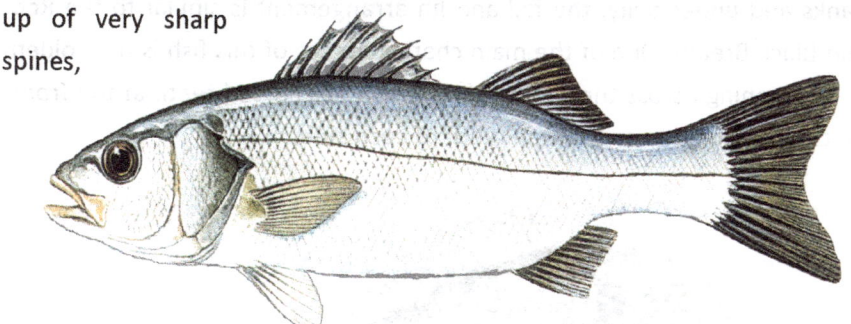

these can cause nasty injuries as can the gill covers. Bass can grow up to 80cm and around 15lbs, although the average size in Cornish waters is around 3 - 8lbs with double figure fish being caught, however this is uncommon.

BREAM, BLACK.

The coloration of the Black Bream is a purple grey with vertical bars of darker grey running up to the top of the fishes back, the fins of the fish are a dark grey in colour, the mouth of the fish is quite small and the top jaw is lined with small needle like sharp teeth. The dorsal fin is long with 11 spined rays and 12 - 14 soft, branched rays. This fish can grow up to 7lbs in weight, however the average size is around 8ozs - 1lb 8ozs.

BREAM, GILT HEAD

Although this species of Bream is mainly caught in Mediterranean waters it is occasionally taken by boat anglers off the Cornish Coast. Coloration of this fish is from blue - grey along the back turning to bright silver on the flanks and under belly, the tail and fin arrangement is similar to the Red and Black Bream. One of the main characteristics of this fish is the golden stripe running across the forehead. This fish has curved teeth at the front of its powerful jaws and flatten teeth to each side.

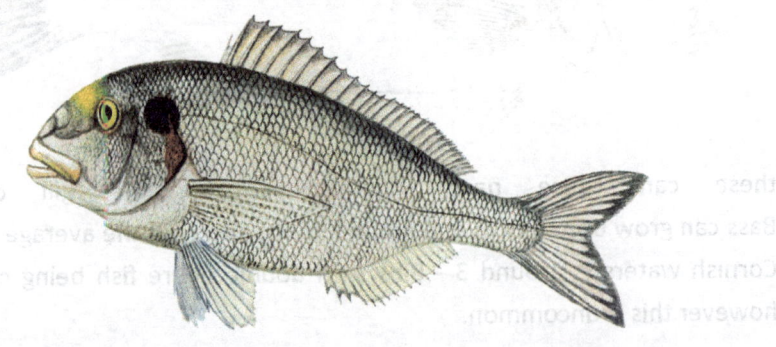

BREAM, RED.

The coloration of the Red Bream is from silver on the under belly to a deep reddish colour at the top of its back, this is broken by a thin black lateral line. The fins of the fish are a dark red to grey in colour. The Red Bream has a dark shoulder patch, to the rear of its head, this is around the same size as the fishes eye, which unlike the Black Bream, is rather large compared with the size of its head. The jaw of the fish is lined with small needle like sharp teeth.

COD FAMILY, COD

Like other members of the same family the Cod has three dorsal and two anal fins. The lateral line on the Cod is white bowed over the pectoral fins. The barbell on the chin is normally shorter than the diameter of its eye. The coloration of the Cod can differ from mark to mark as its habitat has an influence on it, from a light orangey yellow to a dark orangey pink however, the lateral line remains white. The Cod can grow in excess of 45lbs, however, the average size in Cornish waters is around 2 - 8lbs, caught from the shore.

COD FAMILY, COALFISH

The Coalfish is similar to the Pollack in appearance, however it's upper and lower jaws are approximately the same length. The lateral line on the Coalfish is white and only slightly curved, coloration of this fish is a very dark greeny black across the shoulders and back, turning to almost white on the under belly. As with most of the Cod family the Coalfish has three dorsal and two anal fins.

COD FAMILY, HADDOCK

The haddock is easily recognized by a black lateral line running along its white side (not to be confused with coalfish which has the reverse, i.e. white line on black side) Haddock have a distinctive dark blotch above the pectoral fin often described as a thumbprint, Devil's thumb print or like the john dory St. Peter's mark. These fish tend to be few and far between, like the Hake and other members of the Cod family these have been over fished and now where once they were prolific they now are an unfamiliar species.

COD FAMILY, HAKE

Hake are deep-sea members of the Cod family, found on the continental shelf and slope to depths over 1,000m and are popular throughout Europe and America. They migrate southward in the spring and northward in autumn but breeds throughout the year peaking in reproductive activity during August and September. Ranging from 1kg to 5 kg, Hake has a long, round, slender body and is mainly grey and silver in colour. Although these can be caught from the shore, the majority are taken by the boat angler.

COD FAMILY, LING.

The Ling is mainly caught from the boat, however it is possible to catch this species from the shore, off deep water headlands. The Lings coloration can varies from venue to venue, as it's habitat can be a main factor to it's colour scheme, across the back and shoulders the fish is a dark brownie orange and can be slightly mottled, the under belly being from a white colour to an almost pink. The lateral line of this fish is a dark grey to black and is almost straight, the Ling has two dorsal fins and one long anal fin, all of which has a white margin around the outer side.

COD FAMILY, POLLACK

The Pollack has the same fin arrangement as the Cod but has no barbel and the lower jaw protrudes past the upper jaw. The lateral line of the Pollack is very curved, over the top of the pectoral fins. Coloration of the Pollack is a dark green to a yellowy green across the shoulders and back and to almost white on the under belly. The average size of the Pollack in Cornish waters is around 1.5 - 7lbs, from the shore, however, this size of fish can be greatly improved if caught from the boat, where double figure Pollack can be regularly taken on artificial baits.

COD FAMILY, POUTING

This small member of the Cod family tends to prefer warmer water, therefore it is normally caught throughout the summer months. The fishes body is quite deep in appearance, coloration is of a dark brown across the back of the fish and with darker vertical bars running down it's sides. The fin arrangement is the same type as the Cod, This fish has very large eyes compared to the rest of it's body.

COD FAMILY, ROCKLING

There are five species of Rockling, however, this book only covers the two main species caught in Cornish waters, these are the Shore Rockling and the Three Bearded Rockling. The shore Rockling can grow up to 25cm and as a dark red to almost black in colour.

The first dorsal fin on the Rocklings fold down in to a groove in its back, apart from the first ray. The Three Bearded Rockling can grow up to 55cm and has a light pink or reddish body with brownish spots covering it. These two fish are the only ones to possess a pair of snout barbells.

COD FAMILY, WHITING

The Whiting is very similar to the Pollack and Coalfish in it's appearance, however this fish is considerably smaller and lighter in colour. The lateral lines only slightly curved and is white in colour. The lower jaw is the opposite to the Pollack as it recedes slightly in below the upper jaw. The Whiting has a number of very sharp needle like teeth, fin arrangement is similar to the Cod. Coloration of this fish is a yellow to gold colour across the back and shoulders, and blending to almost pure white on the under belly. Average size caught in U.K waters is around 12oz - 2.5lbs, however larger fish are caught from the boat.

DOGFISH

The two main species of Dogfish caught around Cornwall are the Lesser Spotted Dogfish (L.S.D.) and the Greater Spotted Dogfish (Bull Huss), the main differences are the size, weight, fins and nostrils. L.S.Ds grow to around 100cm and about 4lbs in weight, although the majority of fish caught are around the 2-2.5lbs size range.

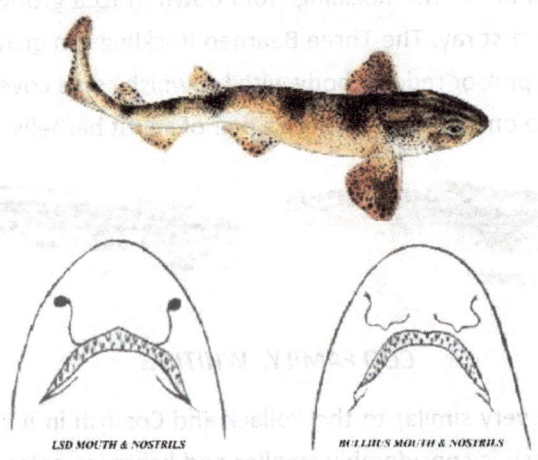

Bull Huss can grow to around 16lbs, although the average size range is in the 8 - 12lbs bracket. The coloration of both fish is a silvery grey, however it is not uncommon to catch fish that have a pinkish or brownish tinge to their colour, both fish have a large amount of dark spots over the body and fins. The Bull Huss has larger spots than the ones on the body of the L.S.D. The skin of these fish is very rough and can cause injuries if the fish twists up ones arm, the best way to avoid this is to hold the fishes head and tail in the same hand, or use a towel.

EELS, CONGER

The Conger Eel can grow up to over 100lbs in weight and over 3 meters in length, however the average size of fish caught in Cornish waters is from 10 - 65lbs. The Conger Eel has a dark fringe to it's dorsal and anal fins, the dorsal fin starts from just behind the pectoral fin and runs the length of the body, the coloration of the Conger Eel can vary from eel to eel, from almost black to almost white. The Conger Eel has very sharp teeth, do not remove any hooks by hand.

EEL, SILVER

Silver Eels are mainly found in estuaries around Cornwall, however, they can be caught on beaches. The Silver Eels dorsal fin starts about one quarter of the way down its body, unlike the Congers. Coloration is a silvery grey, these eels can grow up to 100cm.

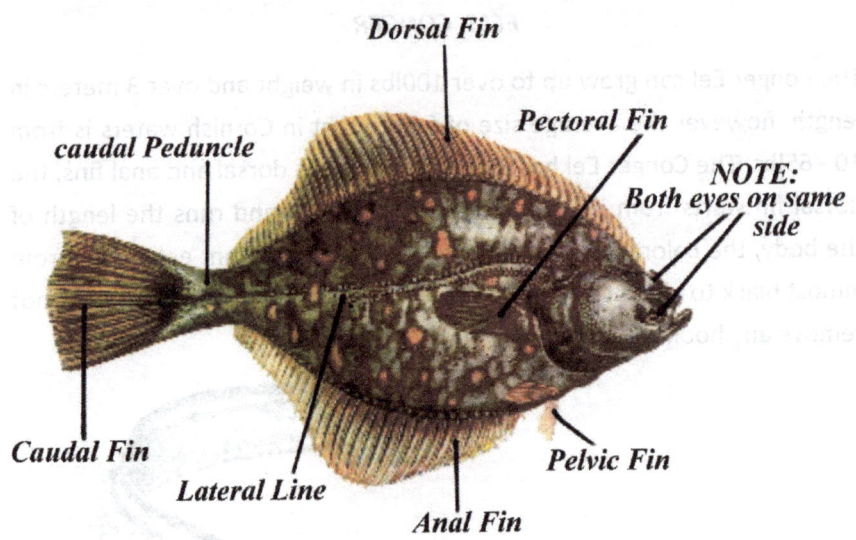

Although flatfish have the same fin configuration as the other species many anglers do get confused, hopefully these fish identification charts will help.

BRILL

A close relative to the Turbot, this flatfish can be found in the same habitat. Coloration of this fish is a mottled grey and brown, the skin of the fish is covered with minute scales and the underside is a off white colour. Brill feed on small crustaceans and small fish.

DAB

The Dab is the smallest flatfish caught in waters around the United Kingdom, it has a semi circular curve above the pectoral fin, the scales on the eyed side of the fish are rough when rubbed light brown to dark brown in colour and the underside is normally an off white colour. The Dab grows to about 25 - 30cm and weigh up to 1.5lbs, however average size is more between 8ounces to 1lb.

DOVER SOLE

This species of fish is found on sandy sea beds and tend to turn up in sand eel nets. coloration of this fish is a medium brown body with light and dark irregular spots, the under side is a creamy white.

FLOUNDER

Average size of this fish is around 1 - 3lbs, the body surface is rough particularly along the lateral line which is only slightly curved above the pectoral fin. Flounders usually have their eyes on the right side of the body, however in some areas about 20% of these fish have the eyes on the left. Coloration of the Flounder is a light yellowy brown to dark brown, it is not uncommon to find orange spots on the top side of these fish, these are normally hybrids due to interbreeding between flounder and plaice.

HALIBUT

The Halibut is the largest of all flat fish, with an average weight of about 25 - 30 lbs. (11 - 13½ kg), but they can grow to be as much as 431 lbs. (196 kg) The Halibut is blackish-grey on the top side and off-white on the under belly side. When the Halibut is born the eyes are on both sides of its head, and it swims like a Salmon. After about 6 months one eye will migrate to the other side of its head, making it look more like the flounder or Plaice.

This happens at the same time that the stationary eyed side begins to develop a blackish-grey pigment while the other side remains white. Many anglers treat this fish in the same way as the Carp, going to extraordinary lengths to catch this species, although the Halibut can be taken from the shore, most are caught around the northern reaches of the country and when you are lucky enough to land one they tend to be very small for this species. All the larger fish are taken from the boat.

HALIBUT

LEMMON SOLE

The lemon sole is a right eyed flatfish with a small head and mouth. This fish has slimy skin, the upper surface of which is reddish brown in colour but also mottled with pink and orange with added flecks of yellow and green, this fish also has a prominent orange patch behind the pectoral fin. The underside of the fish is white, the lateral line of this fish curves sharply over the pectoral fin.

Adult fish can reach up to 65 centimetres, 26 inches in length, however the average size of fish caught is more in the 20 to 30 centimetres, 8 to 12 inches.

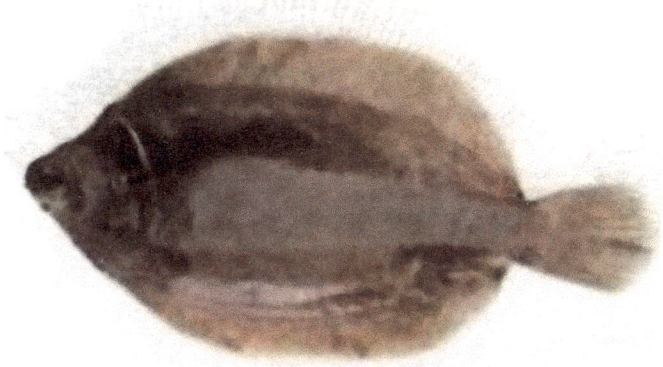

MEGRIM

This species of flat fish is an uncommon visitor to the Southwest of the United Kingdom. The coloration of this fish is a light brown with lighter patches over its body, however at times this fishes body almost seems transparent. The scales of this fish are quite rough and are easily removed.

PLAICE

Similar in appearance to Flounder, the plaice only has bony knobs running from the eyes and over the head, between 4 to 7 in all. The body of the Plaice is smooth with small scales, coloration is light brown with reddish orange spots. Average size in U.K. waters is up to about 2.5lbs however, this fish can grow up it a minimum length of 85cm and 6.5kg, although this is very uncommon.

SAND SOLE

The Sand Sole live on sandy or chalky sea beds, these fish move in to shallow water during the summer months. Coloration is a mottled light and dark brown, there is a large dark spot in the centre of each pectoral fin.

TURBOT

This is the largest of the flatfish caught around the inshore waters of the United Kingdoms Coast, this fish swims on its right side and the body is studded with small bony knobs. The body of the fish is almost circular and a very dark brownish colour. The Turbot can grow up to 100cm although the average size is around 40 - 50cm.

GARFISH

This fish is built for speed with a very long sleek body, the head of the fish has a long beak armed with small sharp teeth. The single dorsal fins are set far back near to the forked tail fin. The bones of this fish are bright green in colour, however, the flesh is of a white colour. The Garfish can grow up to around 95cm and about 2.5lbs although the average size is around 12oz - 1lb 10oz.

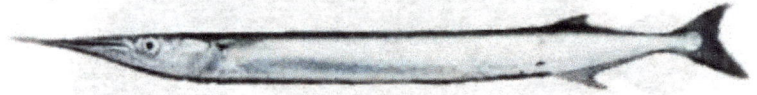

GURNARD (GREY)

The Grey Gurnard is typically grey with small white spots and has a lateral line of sharp spines, as with the other species of Gurnard this one has quite large eyes. The pectoral fins do not reach past the start of the anal fin. Average weight and length is around 20 - 30cm and about 8oz to 1lb.

GURNARD (RED)

A Dark red in colour with a paler underside, the snout of this Gurnard has 3 to 4 spines around its top lip. The lateral line has bony ridges that extend up to the dorsal fins. Maximum length is around 30 - 40cm and like other members of the Gurnard family it has two dorsal fins.

GURNARD TUB

Also red to reddish brown, the Tub Gurnard is easily recognised by its bright red pectoral fins marked with blue and green tips. The lateral line on the Tub is smooth and not raised in the same way as the Red Gurnard, Maximum size is around 60cm, although 35 - 45cm are more common.

HERRING

The Herring can still be caught around the British Isles and seem to be turning up in larger numbers, that is caught with rod and line from the rocks, this is a very oily fish and when caught fresh, makes an excellent bait. Colouration is a deep steel blue or greenish blue on the back with green reflections; the sides and belly silvery; the change from dark belly to pale sides are often marked by a greenish band. The gill covers sometimes glisten with a golden or brassy gloss; fish just out of the water are iridescent all over with different hues of blue, green, and violet; but these colours soon fade, leaving only the dark back and silvery sides. The ventral and anal fins are translucent white; the pectorals, are dark at the base and along the upper edge; the caudal and dorsal fins are dark grey shading into green or blue. The Herring can grow to a length of about 17 inches and to a weight of about 1.5 pounds, although this is rare for a line caught fish.

JOHN DORY

A striking fish of unique shape and coloration, the John Dory has a very tall body that is laterally compressed, the mouth of this species is capable of being protruded far forwards, and being used as a suction tube.

This species of fish has a dorsal fin the first half of which is supported by eight long stiff spines, there is a slight division in the fin and the second half is shorter and soft. The anal fin is very similar to the dorsal fin in its make up but with only four spines.

The John Dory has a dark blotch on either flank encircled by a gold ring where St Peter reputedly left his finger prints whilst removing a gold chain from its mouth. Although this fish is seldom caught from the shore it is possible to hook into one, the average size is around 25 - 30cm and up to 3.5lbs in weight.

MACKEREL

This fish has a coloration unlike any other fish found in Cornish waters. Built for speed this fish has a very streamlined body with small fins and the tail being deeply forked. Mackerel can grow up to 40cm and about 2lb in weight, although the average is around 1lb. coloration of the Mackerel is a metallic greenish blue with twisted thin black lines running across the shoulders and back. The under belly is a silvery light green almost like pearl in colour.

MULLET GOLDEN GREY

The Golden Grey Mullet has a thin top lip, as does the Thin Lipped Mullet. This species of Mullet has two dorsal fins the first being made up from the four spines that can be sharp. The ventral fins are about two thirds the length of the pectoral fins. The head and front of the body has a golden sheen and there is a goldish yellow marking on the gill covers. The Golden Grey can grow up to 50cm and around 3lb, although the average is around 35 - 30cm and 1 - 2lb in weight.

MULLET RED

Red Mullet are totally different from the other three species of Mullet, coloration varies between red with yellowish stripes ion the day light to a mottled red at night. This Mullet has two chin barbells and can grow up to 3lb in weight.

MULLET THICK LIPPED

The Thick Lipped Mullet has a swollen top lip, sometimes with warts on it, the throat slit is very narrow. This Mullet as with the others have two dorsal and one anal fin. The coloration is a dark silvery grey across the back and toning down to and white down the sides and under belly. The Thick Lipped Mullet is one of the largest of the Mullet family caught in Cornish waters and grows to around 60cm and average about 5lb in weight.

MULLET THIN LIPPED

The Thin Lipped Mullet has a very thin lip without and warts on it the first dorsal fin is the same as the others with four spiny rays. The ventral fins about four fifths the length of the pectoral fins, this species of Mullet has a much broader throat slit. This Mullet can grow to 70cm, however, the average is quite smaller.

Pectoral Fin

Spiracle

Caudal Fin

Thorns

Dorsal Fin

Tail

Pelvic Fin

Eye

Disk

RAY BLONDE

These Rays are most common in the Southern and Western sea areas, and can be caught both from the shore or boat. In Cornwall shore caught specimens commonly average between 2 - 9lbs although larger specimens are caught. The upper body colour can vary between a greenish yellow and a fawn brown, covered with small dark brown spots which extend to the extreme margins of the wings. In this species thorns are generally confined to the tail.

RAY SMALL EYED

This Ray is also known as the Painted Ray. This species is found in the South West of England and is rare in waters North of this area. The eyes are much smaller compared to the other Ray species. Coloration of the upper surfaces is a pale cream to yellow with a mass of light coloured marbling which appears painted hence the name.

RAY THORNBACK

A common inshore fish which varies in colour, it is usually a sandy brown to dark brown with darker markings on it, the under side like all Rays is a pale whitish colour.

The Thornback Ray has a pronounced wave to the leading edge of its wings and is more angular than other Rays, this Ray has two dorsal fins placed far down near the end of its tail. The Thornback Ray has a number of spines placed over the top side of its body and three rows down its tail, one down its centre and on each side of the tail.

There may be a small patch on the under side of the wings, however, this is not found on all the Thornback Rays. The size differs from male to female with the male growing up to a maximum of 70cm and the female growing to 120cm.

RAY SANDY

This larger member of the ray family is mainly caught in deeper waters off the western coast of Cornwall. Coloration of this fish is a rich brown with perfectly symmetrical white spots on the upper side of the wings, the upper surface of the fish also is covered with small patches of fine spines and two rows of curved spines running down either side of the tail.

RAY SKATE

The commonest and largest of the Ray family this fish is only occasionally caught from the shore. Coloration is a dark cinnamon brown, usually with light and dark patches irregularly spread over its body. The skin of this fish is very smooth with only two pairs of spines around the eyes.

RAY STARRY

This Ray can be distinguished from other Rays by the number of large spines running down the centre of it's tail, normally around 12 - 19 in all, there are a number of smaller spines covering the upper side of it's body. Coloration is a light brown with a large number of lighter and darker spots covering the upper side, the under side being almost white.

RAY UNDULATE

This fish is similar to the Small eyed Ray with the same kind of markings, only the Undulate Ray has a dark marbling and is a light to dark brown colour over it's main body. Most of these fish when caught are a lot smaller than other members of the Ray family, as with the Small eyed Ray the average size is around 5 - 9lbs in Cornish waters.

SCAD

This fish has a large keeled scales on the lateral line and has separate spiny and soft dorsal fins. A greenish silver in colour this fish has a deeply forked tail and a row of 70 - 80 narrow bony plates along the side of the body. Average length is about 20 - 30cm and weight around 12oz to 1lb 12oz.

WEEVER FISH

Weever fish , Lesser and Greater are not normally fished for, although if fishing on a sandy beach for Bass there is a probability of pulling one of them in, if you have the misfortune of catching one of these fish, be very careful how you handle it. The lesser Weever fish is one of the most venomous fish in Europe. The spiny rays of the first dorsal fin and the very sharp spines on the gill covers have deep grooves in them that contain venom, if stung this can be very painful and cause inflammation seek medical advice. Be very careful when walking across beaches barefoot. Coloration of both fish is dark to light brown with dark spots or greenish markings on the main body. The Lesser Weever fish has longer pectoral fins than the Greater Weever.

Lesser Weever   **Greater Weever**

WRASSE BALLAN

This species of Wrasse is found around the rocky coastlines its coloration varies tremendously with green, brown and red predominating, under the throat, there can sometimes, be found an orange patch. Some fish display a lattice type pattern of red and brown lines across the back and shoulders, as the Wrasse family mainly feed on limpets and other molluscs, they have a set of very large teeth and although they are not sharp they can still cause a nasty injury. All the Wrasse family have only one long dorsal fin and one anal fin, the tail is rounded off at one end. The average size of the Ballan Wrasse is around 3 - 6lb.

WRASSE CORKWING

The Corkwing Wrasse has a similar coloration to the Ballan Wrasse, however, the coloration varies from male to female, the male being a greenish blue and the female a brownish yellow. The Corkwing has two dark spots, one on its head behind the eye and the other at the base of the tail. The average size of the Corkwing is about 15 - 25cm, a fish of 10ozs would be a very good fish.

WRASSE CUCKOO

Although this species of Wrasse is normally found in deeper water it is possible to catch them from head lands around the Cornish Coast. The coloration of the male fish is unlike any other Wrasse, bright blues, oranges and yellows, the female of the species are an orangey yellow and are not so brightly marked. This species grow up to 2lb shore caught, however you may need to find a quiet mark with deep water to find this fish.

WRASSE GOLDSINNY

This smaller member of the Wrasse family is found in the same kind of surroundings as the main members , coloration is a browny orange with a dark spot at the leading edge of the dorsal fin and on the end of the body near the tail

WRASSE ROCK COOK

Similar to the Goldsinny this member of the Wrasse family is also small, coloration is green to brown and lightish yellow on the under belly, this fish has red and blue markings around the facial area.

The following chart is for spot recognition only

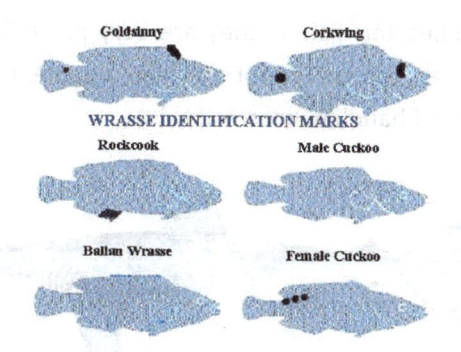

WRASSE IDENTIFICATION MARKS

Goldsinny | Corkwing
Rockcook | Male Cuckoo
Ballan Wrasse | Female Cuckoo

MONK/ANGLERFISH

Monkfish is the English name of a number of types of fish in the northwest Atlantic, most notably the species of the angler fish. Monkfish has three long filaments sprouting from the middle of the head these are the detached and modified first three spines of the anterior dorsal fin. As in most anglerfish species, the longest filament is the first, which terminates in an irregular growth of flesh, (the esca), This modified fin ray is movable in all Directions, and is primarily used for attracting its prey.

SHARKS

Although the Dogfish are the same family as the Shark, these have been placed separately as they are not as common and are mainly caught from the boat. With most members of the Shark family being caught off shore, much of the fishing is from boats that run specialist trips, from various ports around the Cornish Coast.

SHARK BLUE

This member of the Shark family is unmistakable with it's bright blue and white coloration. As with all the members of this family you must be careful when handling this fish as they are very powerful and have very sharp teeth, although not known for attacking people, these fish can and would be dangerous if handled incorrectly.

SHARK PORBEAGLE

This is a heavy set fish with a rounded snout and large tail, it has five prominent gill slits just to the front of the pectoral fins.

SMOOTH HOUND

This fish is a thick set Dogfish with larger fins and a total absence of spots. Coloration is a lightish brown with a white under belly.

SPURDOG

This is the most common member of the Shark family to be found around the coast of Cornwall, this fish has a sharp spine at the leading edge of it's dorsal fins.

TOPE

The tail of this fish is deeply notched, so it is easily recognised, coloration is a browny black with a grey to white under belly. Please note Tope are covered by conservation rules and should be returned to the sea.

TRIGGER FISH

The Trigger fish is becoming a regular visitor to the Southwest of England particularly the Northern coast where this fish has been caught in quite large numbers by anglers fishing mainly for Pollack and Mackerel, using small fish baits fished fairly deep. Coloration of this fish is greenish blue on the dorsal fins, the lower head and abdomen is orange to yellow.

The cheeks have two broad curved bands of blue with narrower bands above and a broad band of blue across the tail stalk. The body is a diamond shape that has been laterally compressed, the eye of the fish is set well back from the snout.

SUN FISH

The Sun fish is a protected species and should not be removed from the water, if you have the misfortune to hook in to one of these fish ,it is best to cut your line do not try to land it as these fish are protected and can grow up to 1000Kgs in weight, however the average size seen in Cornish waters is around 20 to 35lbs. Coloration is is often dark grey to a greyish brown with silvery reflections, the under belly is a dirty or dusky white. This fish cannot be mistaken for any other as the dorsal and anal fins stand up from the body and are very large. The Sun fish has no lateral line on it's body and also has an absence of scales, the skin of this fish is thick and leathery.

SALMON

Atlantic Salmon can be found in the open sea as well as in estuaries when they migrate into fresh water rivers to spawn. Salmon appear similar to Sea Trout but can be distinguished by its forked tail fin, the base of its tail is thinner and the upper jaw is shorter. The male Salmon often show a protruding lower jaw with an upwardly curved end. A typical Salmon has a dark grey to black back with dark vertical bars over bright silver scales dotted with reddish brown and black spots. These fish are designated as Game fish and must be returned to the water unless you are in possession of a current game licence. This applies whether the fish is caught in the sea or river.

SEA TROUT

The Sea Trout is the migratory form of the Brown Trout, and resembles the Atlantic Salmon, although the tail end is sharply squared off and not forked. Coloration is a dark silver grey across the shoulders and back turning bright silver to the under belly, the Sea Trout has a number of dark spots over its body and smaller scales than the Salmon. If you happen to catch one of these fish you must return it to the water, unless you hold a current Environment agency game fishing licence. The environmental agency. will prosecute anyone found not holding a currant license with one of these fish or any member of the Salmon family and heavy fines can be imposed.

SALMON

Atlantic Salmon can be found in the open sea as well as in estuaries when they migrate into fresh water there to spawn. Salmon appear similar to Sea Trout but can be distinguished by its forked tail, the base of its tail is thinner and the upper jaw is shorter. The male Salmon often shows a protruding lower jaw with an upwardly curved end. A typical Salmon has a dark grey to blue back with dark vertical bars, clear bright silver scales tinted with reddish brown and black spots. These fish are endangered in some fish and must be put back in the water. Unless you are in possession of a current permit. These permits for catching these fish are difficult to get by most areas.

Camel Estuary Flounder

Sea Trout scales are smaller .... and resembles the Atlantic Salmon. .... overhead and not below. Fisherman .... lighter and back turning bright silver. .... a number of dark spots over its .... salmon. If you happen to catch one of .... fresh water, unless you hold a current .... a licence. The environmental agency will prosecute .... holding a current licence with one of these fish or any member of the Salmon family and heavy fines can be imposed.

Rigs
And
Descriptions

RIGS & TRACES

The main rule for making rigs or traces is that you use the same strength shockleader for the main body as you would have on the end of your main line, for safety reasons for your self and other anglers that may be fishing in the same area, this rule is printed below.

- 1oz lead = 10lbs strength line.
- 2oz lead = 20lbs strength line.
- 3oz lead = 30lbs strength line.
- 4oz lead = 40lbs strength line, and so on.

There are a few items that you will need to gather to build the rigs in this book, these are as follows.

- A spool of shockleader up to 60lbs depending on weight being used.
- An assortment of floats complete with weights.
- An assortment of hooks, sizes 2 - 6/0.
- beads large and small.
- An assortment of swivels, rolling and barrel, sizes 8 - 4.
- Bait shields or clips.
- Snap links, these can be purchased complete with swivels.
- Crimps, these help to cut down the tying of knots.
- Material for making stop knots, e.g power gum.
- Line for making hook lengths.
- Zip sliders or other booms.
- Lead lifts for rough ground fishing.

If you have followed this list then you should have enough materials to make the rigs, or variations of the same in this book. The art to making a good rig is to be able to tie a good knot and to tie the correct knot in the correct place, the use of crimps will work well on the right line, however if these are put on to tightly these can cut through the line, so although these may cut down on the tying of knots, these are not always practical. The type of lead used with a rig is also very important, if you are fishing for flat fish it is best to use a dumpy lead as this will roll around the bottom and cover more ground, if fishing a storm beach with a lot of current it is probably best to use a grip lead as this will hold the bottom and save the bait and weight from being washed in to the shore. When fishing rock marks or places with a rocky bottom, the best weight to use is a plain lead possibly with a lead lift, this will help to retrieve the end tackle from rough ground. If the rig being used is for long distance fishing ,use a bait shield, this will help keep the bait intact during the cast.

SHOCKLEADER KNOT

Tie a half hitch in the shockleader, now push the end of the main line through the loop and pull slightly up. Now make a five loop UNI knot and using a little spit pull the two knots together and trim the ends.

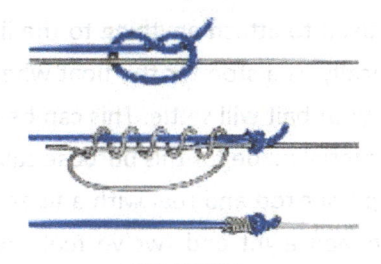

UNI KNOT

Push line through hook or swivel eye, pull 5 - 7 inches line through and make a loop, wrap through the loop 4 - 6 times. Now pull the line tight and trim end.

TUCKED HALF BLOOD KNOT

Push the line through the hook loop, wrap around 4 - 6 times, push end of line through loop "A" and then loop "B", pull up tight and trim the end.

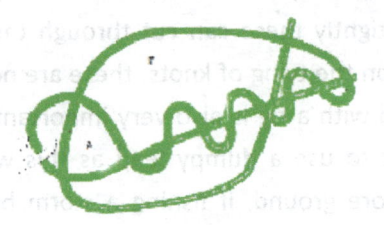

CLINCH KNOT

Push line through hook loop twice, wrap line around it's self 3 - 4 times, push back through first two loops, now pull up tight and trim ends.

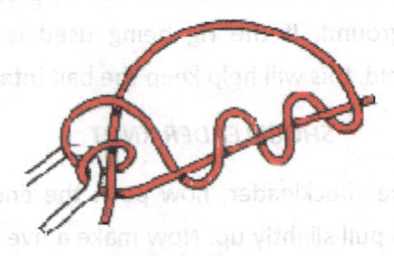

Stop Knot

The stop knot is not used to attach anything to the line such as a hook or swivel, it is used basically as a stop for the float when used and foremost to set the depth that your bait will settle. This can be made from 15lb line, however there is a material made for this purpose called power gum, to tie this knot firstly set up your rod and reel with a float system, take a rough measurement of between eight and twelve feet and that is where you need to tie the knot.

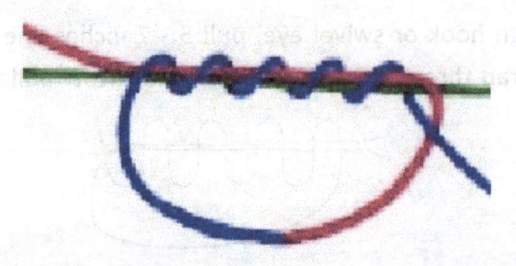

First of all lay about eight inches of the power gum down the shockleader, then whilst holding one end about an inch in, take the other end and take it back towards the end being held so that you have a loop, now wrap the power gum around the shockleader and one side of the loop, you must do this at least four times but as many as eight, you must however wrap it around an even amount of times otherwise the knot will come undone. Once this has been done moisten the knot and pull up tight, trim the ends and now this knot should be able to be adjusted up or down the line but will hold firm enough to fix the float depth.

RIG TIPS

The number, and different variations of rigs used by sea anglers can often be bewildering to the novice or beginner. Ready made versions of many popular rigs can be purchased from most sea angling retailers, however, making up your own rigs, not only provides knowledge and experience but also immense satisfaction, they can also be repaired or rebuilt whilst out on a fishing trip. The most basic of rigs are the Running ledger and the Paternoster designs, once mastered, these are the key to making the more complicated set - ups, however, bear in mind that the simple rigs are usually more trouble free and productive in most situations.

GENERAL

Before starting to make any rigs, try tying a few practice knots. A third hand or a handy nail to hang the rig from as it is being made can simplify the process. Use a pair of nail clippers for trimming end tags as these cut the line clean and close. When tying Paternoster rigs with bait clips or shields, try to use beads and crimps instead of 3 way swivels, totally build the rig, but do not crimp up the crimps until all is together complete with hook. Now pull the swivel up the main body of the trace and crimp in place. this will make sure that the hook length is the correct size for the bait clip or shield. Never over tighten crimps as this can weaken or even cut through the line.

When using crimps to fix hooks to heavy snoods, loop the line through the hook and crimp twice for a stronger connection, it is best to use crimps when making up wire traces.

SNOODS

The strength of a snoods is very important and should be selected to suit the tide and weight of fish being sought e.g. many anglers use a snood of 4 - 8lb, breaking strain when fishing for Mullet, snoods of between 80 and 200lb are commonly used when fishing for Conger eels. The snood length, can also be of great importance for example, Cod tend to take a bait more easily if the snood length is between 24 and 40 inches. One of the best rigs for this is the up and over, or the beach Cod rig as the length of the snood can be tremendously varied.

Bass can react in the same way, however, many are taken on running ledgers or plugs. If making Whiting or Mackerel traces it is best to have a snood of between 6 and 9inches.

When making snoods, try to use a line which is not prone to tangle or twist, a good example of this is "Amnesia" (this is available in various sizes). In many cases other than heavy rock fishing it is best to use a snood length that is a lighter breaking strain to the main line that you have on your reels, this is so that if your hook gets stuck in any underwater snags you are more likely to loose just the snood length. When making separate snood lengths it is best to attach a small swivel and clip to one end as this makes it easier to change snoods quickly, one example is using a snood suitable for a Dogfish for a period of time and then changing it for a beaded snood for flatfish. This method works very well when scrambling over rocks or covering a lot of ground on the coast paths.

TRACES

When making traces the shockleader rule applies as the trace has to withstand the full casting weight of the lead. The body of the trace includes all of the main line from the top swivel to the bottom, at the lead link. When making traces from this book, there may be a necessity to use crimps, these should be put on with care and only crimped with enough force to slightly close the crimp on to the line, if to much force is used, the crimp can and probably will cut through the line. If you do not feel confident enough to use these, or cannot acquire these, there is an alternative, this is a stop knot or, a piece of old telephone wire coiled, tightly around the line will work in the same way as a crimp or stop knot, these are adjustable. Many of the traces shown are for use at marks that have more than enough room to swing a lead out from the end of the rod, for long distance casting, however many of these traces can be considered dangerous if used in areas with little room. For confined areas there are shorter traces, use these.

DIY Rig/Trace Making Board

A rig / Trace making board can be one of the best things that you ever manufacture and can be an indispensible piece of kit enabling you to make rigs and traces of all lengths and types.

One of the easiest ways to make this is to first find an old plank of pine, like an old floor or skirting board approximately 36 inches in length and around 4 inches wide, the reason for pine or similar types of wood is that the pins used in this board are not fixed and can be moved between the holes, these will pull out and wear in chipboard etc. Any way you have your board, now all you need is an electric or hand drill with a 2mm wood drill bit, drill a hole about 10mm deep at one end of the board about 25mm from the end and approximately in the centre, now leave a gap of 150mm and drill a line of holes about 20mm apart and 10mm deep all the way to the other end. Now drill a further two rows as shown below. The pins used in this board are 2mm x 25mm round wire nails, this is the reason for the 2mm holes. When finished use a pin to secure a 3 way swivel in the top hole, work out the length of trace you require and fix a swivel of lead link using a pin in a hole down the other end of the board, now tie a length of line between the two swivels held in place, this gives you the trace or rig body, now whilst this is still attached tie a hook length to the top swivel and work out how long you want the hook length to be, use a pin in one of the side holes to hold the hook whilst you tie it on, remember to use a bit of spit whilst tightening knots etc.

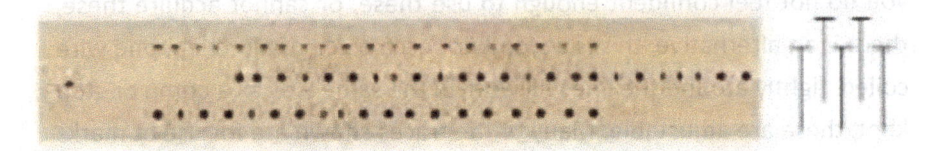

MAKING YOUR FIRST SIMPLE RIG

After reading the first few pages you should have gained a basic knowledge of rigs and the components used, now follow this simple set of instructions and make your first rig, a single paternoster with a bait shield, note the bait shield is optional. You will need the following parts: 1, snap link, 1 lead link, 2 x swivels, 1x 3 way swivel, 1 bait shield optional, 1 x bead, 1 x crimp, 2 x 18" shockleader material, 1 x 14" hook length material, 1 x hook. First of all connect the snap & lead links one to each swivel, now tie the free end of each swivel using a clinch knot to the 2 lengths of shockleader material, you should now have 2 swivels with links attached to the 2 shockleader lengths. Attach the 3 way swivel to the free end of the shockleader on the swivel with the snap link.

Now feed the free end of the other shockleader through the rubber tubing and bait shield if used, make sure that the shield is the correct way up i.e. the cone is facing the lead link end, now slide on the bead followed by the crimp and let it run freely down the line DO NOT squash the crimp at this time, tie the free end of the shock leader to the other side of the 3 way swivel.

It should now look like the picture on the right. If you are using a trace making board stretch out the trace between two pins so that it is taught, this will make it easier to set the hook length. All you should have left at this point is the hook and the hook length material, now attach the two with a clinch knot and then making sure that

The hook length is now shorter than the distance between the 3 way swivel and the lead link, attach the length to the 3 way swivel. If used push the rubber tubing up on to the bottom of the bait shield, put the hook in place so that the hook length is taught, let the bead slide down to the top of the shield and then squash the crimp up behind the bead. There you have it your first rig and remember practice makes perfect.

BASIC ANTI TANGLE SLIDING FLOAT END TACKLE

This is a very simple and effective piece of end tackle and as long as you keep the hook length shorter than the rig body, it is 99.9% tangle free, using this with a sliding float can also greatly increase your casting distance.

The parts needed for this are as follows: 18" Shockleader material, two medium barrel swivels, four beads and two short pieces of silicon rubber tubing, this acts as a type of shock absorber during the cast.

To put this together first tie a swivel to one end of 20lb plus shockleader material using a clinch knot, now feed a bead followed by a piece of silicon tube and another bead, now feed on the float weight followed by a bead, tube and bead, now tie the other swivel to the free end.

trim the knots and apart from the hook length you are done. Use this by feeding a bead up the main line followed by the float, then attach this and a hook length of about 12"16" long, tie a stop knot as shown in the knots section of this chapter.

SLIDING FLOAT

This basic system of float is mainly used for long distance casting for Mackerel, Pollack, Garfish, Scad, Whiting, Bass and Wrasse. The float below is available in various sizes from local tackle dealers. Use this float system on a suitable size shockleader.

PARTS LISTS.

1 Sliding Float. 1 Ball weight to suit. 2 Beads. 1 Swivel, Medium. 1 Hook, size 1 to 2/0. 1 Rubber Stop Knot.

SLIDING FLOAT

Unlike the first float system, this one is mainly used for closer fishing for Wrasse, Pollack, Mackerel, Scad, Bass and Garfish. It can be very difficult to cast this system any great distance without it getting tangled. Use float system on suitable shockleader.

PARTS LIST

1 Sliding Float, as above. 1 Ball weight to suit. 2 Beads. 1 Swivel, Small. 1 hook, Size 1 to 3/0. 1 Rubber Stop Knot.

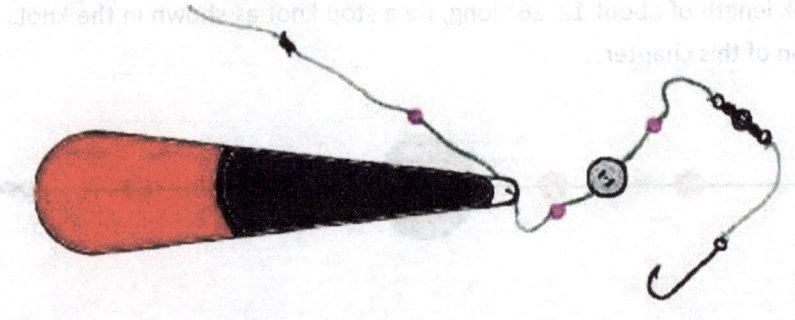

SELF COCKING FIXED FLOAT

This float is ideal for shallow fishing, and is a very simple float to set up, particularly good for younger anglers. A good float for Garfish and Mackerel. Tie the end of shockleader directly to the top of the three way swivel incorporated in the float.

PARTS LIST

1 Self Cocking Fixed Float as Above. 1 Length of hook snood, Approx. 6 - 8 feet, 8 - 10lbs. 1 Hook Size 1-2/0.

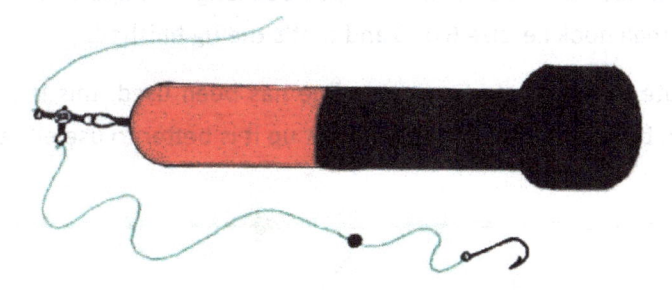

SELF COCKING MULLET FLOAT

This Float system is used mainly for light float fishing for Mullet, although it is also very common in the fresh water tackle box. The float depth can be adjusted by pulling the line through the holes provided, best fished in calm weather with a depth of around 12 feet. This float goes straight on to the main line.

PARTS LIST

1 Mullet Float. 2 - 4 "BB" Lead Shot. 1 Small Hook Size 10- 6 .

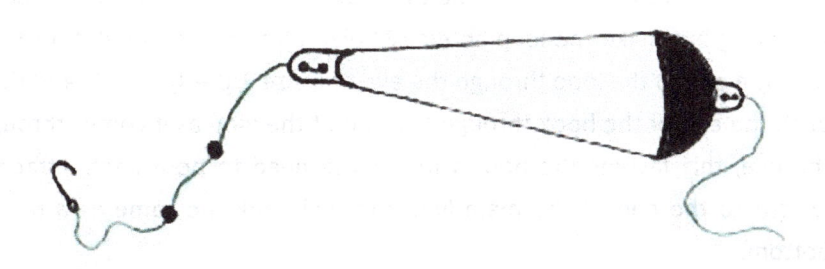

BASIC MULLET RIG

This is one of the most basic rigs/ end tackle to set up, you need no Shockleader, no hook length material, nor the use of beads or swivels, you just simply take a measurement of about 18" from the end of the main line, then form a loop of about 6" diameter, tie this in a tucked half blood knot so that you now have a loop of line tied in the main line approximately 18" from the end. Now attach a small 1/2 — 1oz lead to the bottom end, once this is done, cut one side of the loop near to the knot, this should now leave you with a single hook length of approximately 12" attach a small hook i.e. size 6 or 8 and that's the rig finished.

Please note in the illustration green line has been used, this is solely so that it can be seen, when making this set up it is better to use either clear, ghost, chameleon or grey line as the species this is primarily used for tend to get spooked very easily.

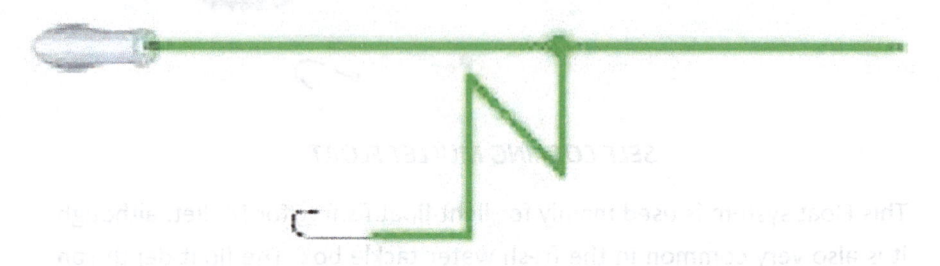

This piece of end tackle can also be adapted to catch Wrasse etc, many anglers use a heavy main line for catching this species and therefore do not have to attach a Shockleader to the end of the main line.

In this case if using up to 25lb line then follow the steps to make the basic Mullet rig but make the loop about 12" diameter and don't cut it, instead feed the end of the loop through the eye of a size 3/0—4/0 hook and then push the end of the hook through the end of the loop as it comes through the eye, this fastens the hook without the need to tie a knot. Attach a weight to the end of the main line, this will work the same as a rotten bottom.

RUNNING LEDGER

This rig can be very versatile, catching most species of fish, particularly good for flatfish , Bass , Cod and Gurnard. This rig is made on the shockleader, this gives the fish a long length of line to run with, before the lead strikes out of the bottom.

PARTS LIST

1 Zip Slider, with clip. 2 Beads. 1 Medium Swivel. 1 Hook, Various sizes to suit 24 inches of Hook Length.

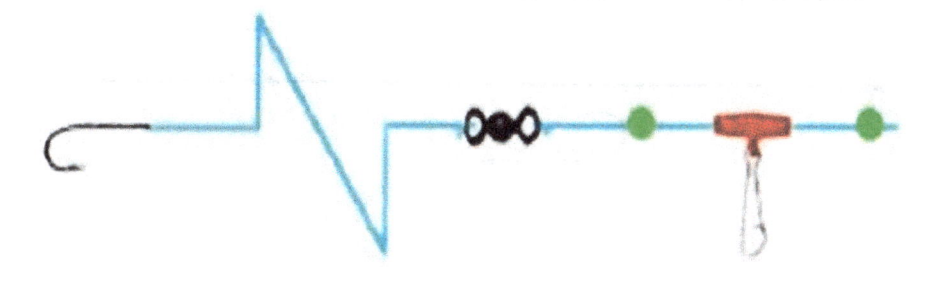

TWIN RUNNING LEDGER

This running ledger rig is similar to the first, however this can be more effective used with worm baits in estuaries for flatfish. Tie trace directly to the end of the shockleader.

PARTS LIST

1 Zip Slider. 1 Three Way Swivel. 2 Beads for trace & 6+ for Hook Lengths. 2 x Hook Lengths 12 inches & 24 inches. 2 Hooks Sizes 1/0 - 2/0.

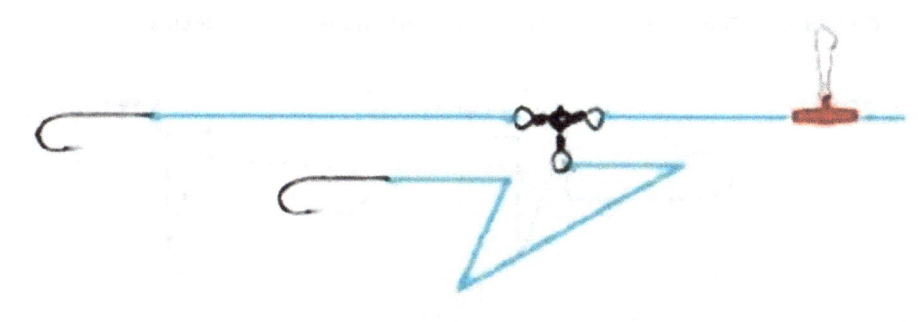

PATERNOSTER SINGLE

This rig is one of the simplest ones to make and use, best for gentle casting, this rig catches most species of fish. The rig is tied directly to the end of the shockleader, by using the three way swivel at the top of the rig.

PARTS LIST

1 Three Way Swivel. 8 - 18 inches of Hook Length.
24 inches of Shockleader
1 Hook, Size 1/0 - 6/0. 1 Lead Clip.

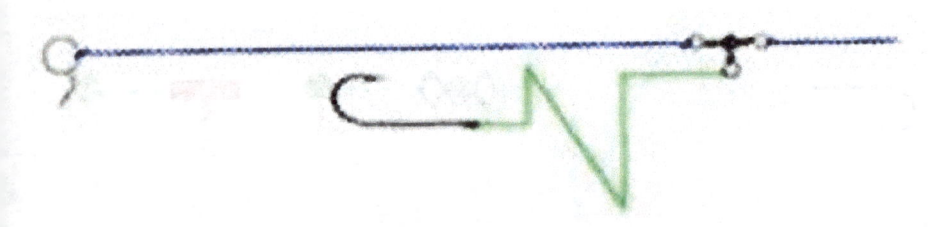

PATERNOSTER TWIN

This rig is slightly more complicated than the single paternoster, however this rig has the added advantage of having two hooks, these can be different sizes and be baited with different baits.

PARTS LIST

2 x Three way swivels. 2 x Hook Lengths 8-13 inches. 2 x 14 inches of Shockleader. 2 x Hooks, Size 1/0-6/0. 1 Lead Clip.

Add beads to these rigs as attractors for flatfish and other species.

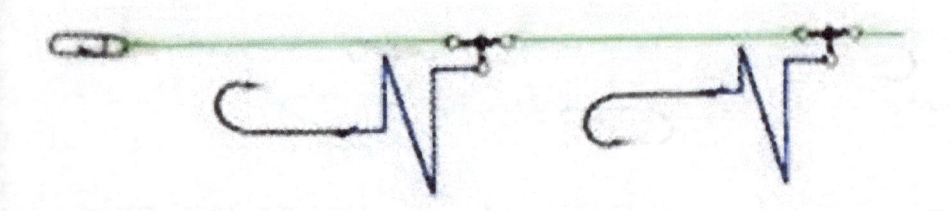

ONE UP ONE DOWN

This rig can be used for attracting more than one species of fish, it is best to use a plane lead with this system. this rig is mainly used for close to medium casting for most fish.

PARTS LIST

2 x Three Way Swivels.1 Lead Clip. 1 Hook Length 12". 1 Length of Shockleader 18". 1 Hook Length 12" +. 2 Hooks Various Sizes.

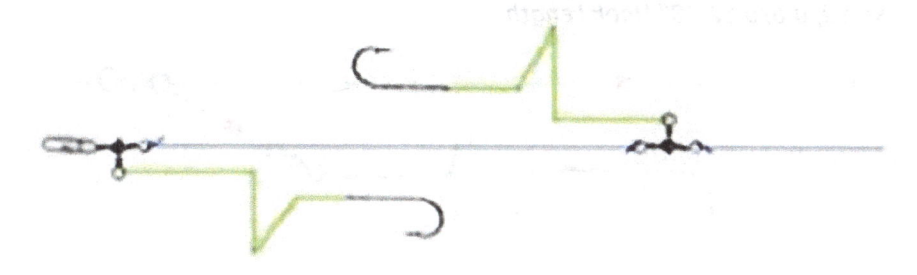

WHITING RIG

Although this rig is primarily a rig for catching Whiting , it can be adapted for many forms of fishing, This trace is connected to the shockleader by the three way swivel at the top of the trace.

PARTS LIST

3 X Three Way swivels.3 x 10-18" Shockleader.1 x Lead Clip.3 x 8-12 " Hook Length.3 x Hook, Size 1/0-4/0.

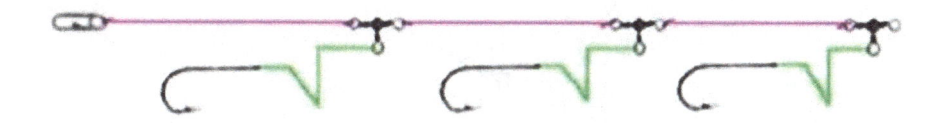

The whiting rig can be adapted by using multi coloured beads on the hook lengths , these make ideal flatty rigs.

PULLEY RIG

This rig can be made at any length that you are comfortable casting with. If made with a long hook length and body this rig is ideal for Cod, Coalfish, Pollack and Bass, and a short body and hook length for Mackerel, Scad and whiting.

PARTS LIST

14-30" Of Shockleader. 2 x Beads. 2 x Medium Swivels. 1 Rotor Clip. 1 Hook, Size 2/0-6/0. 12-18" Hook Length.

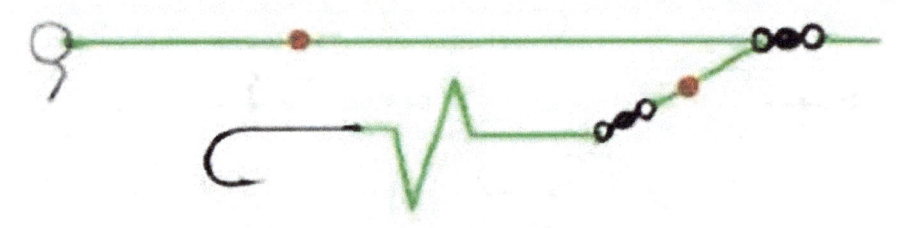

WISHBONE PULLEY RIG

This rig is similar to the first pulley rig, however, having two hooks can help if the fishing is slow, if you use two different sized hooks and baits, the chances are that you may contact more than one species of fish.

PARTS LIST

14-30" of Shockleader. 2 x Beads. 2 x Medium swivels. 1 Rotor Clip. 2 x Hooks, Size 2/0-6/0. 2 x 12-18" Hook Lengths.

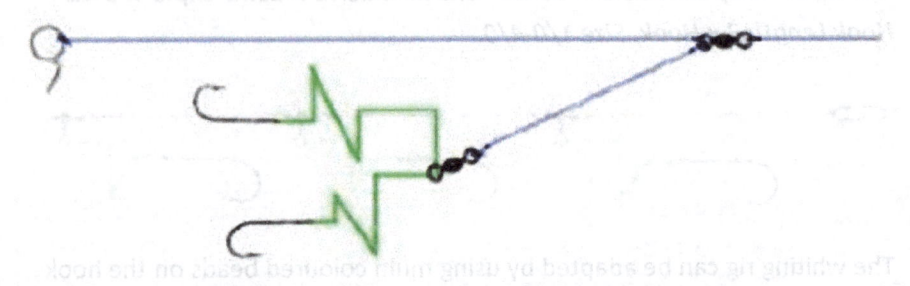

Use thicker line for the hook length, this will stop it getting tangled.

RUNNING PATERNOSTER

This rig can be very effective for short range beach or rock fishing. Used for Rays, Bass, Dogfish, Cod, Whiting, Pollack and Coalfish. If beads are added to the hook length, this rig will work for most flatfish.

PARTS LIST

24" Of Shockleader. 2 x Medium Swivels. 2 x Beads. 1 Zip Slider. 12-20" Hook Length. 1 Hook, Size 3/0-5/0.

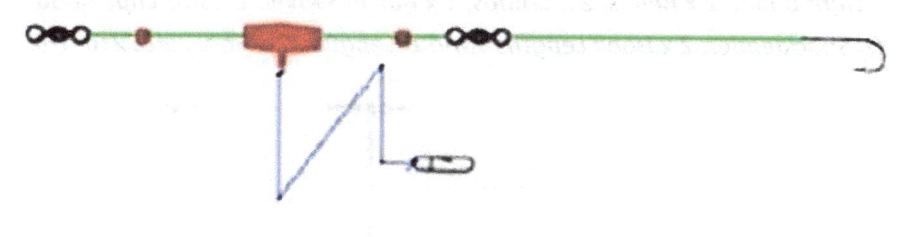

BEACH COD RIG

This can be a very versatile rig, mainly used for Cod, by varying the hook size this rig can be used for Bass, Whiting, Pollack, Coalfish, dogfish and will also catch a variety of flatfish with small hooks.

Attach to main line with a loop and clip or swivel.

PARTS LIST

1 Relay Clip. 1 Rotor Clip. 1 Medium Swivel. 2 x Beads. 2 x Crimps. 24" of Shockleader. 36" Hook Length. 1 Hook, Size 2/0- 6/0.

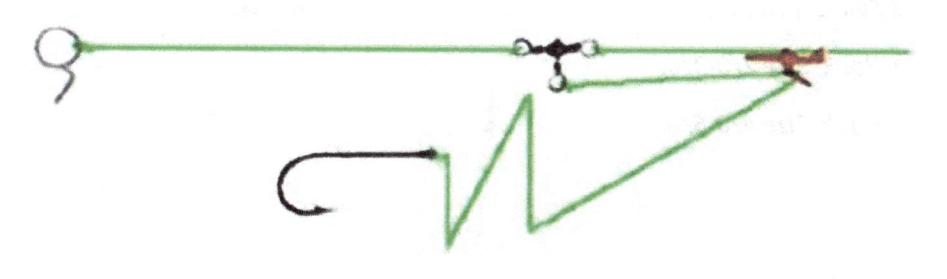

WISHBONE PATERNOSTER

A good rig for catching Bass, cod, Pollack etc, for the medium distance caster, from the beach or rocks, and for use with larger baits. This rig can be Attached to the main line with a loop and clip or a swivel. Both hook lengths can be tied to the boom or tie the second length to the first with a loop.

PARTS LIST

1 Light boom. 2 x Beads, 2 x Crimps. 1 x Barrel Swivel. 1 Rotor Clip. 24-30" Of Shockleader. 2 x Hook Lengths various Lengths. 2 x Hook, Size 2/0-6/0.

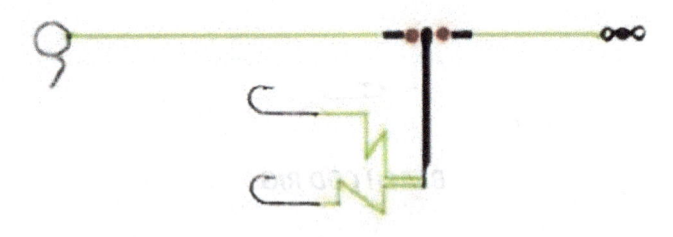

EASY SLIDER BOOM

This can be a very tough rig, used for heavy rock fishing for Wrasse, Cod, Conger Eels and Rockling. This rig is best used at close or medium range. The Pennel hook on this rig is an option and single hooks work just as well. This rig is designed to run up the shockleader.

PARTS LIST

1 Easy Slider Boom. 1 Bead.

1 Swivel (Heavy).

1 Hook, Size 2/0-3/0.

1 Hook, Size 4/0-6/0.

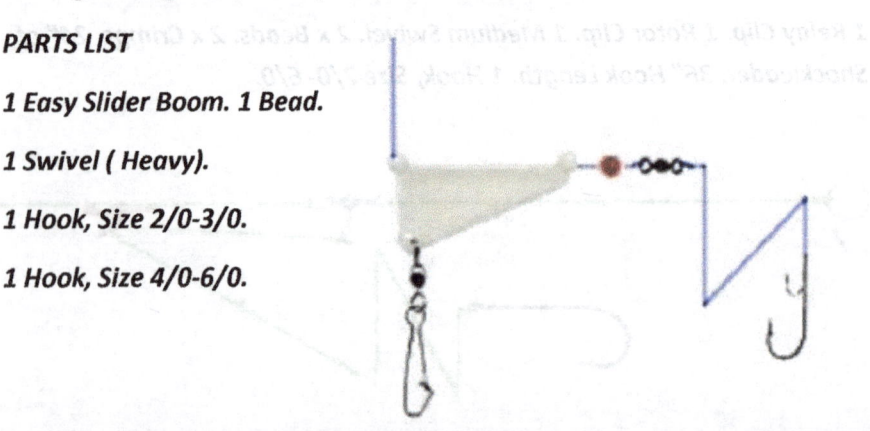

BOMBER RIG

This rig, with a few alterations can make a very good distance casting rig, for putting two medium sized baits out in the same area. various hook sizes can be used.

PARTS LIST

2 x 12 to 24" Of shockleader. 1 x Medium Swivel. 2 x 3 way swivels. 1x Crimp. 1 x bead. 1 x Bait Shield & 1 x bait clip. 2 Snoods 1@ 10" 1@ 14". 2 x Hook, Size 2/0-5/0.

ROTTEN BOTTOM RIG

This rig is used for fishing close in to the edge over very rough ground where end tackle losses can be high. An old spark plug is shown, however nuts, bolts etc can be used. Main uses are for Wrasse and Rockling, although this rig can be used for any species.

PARTS LIST

1 Three Way Swivel. 12 -20" Hook Length. 1 Hook, Size 1/0-6/0. 18-24" of line, lighter than that of the hook length for Rotten Bottom.

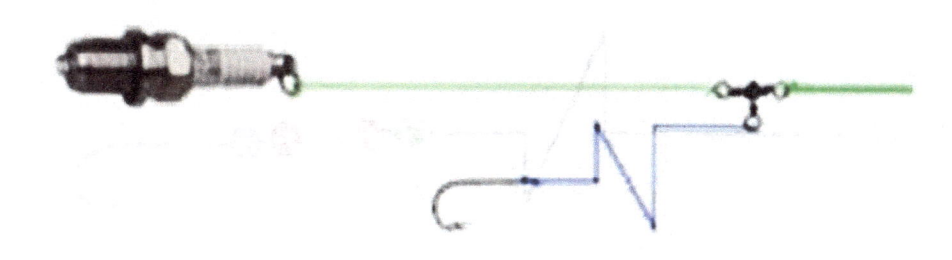

SIMPLE RUNNING LEDGER SPINNING RIG

This light line rig is mainly used for flatfish, in slow moving currents in tidal estuaries, beads can be added to this rig as an attractor. This rig can also be used from the rocks and beach as a light spinning rig. The weight used is designed to run up and down the shockleader.

PARTS LIST

1 Barrel Lead 1.1-3ozs. 1 Bead. 1 Small Swivel. 18-24" Light Hook Length. 1 Hook, Size 1-2/0.

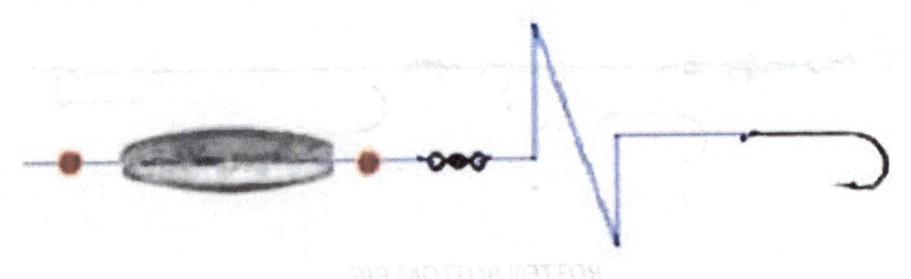

FLATFISH SNOOD

This beaded snood can be used on many different rigs, just by clipping it in place on the main rig body, directly to a swivel. The main use is for Plaice, Dab, Turbot and Flounder.

PARTS LIST

1 x Snap Link. 1 x Crimp. 6-12 Different Coloured Beads. 12-24" Of Hook Length. 1 x Hook, Size 1-2/0.

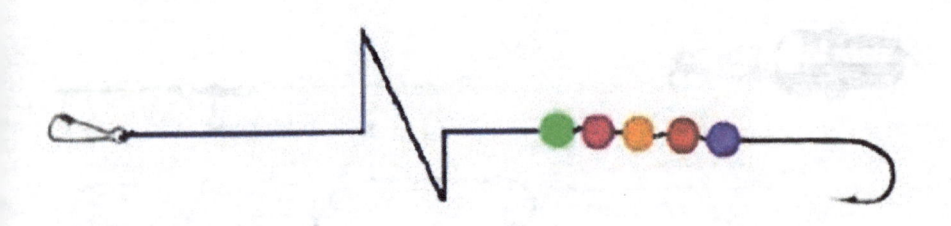

PENNEL HOOK SNOOD

This hook system can be used with most rigs by clipping it to a existing swivel and is mainly used for larger fish such as Bass, Cod, Pollack, Dogfish, Bull Huss and small Conger Eels. Please note this is attached to a paternoster single type rig

PARTS LIST

1 Snap Link. 12-20" Of Heavy Hook Length. 1 Hook, Size 2/0-3/0. 1 Hook, Size 4/0-6/0.

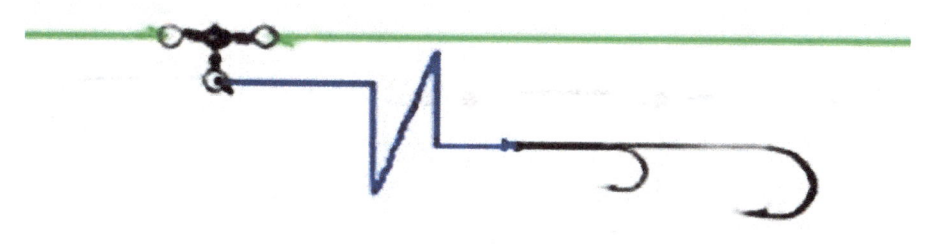

WISHBONE SNOOD

This hook snood can be used in the same way as the Pennel snood, Built with medium to heavy line, this snood can be used for medium to long distance over slightly snaggy ground. Used for catching Bass, Cod, Whiting, Pollack, Bull Huss and dogfish.

PARTS LIST

1 Snap Link. 1 Medium to Heavy Swivel. 2 x 12" Medium Hook Lengths. 2 x Hook, Size 2/0-6/0.

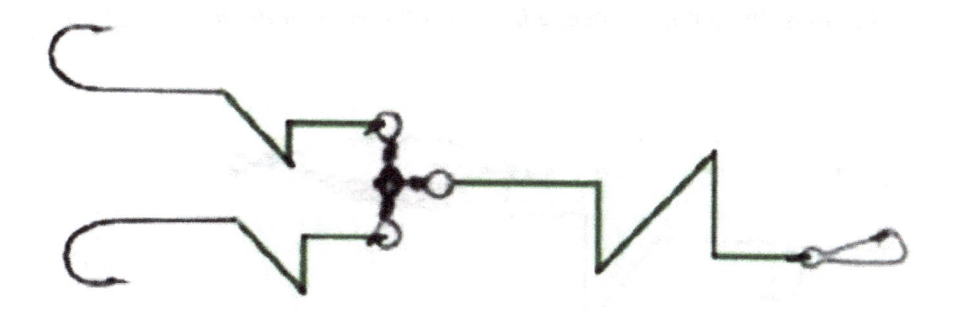

COALFISH SNOOD

This snood can be used, fished deep on a float system or on the bottom, on various other rigs. Placing a starlight in the piece of tube on this rig, helps to attract Coalfish, this snood works well fished after dark, for Scad also.

PARTS LIST

1 Snap Link. 1 Small to Medium swivel. 2 x Beads. 2 x Crimps. 1 Starlight and Tube. 12-20" Of Suitable Hook Length.1 Hook, Size 3/0.

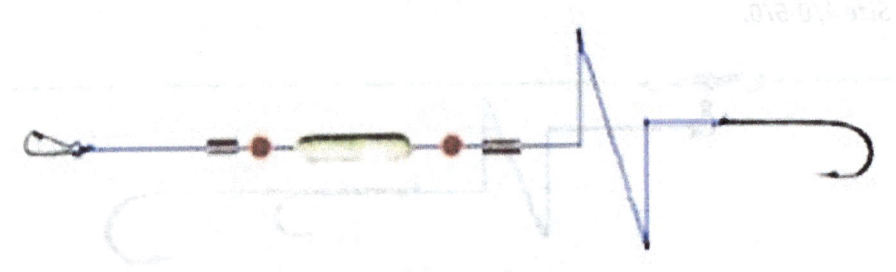

FLATFISH SPOON AND RIG

A variation of a normal flatfish rig, this set up can be used in slight currents and can also be retrieved slowly to help attract the fish. It is always best to remember, to use smaller hooks for flatfish.

PARTS LIST

1 Snap Link. 1 Small swivel. 1 Flatfish Spoon. 1 Three Way Swivel. 1 Weight Clip. 12-24" Of Shockleader. 10-18" Of Light Hook Length. 2 x Split Rings, these may be needed, if not supplied with spoon.

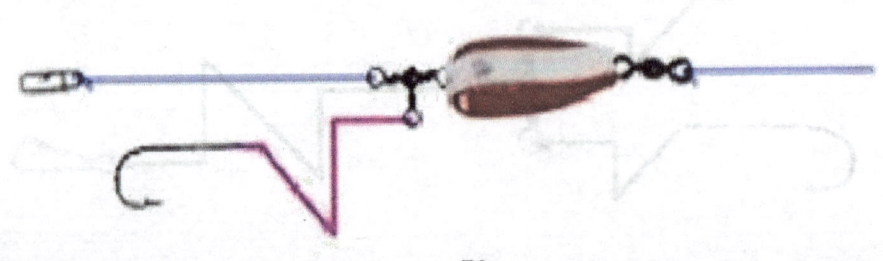

ATTRACTOR RIG

This rig can be purchased as one part, sometimes without the hook length. This rig is ideal for spinning worm baits across the bottom, mainly in estuaries. Mainly used for Flounder, this rig will catch other flatfish, with slight alterations to the hook and length.

PARTS LIST

1 Snap Link. 1 Crimp. 3-9 Beads. 1 Attractor Rig. 18" Of Light Hook Length. 1 Hook, Size 1-2/0.

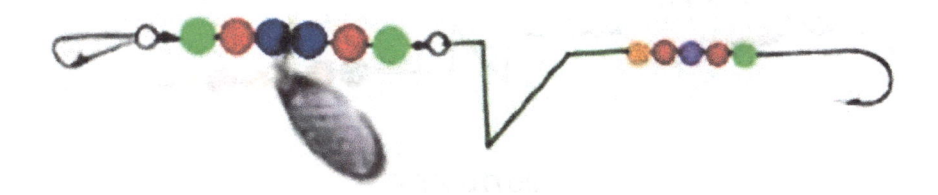

SONAR TYPE ATTRACTOR

The spoon on this rig has slots cut out of it, this helps it to vibrate when it is retrieved through the water, and in doing so helps to attract the fish. This rig will work with most flatfish.

PARTS LIST

1 Snap Link. 3 Crimps. 6-10 Beads. 1 Sonar Attractor. 18" of Light Hook Length. 1 Flatfish Hook, Size 1-2/0.

INLINE FLOUNDER SPOON

Purchased in one piece, these Flounder spoons will work with most flat fish, if the right bait is used. It is often better to change the hook length and hook, these are normally short and the hooks can be blunt, in changing the hook length it is also possible to place coloured beads on this rig to act as an extra attractor.

PARTS LIST

1 Flounder Spoon. 12-18" Of Light Hook Length. 1 Crimp. 3-12 Coloured Beads. 1 Hook, size 1-2/0.

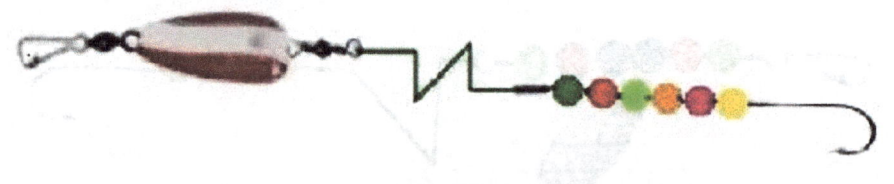

BOTTOM RIG

This rig is mainly used for light bottom fishing, the hook length can be varied to suit casting and fish species, i.e. if the area to be fished has restricted room, then a shorter hook length should be used, however if fishing for Cod etc then this requires a longer trace.

PARTS LIST

1 Medium Swivel. 1 Three way Swivel. 1 Lead Clip. 18-30" of Hook Length. 1 Hook, Size 1/0-6/0.

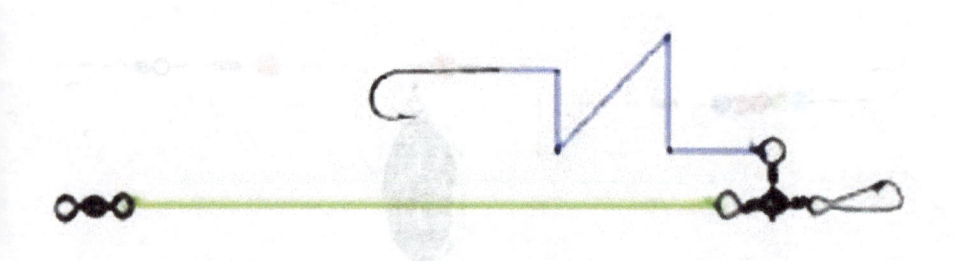

SPINNING RIG

This rig is mainly used for light spinning with rubber lures (Red Gills etc) or Mackerel spinners, however this can also be used with live or frozen Sandeels. Cast out from beaches or the rocks this method can be deadly for Bass, Pollack, Mackerel, Scad and Garfish.

PARTS LIST

4 Beads. 2 bits silicon rubber tubing. 2 x Small Swivels. 1 Barrel Weight to suit. 6-8" Of Shockleader. 12-24" Of Light Hook Length. 1 Rubber Sandeel etc. or 1 Hook, Size 2/0-3/0.

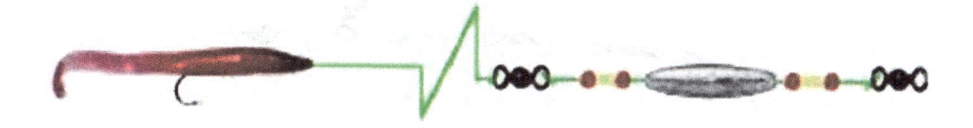

PLUGGING RIG

This is the easiest trace to make and is very basic, having a snap link at either end makes it easy to change plugs at a moments notice. These can be purchased ready made up out of wire trace Material from most good angling shops.

PARTS LIST

2 x Snap Links. Small Swivel. 24" of light line approximately 8-12lbs, for use as the trace body.

HEAVY RUNNING LEDGER

This heavy running ledger is mainly used in conjunction with a heavy main line, and is tied directly to the shockleader at the swivel at the top of the trace. this is mainly used for fishing for Conger Eels.

PARTS LIST

2 x Heavy Swivels. 2 x Beads. 2 x Heavy Crimps. 1 Length of Wire Trace Line. 1 Hook, Size 6/0-8/0.

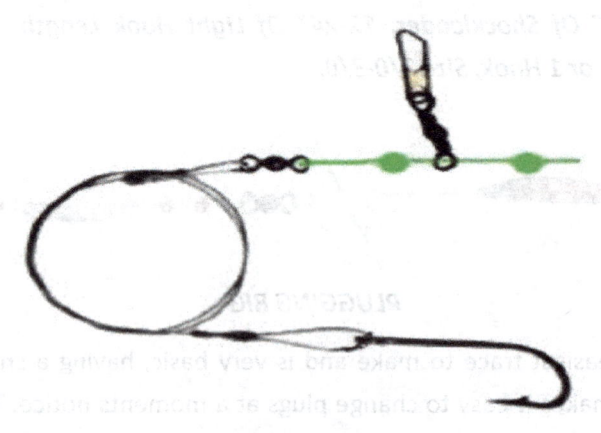

MACKEREL TRACE

Although this trace can be home made, it can be very time consuming, therefore it is probably best to purchase these from your local tackle dealer. This rig comes in many different forms, one of the more popular being the silver shrimp, these come in packs of three and six, if fishing in competition, only three hooks are allowed.

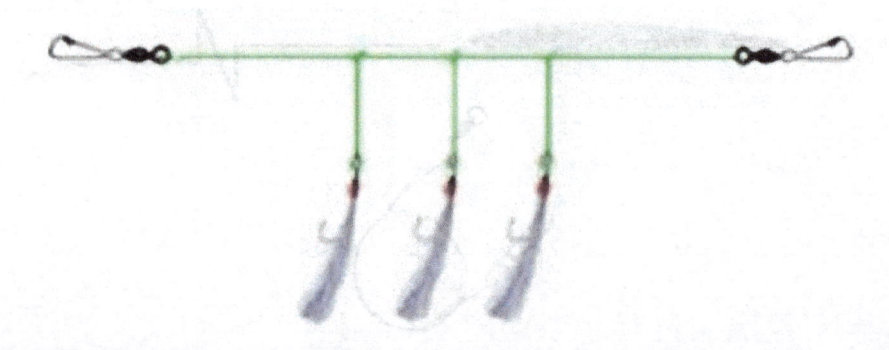

Boat Rigs & Traces

Braided Knot

firstly thread the main line through the eyes up the rod and then follow the diagram below, but pass the braided line through the swivel twice. When finished trim the end of the line but leave about a 5 mm tag, you should end up with something similar to the picture below.

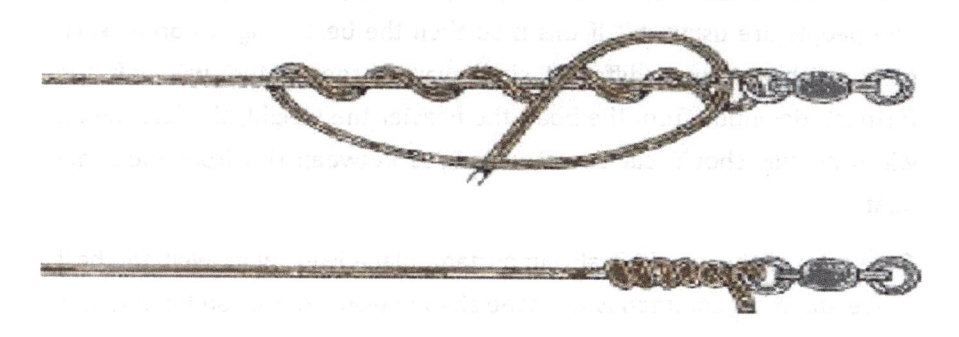

LINES

There are now only two main types of lines used from the boat, these are monofilament and braided line. Monofilament line is quite thick and is best used when not fishing in a current. Braided lines being a lot thinner have less drag in the water and are therefore better in all conditions. Although braided line is more costly, the difference in diameter drag makes it worth while, most braided lines are less than half the diameter of the same breaking strain monofilament line.

TRACES

These are made from various breaking strains of line from a light trace of 10lbs for the smaller species to traces made from 250lb line used for heavy fishing over rough ground for Conger eels. Nylon coated wire can be used however it has to be crimped at either end and as is not worth trying to tie knots in this material. Wire traces are best used for fishing over wrecks and a breaking strain of around 100lbs is recommended.

DOWNTIDE RIG

When using a Downtide rig , there is no need for the use of a shockleader as you are not normally casting the weight but just lowering it over the side of the boat.

This method of fishing accounts for many different species. The Weight used when downtiding can be very important, particularly if more than two people are using this If this is so then the best thing to do is, each person fishing uses a different sized weight, the lightest will drift the furthest downtide from the boat, the heavier the weight, the less the rig will drift, this should cut down on tangles between rigs from the same boat.

The shape of the weight is also important, plane leads work well, the best shape and most common is the cone shaped leads, these can be obtained in a variety of sizes.

PARTS LIST

1 Large Zip Slider.

1 Large Bead, this acts as a buffer between the zip slider and swivel. 2 x Large Swivels approximately size 1/0-4/0. 48" Of Heavy Line, From 25lbs to 50lbs.

36" Of Heavy Line, for use as a hook length, Wire trace line can be used for larger species of fish. 1 Hook, Size 3/0-6/0.

UPTIDE RIG

This method of fishing is a fairly new technique compared with Downtiding, the term Uptiding is exactly what it sounds like.

With this method of fishing a shockleader may be needed depending on the size of weight and strength of main line being used. The use of grip leads are very important with this method.

The idea of uptiding is to cast a weighted rig from the boat so that the lead settles on the bottom , uptide from the boat, and the baited trace moves with the tide. with this method of fishing, if there are three or more anglers on the boat, a larger area of ground can be covered.

This method accounts for many species of fish, as does the downtide rig. The Pennel type hook trace on this rig is optional and works well for the larger species of fish. The clip on this rig is for changing the hook length, to suit different conditions and different species of fish. This type of rig is a type of running ledger.

PARTS LIST

1 Sliding Boom, Although a Zip Slider can be used.

1 Large Bead to act as a buffer. 2 Large Swivels Size 1/0 to 4/0. 1 Clip Link or Snap Link. 1 x 3/0 - 6/0 Hook

18-24" Of Heavy Line, for use as a hook length.

1 Size 3/0 and 1 Size 5/0 hook, if using a Pennel Rig.

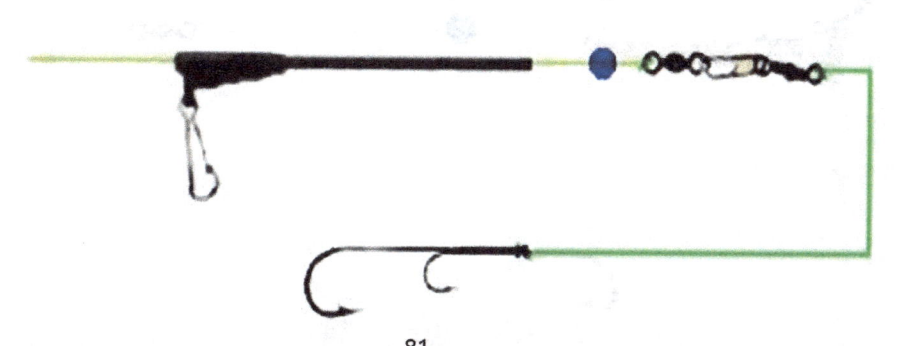

COD RIG

The Cod is the most popular and sought after winter fish to be caught from the boat, although there are numerous ways and rigs for catching this fish, the rig above is one of the more popular ones.

This rig can be used in two or three ways, these are, 1, to lower the baited rig over the side of the boat with a large weight and drift the rig over wrecks and reefs. 2, With the boat anchored lower the baited rig over the side with a 6-8oz lead and use as if downtiding. 3, With the boat anchored, cast the baited rig complete with a grip lead of 6 - 8ozs up tide from the boat, when this settles on the bottom, periodically release a few feet of line off of the reel.

If the latter of the methods are used, there may be a need to use a shockleader, depending on the strength of the main line used. This rig will work with a variety of species particularly Pollack and Ling, by changing the trace line, hook size and bait this rig will work with Conger Eels.

PARTS LIST

1 Medium Eddystone Boom. 1 Large Bead, (2 Beads are used if a shockleader is used with this trace). 1 Large Swivel, Size 1/0 - 2/0. Up To 72" Of Trace Line, Average Size Around 30lbs. 1 Hook, Size 6/0 - 8/0, depending on species. A Pennel Hook can be used with this rig .

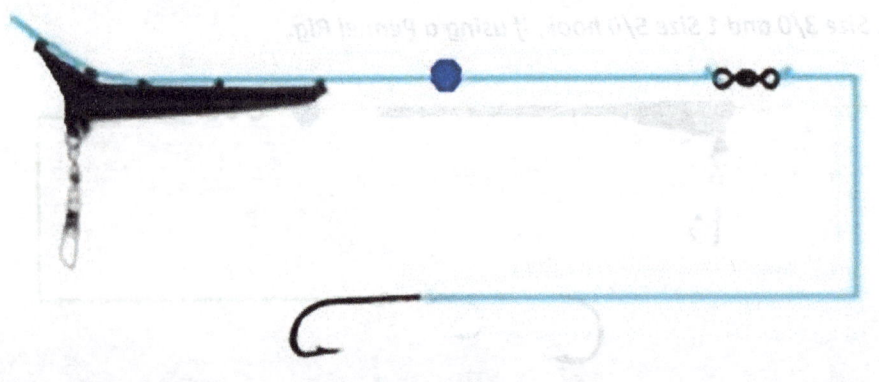

CONGER RIG

This rig set-up is very similar to the Cod rig, however this rig uses heavier line larger hooks and more swivels. Conger fishing from the boat is normally done by, anchoring the boat over a wreck or reef and lowering the baited rig (normally with a whole Mackerel or flapper) over the side, until it reaches the bottom, this can be left where it is, or the reel can be turned two or three turns to raise the boom off the bottom and away from any under water snags, doing this may let the rig drift, however this will cover a larger area.

This rig will often attract Ling and other species of smaller fish, before striking in to the fish, be certain that the bite is sharp or is pulling line off the reel. Up to a 2lb plane weight may be needed for this rig, and a main line of 50lbs plus. When boat fishing for larger species, always make sure that the drag is set properly on the reel, to do this, loosen the drag until line can be pulled from the reel, without snapping, the line should not run off the reel freely.

PARTS LIST

1 Large Eddystone Boom. 1 Large Bead. 2 x Large Swivels, Size 3/0 - 4/0. 24" Of 200lb Mono, between swivels.

48" Of Wire Trace Line or 200lbs mono.

1 Hook, Size 8/0.

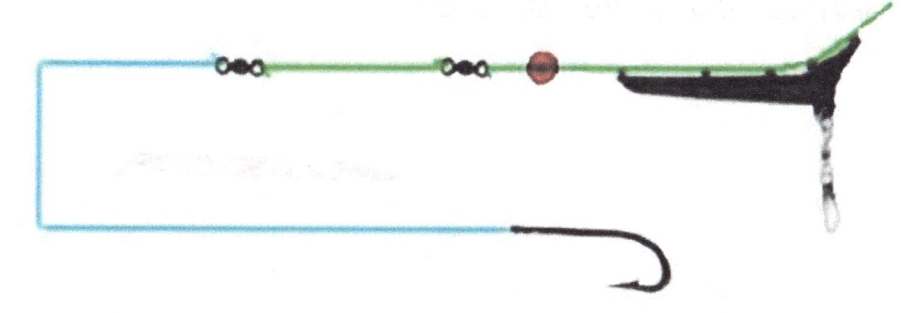

POLLACK RIG

This rig is one of the more popular ones, and is used for a variety of other species of fish, used mainly by lowering the baited rig (with a rubber sand eel) over the side of the boat until the weight hits the bottom, once this has happened turn the reel between 6 and 10 turns to raise the rig off of the bottom, this is about the area in which Pollack swim and feed, however other fish such as Ling and Cod also occupy this area.

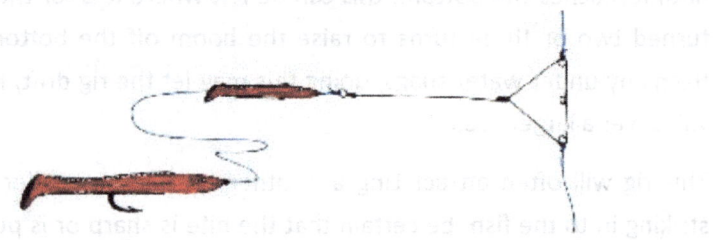

Another method that can be used with this rig is to put a flier at the top of the trace, this helps to attract fish towards the rig and ultimately the rubber eel with the hook inserted in it. Rubber eels come in a variety of shapes and sizes, the way that a flier is set-up is to push the trace line through a smaller eel and then push it up to the end of the boom. The most productive being the red and black ones.

PARTS LIST

1 x 8 - 10" Wire Boom.

20lb Trace Line, Approximately 15 feet.

1 Large Rubber eel (redgill/ eddyston. etc) Jelly worms also work on this rig and are worth a try if the fishing is slow.

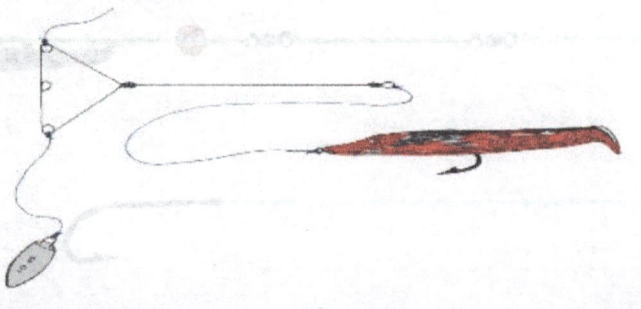

FEATHERED AND PLANE PIRKING RIG

This rig setup is very common, and is used mainly for Cod etc. The feathers on the rig at the top of the page can be of any colour, however the most commonly used and most popular are the white ones. Pirks come in many shapes and sizes normally between 8 and 16ozs. Pirk fishing is normally carried out when the boat is drifting over a reef or wreck. A good

method is to lower the pirk, baited with a whole squid, over the side till it reaches the bottom, then retrieve the pirk about 7 turns of the reel to clear any snags, now raise the rod tip and then

lower it. This is done until the fish are contacted and hooked. Basic pirks are made from a piece of stainless steel tube, filled with lead, however it is probably best to purchase ready made ones from a local tackle dealer.

PARTS LIST

1 Set Of Cod Feathers. 1 Large 2/0 - 4/0 Swivel.

35lb Main Line.1 Pirk Between 8 and 16ozs, there is no set pattern to these.

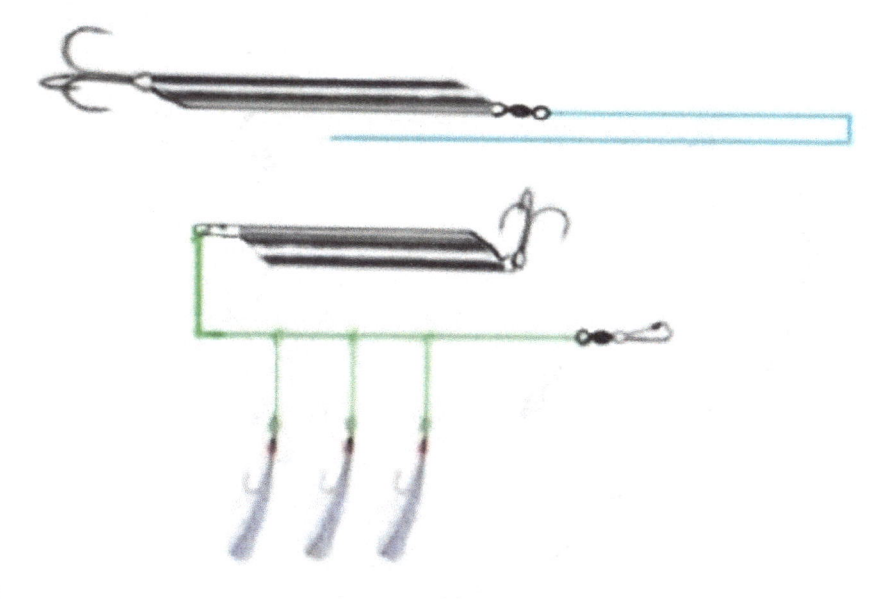

TOPE RIG

This rig can be used with a grip lead for uptiding or with a plane lead for down tiding, although mainly used for tope fishing, this rig can be used for a variety of fish by changing the hook size and weight.

When using this rig it is not unusual to use a whole Mackerel for bait, the tope can take and swallow a whole fish in one gulp. This fish is widely distributed and is found over clean sand, shingle bottoms.

PARTS LIST

1 Sliding Boom, although a Zip slider can be used as a replacement.

1 Large Bead used as a buffer.

3 Large Swivels size 1/0 - 4/0.

48" Of 50lb Line for use as a rubbing Trace.

12-24" Of Heavy Wire Trace Line or 60lb Mono.

2 x Heavy Gauge Crimps, for use if Wire Trace line is used.

1 Hook, Size 7/0.

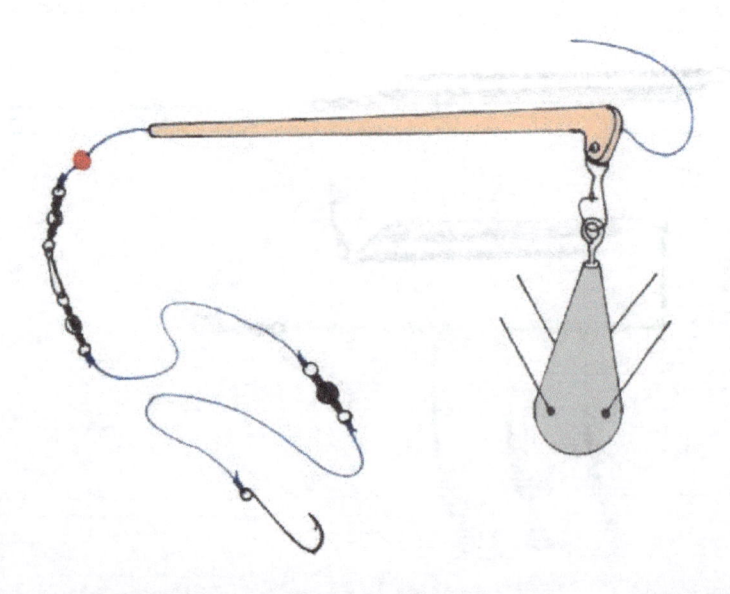

Baits And Presentation

BAITS AND PRESENTATION

Virtually all of the fish sought by sea anglers feed on other forms of marine animal life, many of which can be collected by the angler around the mark that is being fished, the baits shown on the opposite page are just a few in their fresh state.

The art of successful angling is to get the bait in its natural form into the area where the fish are feeding, this book shows you how to put these fresh, frozen and artificial baits on to the hook, however, casting the bait out and keeping it in that state will depend on the type of end tackle or rig being used by the angler.

It can be a waist spending all that time baiting up your hook or hooks just for it or them to get tangled in the main body of the trace or rig and end up scattering the bait over a wider area, this defeats the object of the exercise and bites tend to be fewer and far between, a separate book in the series is available on rigs and traces, however these are more than covered in the previous chapter.

Throughout this book you are shown just what the bait looks like in its fresh condition and what it is supposed to look like when placed or tied on the hook.

The type of hook used can also influence the end result and this is overlooked by many anglers, for instance the use of a worm type bait holder hook sounds great and in principle can work very well, however what no one ever tells you is that these also can cause the angler to use more bait, the main reason for this is that if they are not used properly, these tend to rip the insides of the worm causing it to loose it's juices quicker and get washed out, for this reason and this one alone most of the baits in this book are put on to fine wire Aberdeen type hooks or BLN's, these are simple to use in conjunction with bait needles etc giving you a well presented bait for all types of sea angling.

Lugworm   Ragworm   Peeler Crab

Squid   Shrimp

Cockle   Sandeels

Limpet

Whelk   Razor Fish

Mussel

PREPARATION OF A PEELER CRAB

Many anglers use this bait, however not all know how to prepare them. The following method is one of many and is a very basic one. The first thing to do is, to find or purchase your Peeler Crab, this can be frozen or live, however if you are going to peel this yourself, live Crabs are better than frozen, as many shops freeze these whole, without removing the lungs first. If purchasing frozen peeler, check to see if the lungs are black, as these will deteriorate even when frozen.

The first stage of the operation is to remove the legs and claws, this is done by pulling the leg at the socket, these are removed very easily. Do not discard the legs as these can also be peeled and used for tipping off the bait, or for cocktails.

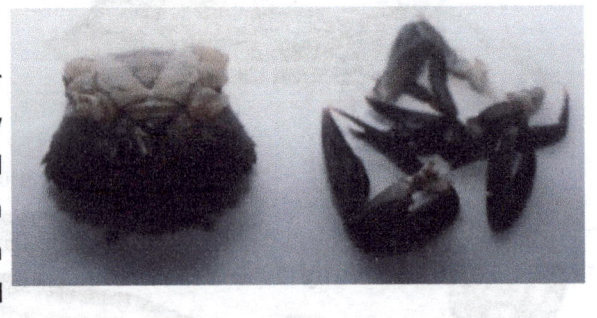

Now remove the under shell, sides , tail and jaw bone, to do this , hold the crab upside down and with the nail of a finger prise up the shell and remove, this normally breaks in to many pieces. with your nail pull up on the jaw of the crab, the bone comes out quite easily, now peel the tail by running your thumb nail down the centre of the tail and applying a little pressure, this will remove the shell from the tail.

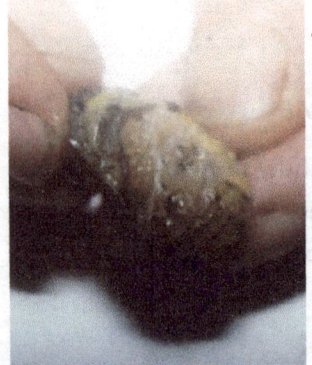

The sides of the crab, by this time are falling off, remove these. With the crab in this stage, pull back the under sides and expose the lungs, these are like thin light brown fingers, behind these is a thin bone the size of the lungs, this must be removed. To do this use your nail and just prise the bone out complete with the lungs.

The final stage is to remove the outer shell of the body, this can be done at the start, however having the main shell still attached, will help to keep the main body in one piece. The outer shell should come off very easily as all the parts holding it have now all been removed.

Before putting this bait on to the hook, the best thing to do is to wash it, this removes any broken shell that still remains on the peeled Crab.

It is always best to obtain and use bait in it's fresh state, even live in some instances, however, properly frozen and prepared baits are always a good substitute. Consideration for others and the environment should be uppermost when digging or gathering live baits, in many of the harbours and estuaries around Cornwall it is forbidden to dig bait in and around boat moorings as this can be dangerous to others.

CRAB BAITS

In order for a crab to grow, it periodically sheds it's old outer shell, before this happens the crab develops a new soft shell under it's hard one, when this happens the crab takes in an excess of water which makes the soft shell swell, at this time the hard outer shell splits and comes off, leaving the crab with a soft skin which hardens off over a period of a few days to a week. After a crab has peeled and the shell has hardened off, it will, if female, develop eggs, these are held by the crab under it's tail, these are normally orange to brown in colour.

Crabs with eggs should not be taken, but should be returned to the water or under the rock from whence it came. Crab baits can be one of the most deadliest baits available for a variety of fish, Bass, Cod, Ray, Wrasse, Flatfish and occasionally Rockling, are the more popular.

Crabs in their natural state can be used, if small enough, however these mainly work with certain species like Wrasse and Rays. Crabs that have recently lost their hard shell are known as soft backed, these are a very good bait for Bass, Ray and Wrasse if used whole with a hook through the back, from side to side, and the legs tied up the line and around the hook with bait elastic. There are a variety of different crabs that can be used for bait, most of these can be found on the shore line around the low water mark. If you are collecting crabs yourself be sure to replace any rocks or sea weed that may be disturbed, this will give cover for crabs to return.

EDIBLE CRAB

These crabs can be an excellent bait, however in most areas a minimum size limit is in force, this helps to protect their commercial value. As a consequence the crabs found by anglers are to large to be used as a single bait and must be cut into pieces and whipped on to the hook with bait elastic.

SHORE CRABS

The common shore crabs are a good all round bait for most species of fish particularly when they are about to peel (shed the hard outer shell). These can be purchased from a local tackle dealer, however because of their popularity during the summer months these may need to be ordered, or if you are going to collect these yourself, you will need a small bucket with a small amount of sea water and seaweed in it, this will help to prolong the life of the crabs collected. The common shore crabs are normally found around rocky beaches, under rocks and seaweed of in estuaries under rocks and weed. Best collected around low tide, on dark evenings.

VELVET SWIMMER

The velvet swimmer crabs are considered to be one of the best and most sought after crab baits for Bass fishing. These crabs are normally found on exposed shore lines, best collected on very high spring tides, on or around the low water mark. As with most crabs the claws can be quite sharp, these can cause injuries if handled incorrectly.

HERMIT CRAB

Hermit crabs have no hard shell, as they live in discarded mollusc shells, however the hermits claws are hard. The hermit crab is an excellent bait for Rays, Smooth hounds and Wrasse. Remove the crab from it's shell and present it whole, whipped to the hook, in some instances you may need to remove the claws as these can be rather large, and will have their shell still intact.

Peeler crab tied with bait elastic

Body hooked hard backed crab

Hermit crab head and tail hooked

Soft backed crab tied with bait elastic

Lightly Hooked shrimp

Hard backed crab hooked through the eyes

MACKEREL

This is one of the most popular fish baits, used for catching numerous types and species of fish. This fish is readily caught and available throughout the summer, either fresh or frozen, when out of season. Mackerel can be used whole as a large bait for Conger eels or as a minute strip, with the skin removed as a Mullet bait, it is very versatile and can be used as a bait for most sea fish. Small, live Mackerel can be fatal to Bass. Fresh Mackerel can be purchased whole or filleted from bait suppliers and fish mongers. The other available fish baits can be used in the same way as Mackerel.

HERRING

This is a very oily fish and hence makes an attractive bait for Whiting, Cod, Rays, Garfish, Rockling and Conger. This bait tends to break up during the cast, therefor it is best to use this bait with a bait shield and tie it on with elastic.

POUTING

Small Pouting used as a live bait can be very good particularly for Cod, Bass and Conger eels. Smaller Pouting work better if presented on a pennel type rig with a long flowing trace.

SMELT

These small fish are best used whole the same way as a Sandeel for Bass, a Fillet of Smelt is an ideal bait for Mackerel and Garfish.

SPRATS

The flesh of the Sprat is soft and oily, fine wire hooks and bait elastic are often used to keep the bait secure, a good bait for flat fish.

GARFISH

A very under rated bait, cut into thin strips or chunks can be deadly for Mackerel and larger Garfish. This bait can work very well either frozen or fresh, and will stay on the hook longer than Mackerel or Sandeels.

Mackerel strip

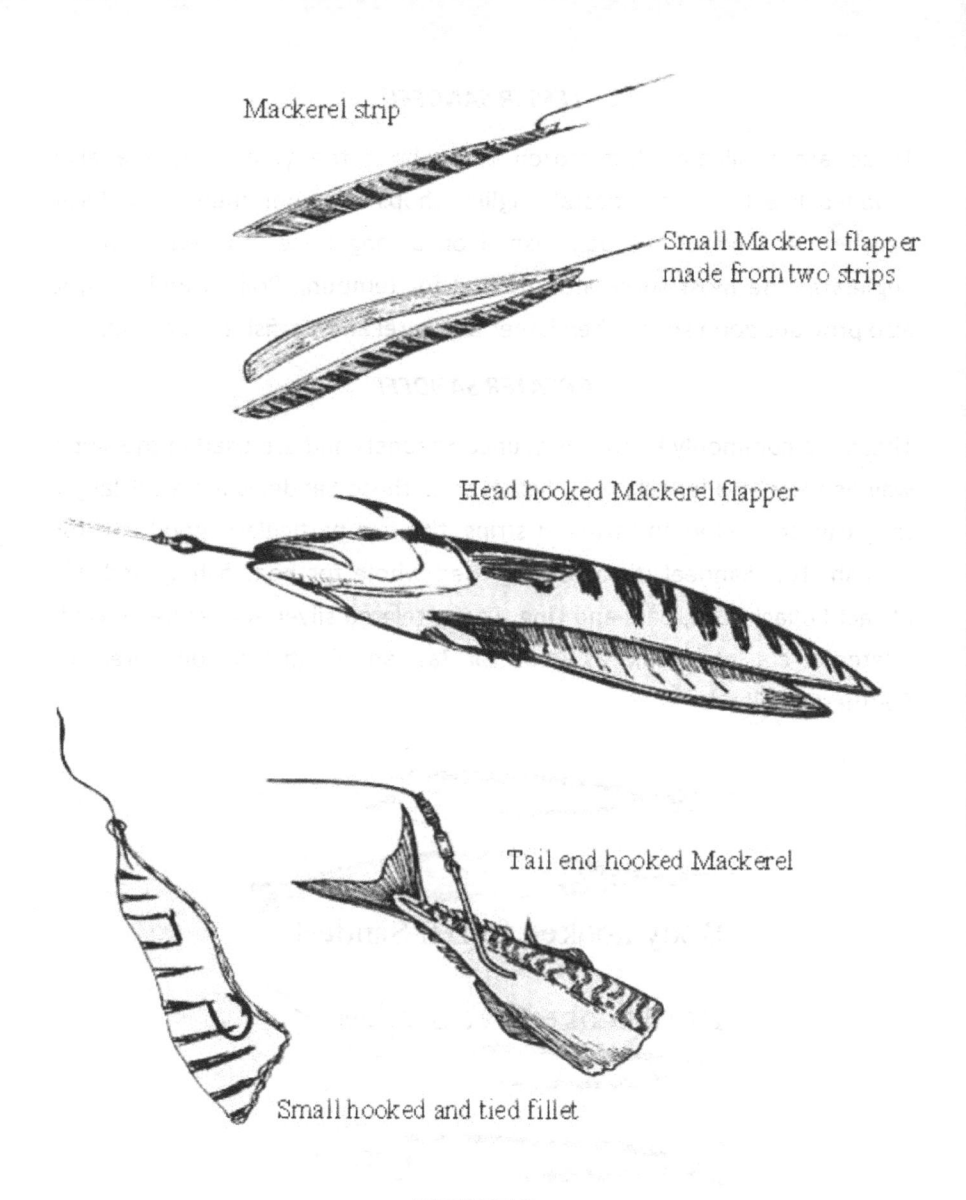

Small Mackerel flapper made from two strips

Head hooked Mackerel flapper

Tail end hooked Mackerel

Small hooked and tied fillet

SANDEELS

Available both live and frozen from most bait suppliers, live Sandeels usually need to be ordered, you will need a bucket and a battery operated air pump to keep them alive and active until required for use as live bait. There are two main types of Sandeel one type is mainly used from the shore and the other from shore to boat.

LESSER SANDEEL

These are available blast frozen throughout the year, they are also supplied live by many coastal angling shops who net them from local beaches. A Sandeel live bait, fished on a long trace is rated by many anglers as the most successful method for tempting Pollack and Bass, it also provides good sport when larger Mackerel and Garfish are around.

GREATER SANDEEL

These are commonly known as Launce Sandeels and are used in the same way as their smaller relatives, however as these Sandeels are a lot larger they can be filleted and used in strips, this is a particularly good bait for Flatfish. This Sandeel is commonly used whole for boat fishing and will attract Pollack, Cod, Bass and Ling. The unrelated silver eel has been used, filleted or cut into steaks as a bait for Bass and Dogfish in some areas of Southern England.

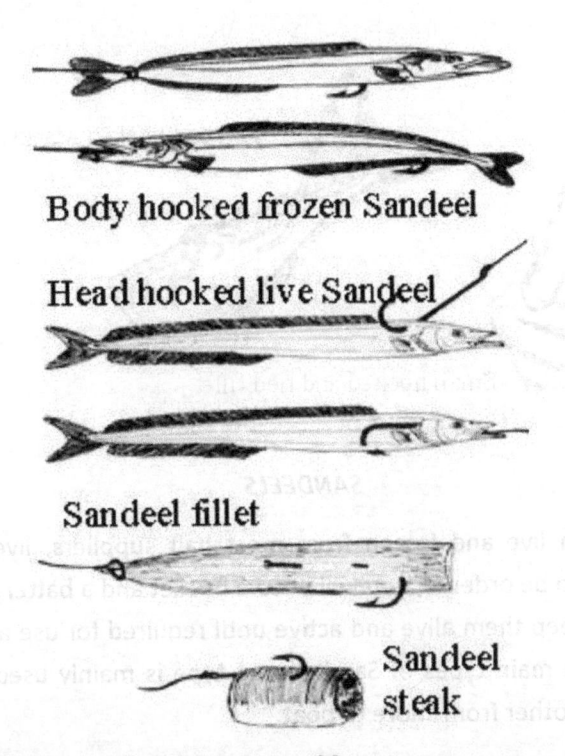

Body hooked frozen Sandeel

Head hooked live Sandeel

Sandeel fillet

Sandeel steak

SQUID

During the summer small from bait shops and local fishmongers, these are usually caught locally, however, most available Squid are sold frozen and are normally imported. The most common type are Calamari Squid. When buying fresh or frozen Squid the flesh should be pearly white, do not be misled by the skin colour which can vary from a pink to a light brown, both with small dark spots. The skin can be removed with ease. Squid can be fished as a whole bait, usually on a pennel hook for Bass, Cod and Conger eels. Squid cut in to thin strips can be very versatile bait used for Mackerel, Whiting and Cod. The Squid head used on a single hook can be a very good bait for Dogfish.

CUTTLEFISH

These can be purchased from most bait shops, and are sometimes caught by anglers using Mackerel feathers. Best cut into strips up to 3 inches long and used from the shore, it is an excellent bait for most flat fish and Bass, small whole Cuttlefish used on a pennel hooked rig will catch Dogfish, Cod and may attract larger Bass. Cuttlefish can be frozen down and used throughout the season.

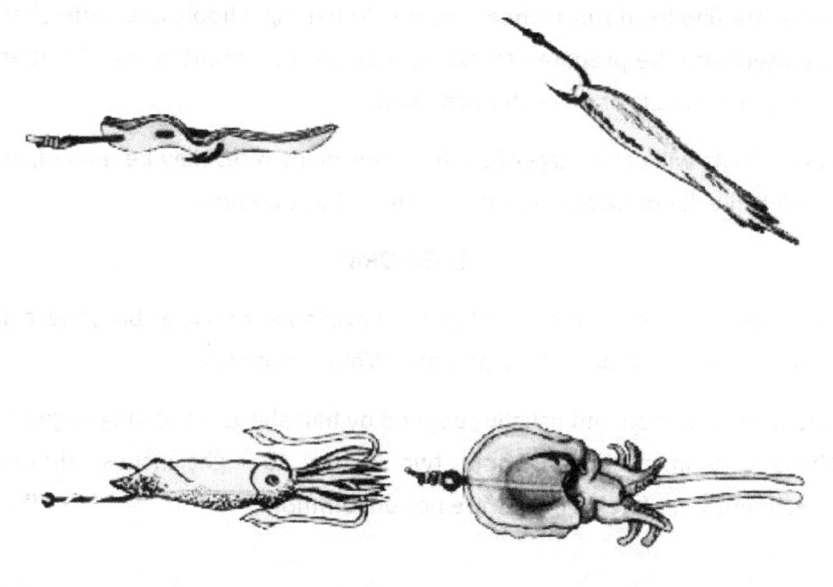

LIVE BAIT COLLECTING

It is always better to dig for live bait as the tide falls, this gives you more time to find casts and collect your bait without the fear of a tidal surge coming up the estuary and either knocking you over or cutting you off, the same goes when collecting peeler crabs, but even more so in the dark, remember a safe fisherman / bait collector is a live one!!!

When digging for Ragworm, King Ragworm or Lugworm, the best practice is to refill the holes dug. Bait pumps work well in a lot of areas, although with deep mud around many of the estuaries the best implement is a wide garden fork.

Always keep bait reserves cool whilst you are fishing, this should help to prolong the useful live. When preparing bait it is best to use a sharp filleting knife, this will cut through the flesh of any fish with ease.

A pair of strong scissors can be used if a filleting knife is not available, these are a lot safer in unpractised hands. The baits in this book are the more common and most popular ones used.

This chapter deals with the bait types and there presentation, however there are few fixed rules when it comes to baiting a hook, and with what it is baited with, be prepared to experiment with different types of bait and different cocktails of more than one bait.

Larger baits will catch larger fish, however many bites may be missed, as a small fish will not be able to take all the bait at one time.

RAGWORM

There are three main types of Ragworm available for use as bait, these are King Ragworm, Harbour Ragworm and White Ragworm.

The most common and usually supplied by bait shops is the King Ragworm, these vary in size from about two inches, to eight inches, although specimens over twelve inches are not uncommon.

HARBOUR RAGWORM

Harbour Ragworm are the smaller variety of Ragworm usually dug from heavy mud estuaries and harbours. These are a recommended bait for Mullet, Flounder and Wrasse, these are usually fished live in bunches on fine wire hooks either on the bottom or on float tackle. If harbour Ragworm can not be obtained, for fishing for mullet then Garden worms can make a worth wile alternative.

KING RAGWORM

The best place to find King Ragworm is on mud and shale banks in estuaries King Ragworm can be threaded on to the hook at the head end, pass the hook point through the worms mouth and thread up the hook, leaving only part of the tail hanging. These worms can be used whole or cut into sections and used for more than one bait. Fished live with the hook nicked through the head is a favourite bait for Bass, Flatfish and Wrasse.

WHITE RAGWORM

These Ragworm are similar in size to the Harbour Ragworm but are white in colour, they are found in clean coral sand beaches and sand bars of the sea shore and estuaries. The favourite use for White Ragworm is as a tip for other Ragworm baits on fine wire hooks for Flatfish or singularly on a small hook for Corkwing Wrasse.

All Ragworm will keep in a cool moist place for several days. The best way of keeping White Ragworm is to place them in a tub, approximately half full with Coral sand and about 5 to 10mm of sea water, this should keep these worms healthy for between one and two weeks if kept in a cool place.

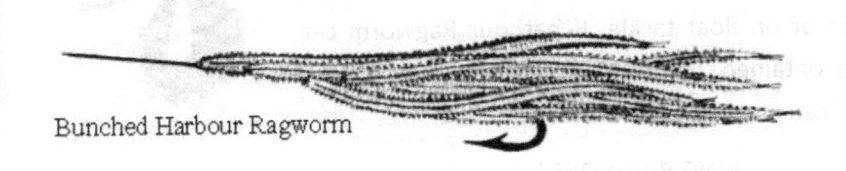

Bunched Harbour Ragworm

King Ragworm

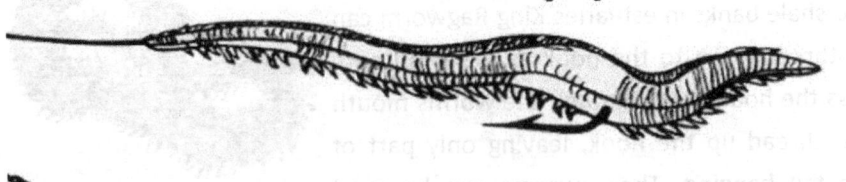

Head hooked Ragworm

Sectioned Ragworm

Head hooked White Ragworm

LUGWORMS

There are two main varieties of Lugworms used by anglers these are Black Lugworm and Blow Lugworm, although there are variations within the main varieties. Lugworm can be located by the presence of their blowhole and cast, in estuaries and on some shallow sandy beaches, only being dug at low tide in estuaries and on low water of the high spring tides on shallow beaches. Dig with a wide blade fork but please fill in any holes or trenches dug, do not dig in or around boat moorings as this can be dangerous to people gaining access to small boats.

BLACK LUGWORM

These are the largest of the Lugworm family averaging from three, to eight inches in length.

This Lugworm is a dark red to almost black in colour, the skin is tougher than that of the Blow Lugworm variety, one of the most sought after Lugworms is the Black Lugworm with the distinctive yellow tail, as these are a prized bait for Cod, Whiting, Bass and Flatfish bait.

YELLOW TAIL

The yellow tailed Lugworm can be found in the same environment as all the others, the distinctive yellow end to the tail is coloured by the amount of iodine found in the worms system, when putting these Lugworm on the hook, you will find, that your fingers get stained with a yellow tinge. this wears off in a matter of hours.

The yellow substance that comes out of these worms can sting a lot if it gets in to a cut, so watch out for this.

BLOW LUGWORM

These are similar to their relative, the Black Lugworm but the skin is a lot thinner and they have a tendency to burst open if cast to powerfully or when feeding the hook through them. Blow Lugworm are very good all round bait accounting for many of the fish species including Rays, Cod, and Flatfish. Worm baits are the best baits to use when estuary fishing as they are part of the natural food chain in this environment.

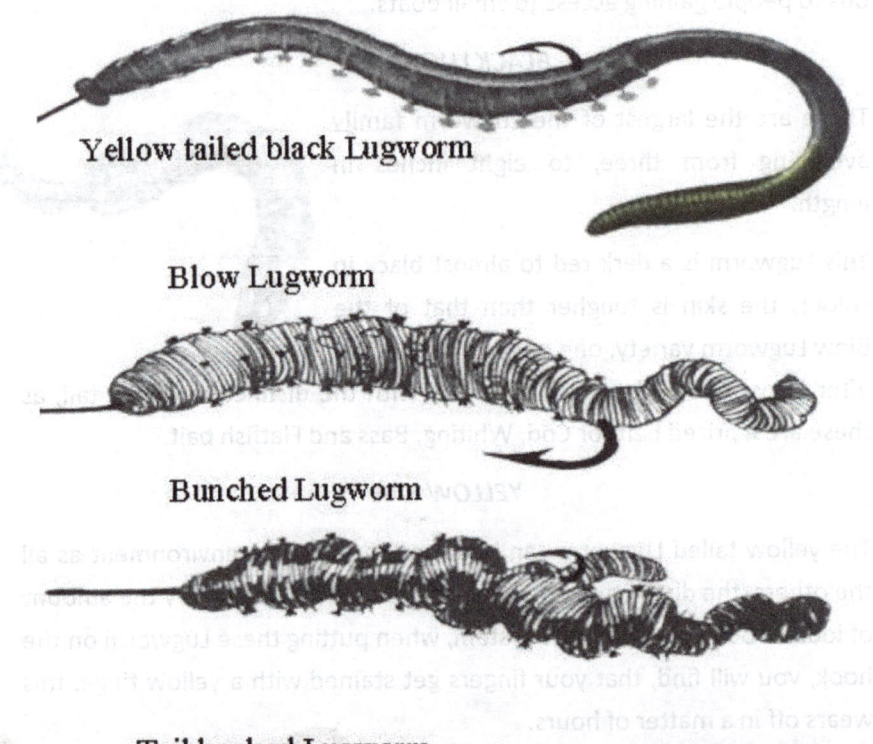

Yellow tailed black Lugworm

Blow Lugworm

Bunched Lugworm

Tail hooked Lugworm

SHELLFISH AND MOLLUSCS

Almost any of the Shellfish, Molluscs and gastropods can be used as bait although, in use only a few of these have achieved popularity. Wrasse feed on virtually any of the shelled marine creatures so in theory most should produce results. however, it is best to look over the area to be fished at low tide and collect a few of the Shellfish and Molluscs etc.

Most of this group of baits are used by many anglers, not as a first bait but as a standby, however these tend to be very under rated, for example Wrasse do not scour beaches for worm baits etc, they do however pick limpets, mussels etc from rocks and crunch them up but then again these are the wrasses natural food and these can be found in abundance around the coast line so try using a natural bait you may be surprised.

LIMPETS

These are found at low water fixed to the rocks, they can be prised off using a strong screw driver and make a good bait alternative to Crab for Wrasse fishing. Once removed from their conical shell the Limpet is quite tough, these should still be tied to the hook with bait elastic.

MUSSELS

Collected fresh Mussels are a very good Cod and Flatfish bait. After removal from their shell they are very delicate and must be secured on the hook with bait elastic, care must be taken when casting this bait as it can break up very easily.

WHELKS

Whelks and similar Gastropods can be collected from the rocks and rock pools at low water. Remove them from their shells and use them as a bait for Wrasse and Flatfish.

As with most of the other types of shell fish these must be tied to the hook for casting.

RAZORFISH

These live in deep vertical burrows in the sand around the low water mark. They can be persuaded into the open by pouring table salt down their burrows.

Once removed from their shell and Tied on the hook with bait elastic these make a very good Bass bait, and will also attract other species.

CLAMS AND COCKLES

These are found in sand and mud on open beaches and estuaries, look for a small blowhole and dig out with a garden fork. Recommended for Bass and Flatfish, remove the shell and tie to the hook with bait elastic., if used fresh, these will also attract members of the wrasse family.

COCKTAILS

A Cocktail is a mixture of more than one bait, these can be used to target a particular species of fish or be used when fishing is slow (bites are far and few between).

There are many advantages to using cocktail baits, for instance if you wish to target more than one species i.e. cod and whiting, these fish will each take squid, worm or fish baits and yet if you are only catching whiting on squid baits, if you add a few lug or rag to this existing bait it will normally attract cod or Pollack to the same bait.

There are a variety of cocktails that can be used and are used in every day sea angling these are, Squid and Mackerel, Squid and Lugworm, Squid and Ragworm, Mackerel and Lugworm, Lugworm and Ragworm, Shellfish and Ragworm and Crab and worm baits.

These can also be made up from fresh bait and a artificial bait, such as rubber worms.

SQUID AND MACKEREL

This mixed bait is made up from up to half a Mackerel and up to a whole Squid, varying in size it will attract and catch Conger eels, Dogfish, Bull huss and Bass in some places.

With a large Squid and Mackerel Cocktail be sure to use a larger sized hook than normal or a pennel type set up as the hook point, if shielded will not bite into the fish this will result in missed strikes. This bait used on a smaller scale will also attract Mackerel, Pollack, Whiting smaller bass, cod and of Coarse dogfish and bull huss.

SQUID AND LUGWORMS

This bait is very effective for Cod and Bass, although it will also take Whiting and Dogfish. There are many ways of presenting this bait but the three best are,

1) First hook the tail of the Squid and push it up the line, then feed between one and four Lugworm on the hook and push up the to tail of the Squid, now hook the head of the Squid. pull all of the bait down towards the hook and secure with bait elastic.

2) Remove the insides of the Squid and fill with Lugworms, wrap the Squid in bait elastic and tie off. Now thread the Squid complete with Lugworm on to the hook, secure with a half hitch in the line.

3) Just using the head of the Squid and either Lug or Ragworm this may sound like the other two bait methods, however this bait can make a substantial difference when fishing for cod or bass. Using a pennel hook system first feed the lower hook through the head of the Squid pushing it up the line and then hooking it with the top hook now feed Lug or Ragworm or even both on to the lower hook, when you have a bunch of worms almost covering the lower hook lightly tie them and two tentacles of Squid using bait elastic, this should keep all the bait and juices intact until it reaches the sea bed. Please note it is best to use either a bait clip or shield with this method.

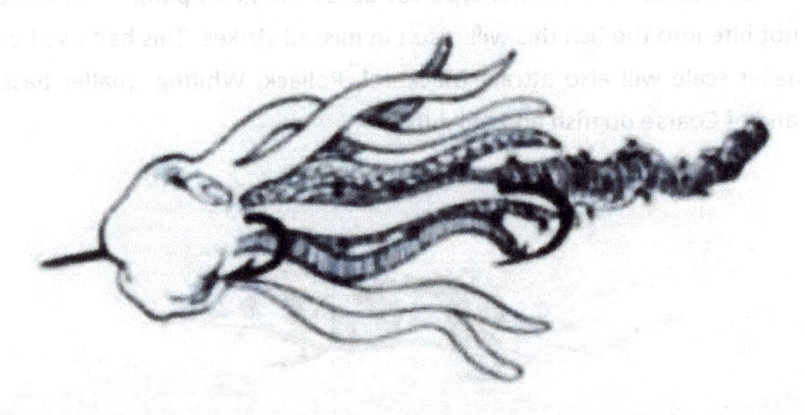

SQUID AND RAGWORM

This is made up and used the same way as the Squid and Lugworm, however, this tends to work better for Cod when the fishing as slow.

LUGWORM AND RAGWORM

All you have to do with this Cocktail is either tip Lugworm off with Ragworm or the other way around. Used mainly for Flatfish and Bass.

SHELLFISH AND RAGWORM

This Wrasse bait is made up from Mussels or cocktails and tipped off with White Ragworm. First remove the Shellfish from its shell and use elastic to secure it to the hook, then place two White Ragworm, hooked through the head only, on to the end of the bait. Please note that with this and many other Worm baits, you cannot put to much power into the cast or you will loose part or all of your bait , however this can be avoided by placing the whole bait in a P.V.A. bag, this dissolves when wet.

SCENTS AND OILS

These can be purchased from most good angling stores, most anglers associate these with fresh water fishing, however there are a few that if used properly can be a deadly additive, the best two for the purpose of sea angling are Pilchard Oil and edible Crab Scented oil, these do work on their own and can even produce better results than fresh baits. The tried and tested way to use these is to wrap and tie cotton wool around a hook now secure with bait elastic, now dip the hook into the oil and allow it to soak for a few seconds, now just cast your line out as Normal, if you use this method on a multi hook trace, you will tend to get more bites on the cotton wool, I have caught Wrasse, Bass, Cod and Whiting using this method and it never ceases to amaze me.

ARTIFICIAL BAITS

Artificial baits (lure and plugs) used alone or in conjunction with natural baits can be deadly for most species of fish, the type, colour, size and shape used depends mainly on the type of fish being sought by the angler. The main lures and plugs described in this book are Mackerel Feathers and Spinners, Rubber eels and Worms, Spoons, Muppets, Bass plugs and Bullets, these can all be purchased from local tackle dealers, for a reasonable price.

FEATHERS AND SILVER SHRIMPS

Mackerel, Cod Feathers and Silver Shrimps can be purchased in ready made form in packets of three to six, these are used by casting out and retrieving slowly, sinking and drawing all the time, this as best done with three feathers and on light tackle i.e. Carp rod.

If entering any competitions be sure to find out how many feathers you are able to use, as in some counties feathers are banned in competition, and in others only three feathers are the amount used. Baited feathers work very well from the boat, these attract Mackerel, Pouting, Cod, Whiting, Ling and Pollack. Used from the shore, baited feathers can account for Mackerel, Pollack, Small Pouting, Whiting and Dogfish.

Silver Shrimps work in much the same way as the feathers, however these produce more fish if used from the boat.

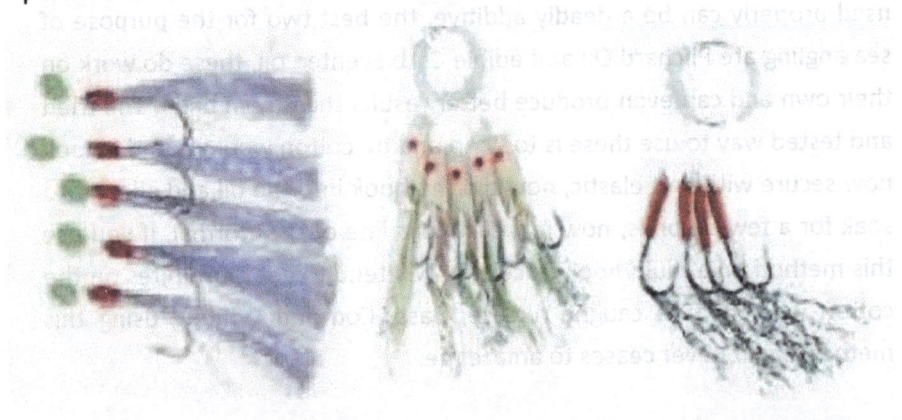

SPINNERS

A spinner is used by casting out, and then retrieving it, varying the speed. Most spinners need a separate weight, however, one can purchase a weighted spinner and this, on light line works well. A spinner has a blade that rotates like a propeller when the lure is retrieved, it is an excellent lure for Mackerel and most predatory species of fish.

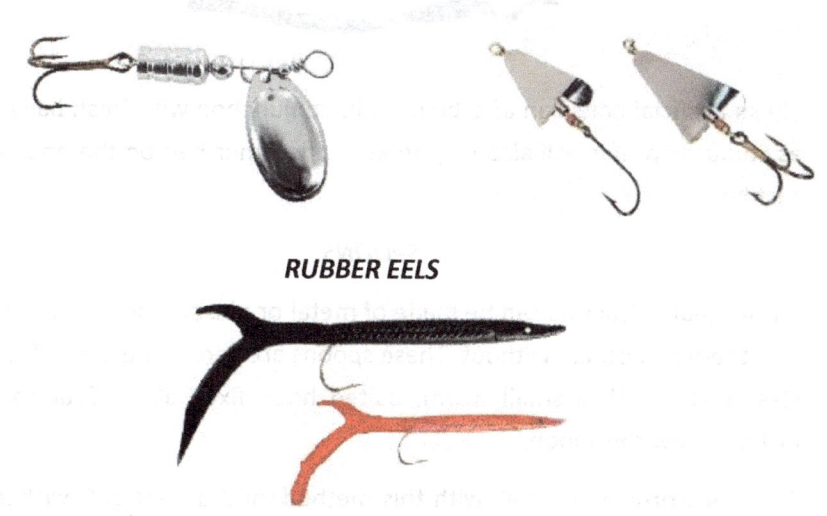

RUBBER EELS

There are many varieties of rubber eels Eddystone, Red gill and Delta, are just a few. These are used the same way as a alive or frozen Sandeel when spinning. The variation between rubber eels is normally in the tail shape and length, however, they all will catch Pollack, Mackerel and in winter Whiting. There is a mass of coloured rubber eels to choose from, black, blue, grey or red tend to work better from the shore. From the boat rubber eels can be very productive with Cod, Whiting, Mackerel, Ling and Pouting being among the fish taken from many off shore wrecks. There are numerous types of rubber eel used from the boat However one type is not better than another although different coloured eels do tend to catch better fish at different times of the tide.

RUBBER WORMS

These are purchased in resealable packs in different sizes, either Ragworm or Lugworm, placed on a hook the same way as a live worm these work well for most Flatfish. At the end of your fishing trip the Ragworm variety can be put back in the pack with the others and will retain its smell.

These artificial baits can also be used in conjunction with fresh baits, such as Squid strip, this will also help to keep the other bait on the hook when casting.

SPOONS

These small attractors can be made of metal or plastic, some with slots cut into them and others without. These spoons are very useful when fished in clear water with a small worm, baited hook fixed about four to eight inches below the spoon.

Artificial worms work well with this method, and do not get washed out like live worms can. Used for retrieving slowly over sand bars these spoons are deadly for Flatfish.

The above pictured is an attractor spoon, the cut slots in these help to cause vibrations simulating an injured fish, in doing so this alerts all the fish in the area and if the right species are around they will home in on the spoon and ultimately the baited hook trailing behind.

MUPPETS

These rubber like Squid first proved their value in wreck fishing, however, baited and used from the shore they have been known to attract and catch Cod, Pollack and occasional Bass. These are best fished on the bottom on a long flowing trace, i.e. a running ledger, these can be very effective when used in the same way as a squid and lug or Ragworm cocktail bait, just feed the Muppet up the line, bait the hook with a worm bait and the pull the Muppet back down so that the head covers the top of the bait and the legs move freely.

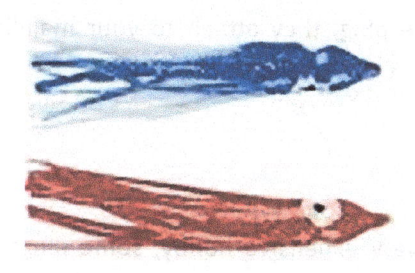

PLUGS & PLUGGING

Let me start this section by stating that this is not a plug directory, there's simply too many plugs to mention, however a few of the better known ones are over the last few pages of the book. Plug fishing can be tremendous fun and does need a bit of skill to be successful, sometimes you are aiming your plug over a narrow gully with weed down both sides, missing the mark could result in the loss of your plug, so target practice is not a bad idea!

You really do also need a light rod and reel, not just for casting purposes, but bear in mind you will be holding the rod for a considerable amount of time, this is not a method where you can put the rod down and wait for a bit you will be constantly moving from rock to rock and always casting out and reeling in your chosen plug and should you have a fish on the end it can be fairly hard work as you have to play the fish, if you just reel in at high speed, the chances are that you could loose your plug and the fish.

So you have your plugging/carp type rod and reel, it should be loaded with between 8 and 12lbs line, however many anglers do use 15lbs and believe it or not this does cut down the casting distance and in turn will cut down the amount of fish you catch, braided line however does not have this effect a 15 to 18lbs braid is around the same diameter as 8lbs mono and once you are use to casting with it, can increase your cast dramatically. If braided line is used refer to the braid knot earlier in the book. Another real money saver is to use a wire trace to attach your plug, these can be purchased at most angling stores and does help in retrieving stuck plugs, these are available in different lengths and strengths and clip direct on to the front eye of the plug, they attach to your mainline by tying to the swivel.

Plugging can be a very expensive hobby, some plugs can cost over £20 each so the best thing to do is try and cut down on losses the best you can. Plugs come in numerous designs, shapes, colours and sizes, one of the most popular and hard to get hold of is the J13 range, this is a jointed lure and comes in many colours however, the best one in the range in my opinion is pictured below.

Plugs come with many different patterns on them, some of the best ones for Bass are the ones with the patternation of the Mackerel, Sandeel or White bait, these are three of the main species ambushed by Bass and Pollack. Not only are there all these different patterns of plugs, but just when you think you have the ones that you want you start to realise that there are a whole range of jointed, floating, sinking, diving, popping, wobbling and rattling plugs as well as numerous others, these all have pride of place in the tackle box, all work well in their own way and we all end up with our favourites.

Jointed plugs tend to act more realistically when being retrieved through the water, the idea is similar to spinning, however you must take note of the action of the plug being used, you don't want to retrieve a diving plug like a bat out of hell, all you will do is get it stuck or loose it in the bottom.

Ultimately, although there are numerous plugs out there all with different actions the only thing you have to do is know your plug and work towards a varied retrieval rate, for instance if it is a floating plug with a diving spoon on the front edge, reeling in fast will make the plug dive where as slowing almost to a stop will allow the plug to rise back to the surface, another important thing to remember is that during the retrieval the tip of the rod is normally pointed towards the water and not the sky, in fact the only time you really need to raise it is when you have reeled in or have a fish on your plug, in which case you start to play the fish letting it take line via the drag system if necessary but at all times you should stay in control, keep the line tight and try to keep the fish from any visible snags such as weed etc.

Surface plugs tend to be semi buoyant meaning that they tend to stay in the top 1meter of the surface water, again you have splashers, poppers rattlers etc.

splasher plugs give off the same effect as a small feeding mackerel type fish gives when chasing sandeels to the surface, in this case a steady medium speed retrieval is best, many of these also make a subtle popping sound as they are drawn across the surface of the water, in doing so helping to attract your target fish.

The popper and splasher plugs all seem to have more or less the same body style with the abrupt angle at the front of the plug, therefore it is almost certain that should you buy a plug of this shape it will either splash, pop or do both. Rattlers can be almost any shape and style, they can be short and dumpy, long and thin and even jointed, they make a rattling sound as they are retrieved, the noise comes from a single or multiple ball bearing rolling around in the internal space of the plugs body.

As a coincidence these tend to be semi buoyant, however you can still get floating, sinking and diving versions of this plug, depending on which style you have will determined the way in which it is retrieved.

Starting and stopping the retrieve in short speedy bursts will make most of these dart downwards and then back to the surface, this will also make the plug rattle, hence the name, these work very well in calm waters, in fact the smoother the sea the better in most cases. The smaller dumpy style above tend to stay roughly in the top two meters of water and neither rise or fall to any great extent, retrieve in the same way to produce the rattle. Floating plugs do exactly what they say on the box, they float directly on the surface of the water and only during the retrieve do they go under, the faster you reel the deeper and sharper they dive, stop reeling and the plug resurfaces.

Sinking plugs however do just that, they sink as soon as they hit the water, these will continue to sink during the retrieval until they reach that natural angle between the plug and rod tip by which time they start to make their way back towards the surface, bear in mind you should continually reel when using this type of plug if you go too slow or stop they will hit bottom and stand a chance of getting snagged.

The hydro pencil plugs are more or less between the floating and sinking ones, they tend to be top water lures and work very well retrieved at medium to high speed, this does depend on just how far you manage to cast them out though, obviously if it's a short distance retrieve slower than normal.

Another plug that has to be mentioned and brings a new meaning to an old saying " throwing a wobbler" is the one shown left, this plug literally wobbles through the water giving out vibrations simulating an injured bait fish and in doing so attracting the target species you are fishing for. This type of lure can be very effective when plugging in very calm conditions where the sea is almost flat to mirror like, these dive when retrieved through the water.

Flexi heads, these are not strictly plugs but are more of a lure, these can sink fairly fast and like some of the plugs must have a constant retrieve, these can be purchased in a wide variety of colours and sizes and work extremely well for bass.

Shads again these are basically a lure and come in a variety of size weight and colour patterns, as with all the plugs mentioned previously colour can be everything when in pursuit of bass, chose the wrong colour and you are more likely to catch pollack and all though this is still sport and fun it just isn't that fine specimen of a bass.

Finally to end this section as it would be almost impossible to mention all plugs and lures made for the purpose of plugging and lure fishing, thank you to all the manufactures that continue to spend time money and effort in the pursuit of our sport.

BAIT CLIPS AND SHIELD

These are a very important part of your every day fishing tackle, there are two main types the sliding bait clip and the bait shield.

Both of these work in more or less the same way except the shield helps more when the bait hits the water as it removes most of the impact, thus helping to keep the bait in one piece.

The bait shield is fixed to the trace by first sliding a crimp, bead, bait shield and then rubber tubing on to the bottom of the main rig body, when the rig has been made and hook length set, all you need to do is to slide the rubber tubing on to the end of the shield and then place the hook under the arm, now with the rig body and hook length taught squash the crimp just above the top of the shield, when this hits the water the shield moves up to the bead, twisting the arm and pushing the hook free from the holder.

The bait clip is used more when you are using either a trace with more than one hook length or an up and over rig, this device just simply slides up the line and is held in place with a piece of rubber tubing, therefore when the bait hits the water the clip slides up the trace causing the hook length to go slack and fall off of the clip.

BAIT ELASTIC

Please note this should not be confused with shearing elastic, Bait elastic is a lot thinner and more fragile, it is a lot weaker and is easier to use when tying bait on a hook.

As Shearing elastic is stronger this will cut through the bait, should it be pulled to tight, when this happens it defeats the object as most of the bait is lost during the cast or will wash out in no time at all.

BAIT TIPS AND SHIELD

There are a variety of these, but of you, every day, fishing tackle, there are two main types, the shield type of the bait shield.

Bait shields are a means to help the bait stay in the whole fishing help from under the bait in the water as it removes most of the time. Thus helping cushion the bait in the line.

The bait shield is placed on the trace by first hold a crimp bead in place, and then held in strong onto the bottom of the main. Then simply cut the fig bat peer trace and hook though set of you need to do is to slide the rubber tubing on top of the washed and then slide the ...

...hook over the top of the body and fig it much tight ... must also on to the top of the shield, when the hook ... wears the shape ...

bushing the hook ...

The bait may be ...

more than one ...

simply slide ...

onto the un-end ...

adding bait ...

BAIT ELASTIC

Please note this should not be confused with sheering elastic. Bait elastic is a lot thinner and more fresh. It is a lot weaker and is easier to use when tying bait to a trace.

As it nearly elastic it stronger this will cut through the bait should it be pulled to tight when this happens it defeats the object as most of the bait is lost during the cast or will wash out in no time at all.

118

Fishing Marks in Detail

*C.F.S.A. Champion 96/97 Paul Hawken
with Bass of 7lb 10oz and 7lb 14oz
taken from the Newquay area.*

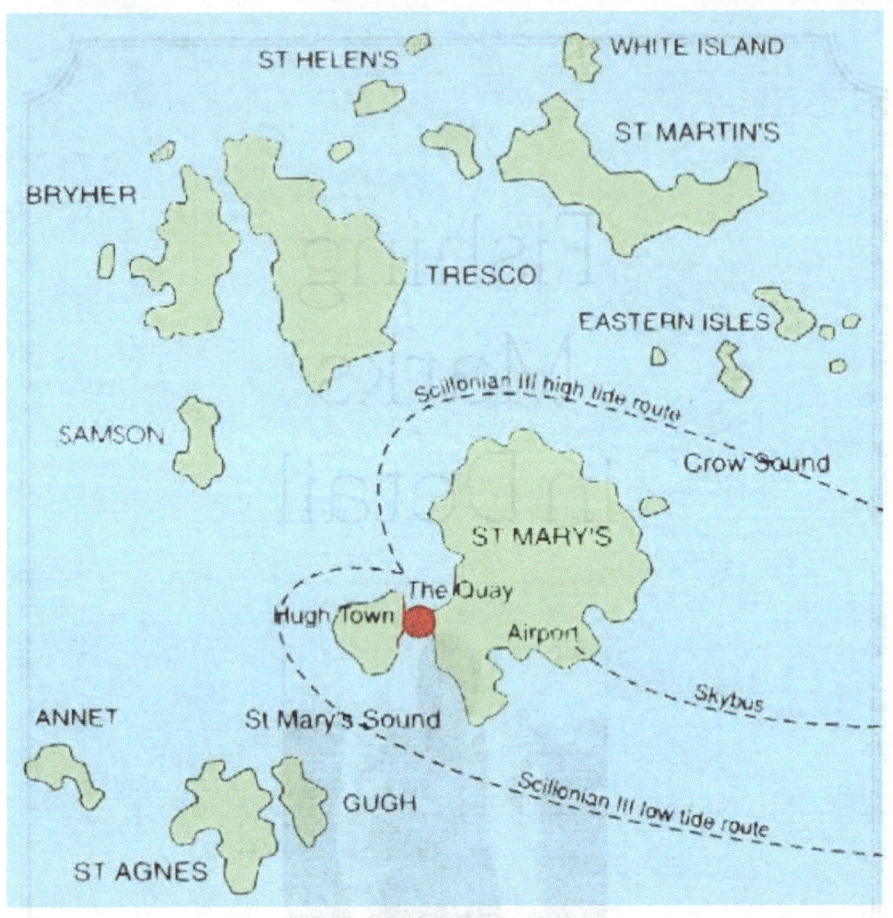

THE ISLES OF SCILLY

Although this large group of islands (145 in all) are not connected to the main land, these are in Cornish waters, therefor many of the Cornish record fish caught, are landed on the Isles of Scilly. The Isles of Scilly can be reached By air or boat to the island of St Mary's, from here boats travel to the other main islands on a regular daily basis. These islands boasts some of the best fishing in Cornish waters, with many species being taken throughout the year, however boat trips are governed by the weather during the winter months. Due to the warmer weather on and around the islands, species such as Bass , Mackerel , Garfish and Wrasse turn up earlier in the year and tend to stay longer. The island of St Mary's has many clean sandy beaches and although these are normally covered with bathers, it is still possible to find a quiet spot and cast a fishing line out in to the surf. the best time to fish these beaches is either early in the morning or late at night. As well as many beaches, there are numerous rock marks around the island, these mainly have a clean sandy bottom and most are snag free. Most of the Isles of Scilly can be fished, either from the shore or charter boat. Although the islands get a lot of calm weather it can be very dangerous to fish rock marks, unless you have fished these before, if you have not, then ask a local or hire a guide as these will almost certainly know the safer marks to fish, and where to fish in adverse weather conditions.

MAIN SUMMER SPECIES

The main summer species to be found around these islands from the boat and shore are not unlike the fish taken from around the Cornish Coast, however these are Bass, Red Bream, Black Bream, Gilthead Bream, Bass, Conger eels, Dab, Dogfish, Garfish, Red Gurnard, Grey Gurnard, Tub Gurnard, John Dory, Mackerel, Megrim, Plaice, Pollack, Turbot, Bull Huss, Smooth Hound, A Variety of Rays, Ballan and Corkwing Wrasse and Tope.

MAIN WINTER SPECIES

During the winter months the weather can get very rough around the islands, because of this the fishing can get very restricted, however the main winter species are, Cod, Whiting, Coalfish, Pollack, Shore Rockling, Three bearded Rockling, Small Ling, Dogfish and Conger eels.

BAIT

Local boatmen catch fresh Mackerel, smelts, Sandeels and Squid to be sold as bait to the angler, however baits like Scad which is a very good bait for on the boat would need to be caught by the angler. With baits, such as Lugworm, Ragworm, Crab and White Ragworm, the angler will probably need to purchase or dig/collect these before leaving the mainland as these can be in short supply and expensive on the islands.

TIPS

If you are thinking of visiting this angling paradise, make sure that you have all the tackle that you need with you. Numerous rigs and leads can be used around these islands, however apart from float tackle some of the favourite rigs are running ledgers, Pulley and paternoster rigs.

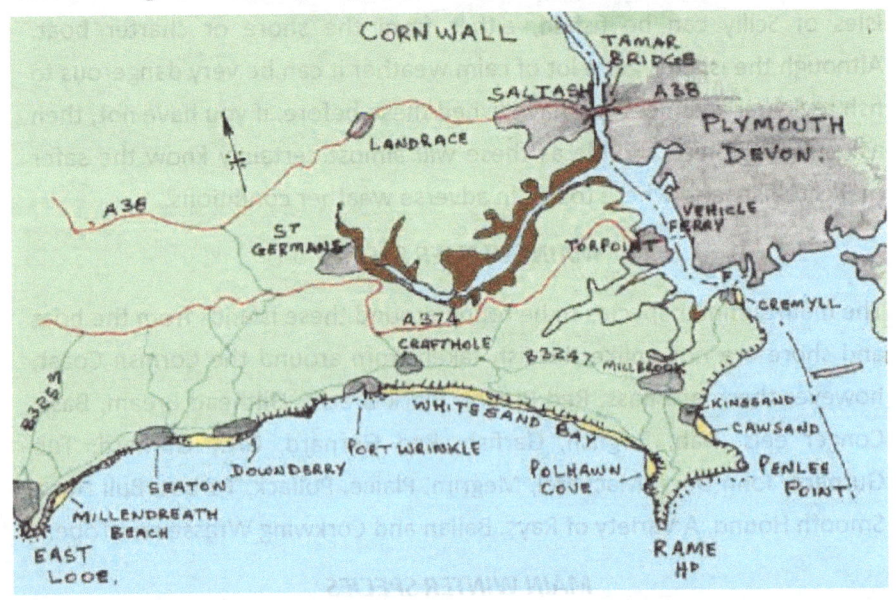

The above map takes in all the fishing marks from Cremyll to East Looe on the south coast of Cornwall, this map covers the following marks.

Only the main fishing marks have been described in detail, the others fish similarly to the marks nearest to them.

Cremyll. Cawsand. Penlee Point. Rame Head. Polhawn Cove. Whitsand Bay. Portwrinkle. Downderry. Seaton. Millendreath Beach. East Looe.

CREMYLL O.S.MAP REF.: 454534 SOUTH COAST

Cremyll is one of the most easterly beaches on Cornwall's South Coast and is situated at the end of the B3247. Turn off the A38 on to the A374 towards Torpoint Ferry, now turn down the B3247 for Millbrock and Cremyll. There is a public car park in Cremyll, approximately 200 yards from the foot ferry and beach. This beach is almost opposite Devils Point on the Devon side of the Tamar (Hamoaze) River. A cast of approximately 60 to 80 yards will reach a very deep shipping channel. Do not fish beyond the block house and red buoy as one, you will be cut off by the rising tide and two, there are very many under water snags, these can be very heavy on end tackle lose. This area can become very congested during the summer months, therefor it is best fished from October through till March, during this time, this venue is well noted for it's larger than usual sized cod and Conger Eels.

MAIN SUMMER AND WINTER SPECIES

During the summer, Dogfish , Pollack , Conger Eels and occasional Mackerel, Garfish and Bass. During the winter, Cod, Whiting, Pollack, Coalfish, Flounder, Rockling, Dogfish and Conger eels.

BAIT & TIPS

Whole or strip Mackerel and squid, live or frozen Sandeels, Ragworm, Lugworm, Smelts and Cocktails of Squid and Mackerel or Squid and Worm baits. It is best to use pulley or paternoster type rigs with plain leads at this venue, vary the hook size for different species of fish.

PENLEE POINT   O.S.MAP REF. : 443478   SOUTH COAST

This popular headland mark can be reached by walking the paths from Kingslaud or Rame villages . The sea bed at this venue is mainly rock and kelp therefore , the best fishing to be done is with float tackle. There are numerous rock gullies that come out from the headland and point towards Rame Head these can be very productive for many species of fish. In the past Penlee Point has produced numerous specimen fish .

MAIN SUMMER SPECIES :

Bass, Wrasse, Mackerel, Garfish, Scad, Mullet, Dogfish, Pollack, Rockling and Conger eel.

MAIN WINTER SPECIES

Pollack, Rockling, Whiting, Cod, Coalfish, Dogfish and Conger Eels, Care must be taken whilst fishing this mark in Winter, as winds can be very strong and the swell can be very high.

BAIT & TIPS

Sandeel live or frozen , live or frozen peeler or soft backed Crab , Mackerel whole or strip, Squid whole or strip , Ragworm , Lugworm and Cocktails of Mackerel and squid or Worm baits and squid. If bottom fishing use heavy line as this venue can be very demanding on end tackle, float or bottom fish for Wrasse using Crab or worm baits can be very productive. The use of a lead lift can be very important, as this may help to land and not lose the fish. Bass take Sandeels or Crab at this venue either fished on the bottom or float fished. Pulley , Paternoster and bomber rigs work fairly well at this venue, however it is best to fix a lead lift to these as this will aid the retrieval of gear. If you are going to be fishing for Conger Eels from this mark, make sure that you are using a heavy main line, large bait tied to a large hook, and the most important thing of all is a very heavy mono or wire trace with at least two large swivels incorporated within. It is also very handy to carry a extendable gaff with you on your trip as this can prove to be very valuable for landing larger fish.

RAME HEAD   O.S.MAP REF. : 418481   SOUTH COAST

This venue can be reached by a narrow lane running from Rame village to the coastguard lookout post , parking is possible near to this area. This headland is one of East Cornwall's premier rock marks, however, all the usual warnings apply . Go prepared for rough walking and rock scrambling, Watch out for abnormal swells, in other words be safety conscious. Deep gullies lined with kelp beds can produce excellent sport either on float or bottom fished tackle, use a main line of at least 20lb and be prepared to loose end tackle .

MAIN SUMMER SPECIES

Wrasse, Bass, Pollack, Garfish, Mackerel, Scad, Rockling, Plaice, Turbot, Dogfish and Conger eel.

MAIN WINTER SPECIES

Cod, Whiting, Rockling, Pollack, Dogfish, Conger Eels, beware of rather high swells during the Winter months.

BAIT & TIPS

Sandeels live or frozen, Mackerel, peeler or soft backed Crab, Squid, Lugworm, Ragworm, artificial plugs and lures. Mackerel, Garfish, Pollack and Wrasse are frequently caught on artificial lures. If using Mackerel feathers, beware of other anglers in the area.

POLHAWN COVE (happy valley) O.S.MAP REF. : 421494 SOUTH COAST

This mark is situated to the extreme East end of Whitsand Bay, at low tide almost 6 miles of beach is exposed, backed by high cliffs. Parking is available at the top of Wiggle cliff, just off the Southwest Coast Path and the Village of Rame, from the car park follow the Southwest coast path to this venue. Polhawn Cove and the area around consists of many low fingers of rock alternating with sand stretching out from the foot of the cliff, this mark has a reputation for large Bass in the summer and early autumn particularly after a strong Southwest storm.

MAIN SUMMER SPECIES

Bass, Mackerel, Garfish, Turbot, Plaice, Dogfish, Pollack, Wrasse, Scad and occasional Dab.

MAIN WINTER SPECIES

Whiting, Occasional Cod, Dogfish, Pollack, Rockling and Conger Eels near and around the Polhawn Cove Area.

BAIT & TIPS

Peeler Crab, Sandeels live or frozen, Mackerel, Smelts, Squid, Ragworm, Razor fish and cocktails of all these baits .A single hooked rig i.e. pulley, Paternoster, running ledger, cast as far as possible beyond the breakers will usually contact the Bass , however many fish are caught within the first 30 yards, fish from low water on the flooding tide .When fishing for flatfish, it is best to use a beaded trace with small hooks.

WHITSAND BAY   O.S.MAP REF.: 393522   SOUTH COAST

This 4 mile stretch of sand and rocky outcrops is situated between Polhawn Cove and Portwrinkle, to reach this venue follow the A374 from the roundabout at the craft centre off the A38, follow this road for approximately 5 miles and then turn to the right, on to the B3247 at Polscoe, towards Crafthole. Follow this road through the Village, until you find the signs for Freathy, drive down the old military road until reaching the car park. From here follow the Coast path and one of the numerous trails down the cliff to the beach. This area is exceptionally good for Bass, casting in to the surf or plugging around the rocky outcrops.

MAIN SUMMER SPECIES

Bass, Plaice, Turbot, dab, Grey Gurnard, Mackerel, Tub Gurnard, A Variety of Rays, Dogfish, Bull Huss and small Conger eels.

MAIN WINTER SPECIES

Fewer species are caught during the winter months, however Cod, whiting, Coalfish, Pollack, Dogfish and Small Conger Eels. Are still present.

BAIT & TIPS

All the usual bait work here, however for bass use Peeler Crab or live Sandeels. The best rigs to use are pulley , running ledger and paternoster coupled with a plain lead, vary the size hook depending on species sought.

PORTWRINKLE   O.S.MAP REF. : 355538   SOUTH COAST

The small Village of Portwrinkle is situated on the B3247 at the Western end of Whitesand Bay, parking is in the Village in a pay and display car park, from here it is a short walk to the rocks and beach. There is a wide expanse of rough ground which lies between the harbour and the beach, This area can be very hard on end tackle at high water. The harbour wall is a good casting site for the angler to put a bait out between the rocky outcrops, rock fishing is also possible at the Western end of the cove. Approximately 1 mile West of Portwrinkle is an area of rock fingers and sand , this area can be very productive in calmer weather.

MAIN SUMMER SPECIES

Bass, Wrasse, Mackerel, Garfish and Dogfish, Small Conger, Gurnard, Scad and Pollack.

MAIN WINTER SPECIES

Whiting, Dogfish, Conger Eels, Rockling and few Cod depending on the weather and tides.

BAIT & TIPS

Sandeel live or frozen peeler or soft backed Crab, Mackerel, Squid, Ragworm, Lugworm, Smelts and artificial lures. Use a main line of around 20lb as you will loose tackle if light line is used. Crab baits can be found at low water among the rocks. A good method here is to float fish with small fish baits or to spin or drift a live Sandeel in the mid water depth of between 10 and 15 feet.

DOWNDERRY O.S. MAP REF. : 315539 SOUTH COAST

This venue is situated on the B3247 to the East of Seaton, a lane runs down the East side of the hotel and on to the beach.

Parking is on a pay and display car park in the village, this beach that backs on to the road is made up from silvery sand, shingle and outcrops of rock to the Eastern and Western ends.

The rock gullies that run out to sea can be very productive during the summer months with Bass and Ballan Wrasse being the top of the list.

Do not park on the beach as the sand can be very soft at times. Picture, left, Small Ballan Wrasse taken from the South Coast of Cornwall.

MAIN SUMMER SPECIES

Bass, Ballan Wrasse, Pollack, Mackerel, Garfish, Scad, Plaice, Dogfish and Corkwing Wrasse present at the Eastern end of the beach, from the rocks.

MAIN WINTER SPECIES

Whiting, Dogfish, Pollack, Cod during or just after a winter storm, however it is best to fish from the beach during this period.

BAIT & TIPS

Sandeels live or frozen, Mackerel, Ragworm, Lugworm, Squid strip, Smelt, peeler or soft backed Crab and Worm, Squid Cocktails.

It is always worth spinning in the surf with Sandeels for Bass, Pollack, Mackerel and Garfish on the rising tide.

Wrasse fall to Worm or Crab baits. Float fish from the Eastern and Western ends of the beach with small fish or worm baits.

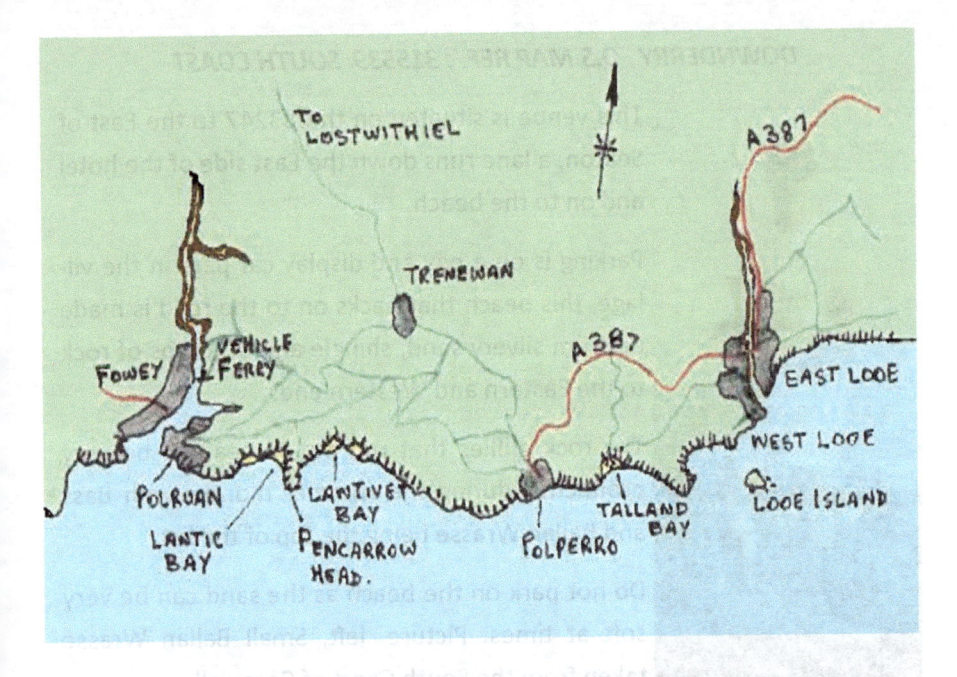

The above map covers the area from Polruan to East Looe and takes in the following marks.

- Polruan.
- Lantic Bay.
- Pencarrow Head
- Lantivet Bay.
- Polperro
- Talland Bay
- West Looe
- East Looe.

Although the above map has all the above fishing marks printed on it, not all of these have been described in detail, however the marks in question fish similar to the marks nearest to them.

POLPERRO O.S.MAP REF. : 208518 SOUTH COAST

This small harbour and village is situated approximately 5 miles Southwest of Looe and can be reached by following the A387 out of Looe, to it's end in Polperro. Due to the narrow streets in this village, summer traffic is banned, although parking is available in a large car park above the village with access via the A38 and A387. This venue has deep water and fishing is possible from both sides of the outer harbour wall. It is best to float fish for most species from here as bottom fishing requires heavier line.

MAIN SUMMER SPECIES

Wrasse, Mackerel, Garfish, Bass, Wrasse, Pollack, Scad, Rockling, Dogfish and Conger eel. Occasional Black Bream can be caught, and have been taken in the past, however these tend to show up more frequently towards the middle of the summer.

MAIN WINTER SPECIES

Whiting, Cod, Dogfish, Rockling and Conger Eels, however the occasional Pollack and Coalfish are caught.

BAIT & TIPS : Sandeel live or frozen, Mackerel strip or whole, Squid whole or strip, Ragworm, Peeler or soft backed Crab, Smelts, Lugworm and Cocktails of worm baits, Squid and Mackerel fillet or Squid and worm baits. Conger eel and Dogfish can be caught on heavy tackle using Squid and Mackerel cocktails tied, with bait elastic, around a size 6/0 to 8/0 hook. Mackerel feathers work well here, however, watch out for other anglers lines that may be bottom fishing. Wrasse can be caught on the bottom or by float fishing with Crab or Worm baits. Spinning with Mackerel Spinners, Artificial rubber eels and Plugging very deep can produce excellent sport with medium sized Pollack, Bass and larger Mackerel, care must be taken, not to go to deep, particularly with plugs as these can be very expensive and easily lost on the rough bottom. Wrasse fishing can be done from this venue, using medium sized line, however you must hold the rod whilst doing this.

PENCARROW HEAD O.S.MAP REF. : 150505 SOUTH COAST

Pencarrow Head lies between Lantivet Bay and Lantic Bay and is reached by a narrow coast road and coastal footpath from Polruan. This venue has rough ground and is considered a Wrasse hot spot by many anglers. The deep Kelp filled gullies have held many specimen sized fish in the past. The best time to fish this mark is between May and October and in the later part of the season for Bass. Fish from rock platforms and cast out, either between or beyond the gullies .

MAIN SUMMER SPECIES

Wrasse, Bass, Pollack, Mackerel, Garfish, Scad, Dogfish, Rockling, Conger eel.

MAIN WINTER SPECIES

Whiting, Cod, Rockling, Pollack, Dogfish and Conger Eel, do not turn your back on the sea during the Winter months, as the water can crash in to these gullies and sometimes cover the area where fishing is to be done.

BAIT & TIPS

Live or frozen peeler or soft backed Crab, Mackerel fillets Squid strip, Sandeel live or frozen. Crab baits fished on the bottom is a favoured method for catching Wrasse , tighten into the fish as soon as it bites.

LANTIC BAY   O.S.MAP REF. : 145508   SOUTH COAST

This bay lies to the West of Pencarrow Head and is reached via the road from Polruan and the coastal foot path . There several sandy coves and rocky outcrops , all except the largest can be cut off at high water on spring tides . A steep path leads down to the main beach which is a steeply shelved bay at the foot of the cliffs. The sea bed in this area is a sand and rock mixture , after strong storms this venue can attract weed, however, this is possibly the best time to fish .The bay is well sheltered from any winds other than Northwest, West and Southwest .

MAIN SUMMER SPECIES

Bass, Wrasse, Mackerel, Garfish, Gurnard, occasional Pollack, Rockling and Dogfish.

MAIN WINTER SPECIES

Winter species can be very far and few between at this venue, with Whiting, Rockling, Dogfish and Cod occasionally showing.

BAIT & TIPS

Sandeels live and frozen, peeler or soft backed Crab, Mackerel, Lugworm and Ragworm. Pulley or ledger rigs with 3/0 to 4/0 hooks cast into the surf work well for Bass. Float fishing with a thin strip of Mackerel, at a depth of around 6ft can be very productive for Mackerel, Pollack or Garfish. Try to avoid very high tides, these can be dangerous during Winter.

POLRUAN O.S.MAP REF. : 124510 SOUTH COAST

This small town is situated across the Estuary from Fowey and is best reached by using the ferry from Fowey Quay or by road from Lostwithiel.

Parking is in the town with a short walk back to the coast, there are many rock marks that can be reached from the town quay and along the South shore, from the coastal footpath. The sea bed varies from sand to rock and kelp in different areas.

MAIN SUMMER SPECIES

Bass, Pollack, Wrasse, Mackerel, Garfish, Scad, Plaice, Flounder, small Conger Eels and Dogfish.

MAIN WINTER SPECIES

Dogfish, Flounder, small Conger Eels, Pollack, Coalfish, Cod have shown up at this mark in the past, however numbers have greatly reduced over the years.

BAIT & TIPS

Sandeels live or frozen, Mackerel strip, peeler or soft backed Crab, Squid, Lugworm and Ragworm.

Although the sea bed looks fairly clean, there are a number of hidden underwater snags in the area.

A long distance cast from the shore into the mouth of the Estuary can be very productive for flat fish. Watch out for boats long lining close to the shore, make shore your drag is set on your reels.

The best rigs to use at this mark are Pulley, Paternoster type, running ledgers and Whiting or Mackerel traces, however a large variety of fish are taken on float tackle.

Ballan and Corkwing Wrasse are taken on float tackle baited with Peeler or soft backed Crab or bunches of harbour Ragworm, tipped with a single White Ragworm.

EAST AND WEST LOOE   O.S. MAP REF.: 252537   SOUTH COAST

Looe is situated between St Austell and Plymouth, to reach this venue turn off the A390 to the right at East Taphouse and follow the B3359 until it reaches the A387, this road will take you straight in to Looe. Parking is available in the car parks around the Village. The Village of Looe is very commercialised, therefor fishing this venue can be very difficult and restricted as the boat traffic can be very heavy. Looe is the centre of British Shark fishing, from various charter boats, Blue Sharks, Mako, Thresher and Porbeagle being the main species caught. The foreshore at East and West Looe can also Produce a large number of different species, caught from the beaches and rock marks, species listed below.

MAIN SUMMER SPECIES

Bass, Mackerel, Pollack, Garfish, Plaice, Turbot, Dab, Tub and Grey Gurnard, Rays, Rockling, Dogfish, Mullet, Ballan and Corkwing Wrasse, Conger eels and occasional Red and Black Bream.

MAIN WINTER SPECIES

Cod, Whiting, Rockling, Pollack, Coalfish, Flounder, Dogfish and Conger eels, are all possible from the shore in calmer weather conditions.

BAIT

Main baits are Ragworm, Lugworm, Peeler or soft backed Crab, Live or frozen Sandeels, Smelts, Mackerel whole or strips, Squid whole or strips, Mackerel flesh or bread for Mullet. If fishing for Flounder during the winter months, one of the best marks to fish, is just up from the road bridge in the Looe Estuary, it is best to use plain leads as these roll around with the tide and cover more ground. Use a Flounder spoon baited with harbour Ragworm, retrieving it slowly, as an alternative to a baited rig. The East Looe Quay and all around the harbour can be very productive, however fishing can be very restricted as this harbour can be very busy. The foreshore around Looe can be very good for winter species, however anglers must keep an eye on the weather and the sea as this can rise quite quickly.

The above map shows a the area from Golant to Dodman on the South Coast of Cornwall and incorporates the main roads, beaches and following marks,

- Golant.
- Fowey.
- Gribben Head.
- Polkerris.
- Carlyon Bay.
- Charlestown.
- Black Head.
- Pentewan.
- Mevagissy.
- Chapel Point.
- Gorran Haven.

GOLANT O.S.MAP REF.: 123547 SOUTH COAST

Golant lies on the Fowey Estuary approximately 4 miles from Fowey. To find this mark follow the A3082 and B3269 from Fowey to the cross roads at Castledore, turn right here and follow the narrow road down to Golant, parking is available on the left hand side of the road, from the toilet block to the railway crossing. From here either walk down the slip way and turn left up to the top of the old boat house and fish from here or follow the path down the side of the railway line and fish from the foreshore. Golant is one of the areas that digging your own bait and gathering Peeler crabs is permitted, however this must be done away from the end of the slipway and boat moorings, signs are visible stating that any person or persons caught digging around the above areas will be prosecuted and fined. Fishing in this area of the estuary is limited to the tide, at low water there is very little or no water at this mark.

MAIN SUMMER SPECIES

There are very few species to be caught at this venue, however Bass can be taken here in large numbers.

MAIN WINTER SPECIES

Fishing from the old boat house and slightly down stream can be very productive for Flounder during the winter.

BAIT & TIPS: Sandeels, live or frozen, Lug and Ragworm, Peeler or soft backed Crab, Mackerel strip and Smelts during the summer months and Ragworm, Lugworm during the winter. If fishing from the boat house it is better to use a grip lead as there are numerous mooring rope's and chains, using a grip lead should stop the lead drifting up or down stream and getting entangled with these. The best time to fish this venue is on a neap tide as there is not as much water movement. As most baits can be dug or gathered in this area it is best to use these for your fishing trip.

FOWEY   O.S.MAP REF. : 118511   SOUTH COAST

The river Fowey is situated approximately 8 miles East of St Austell and offers a wide range of species, caught from rock marks, little harbour walls and town quay areas. There are many car parks in and around the town of Fowey. Most fishing is done at the mouth of the river at St Catherine's Castle. Readymoney beach is enclosed with rocks on both sides, at low tide walk along the right hand side to gain access to the river mouth, however the climb back up to the castle at high tide can be difficult.

Fowey Estuary

MAIN SUMMER SPECIES

Plaice, Mackerel, Garfish, Pollack, Ballan and Corkwing Wrasse, Scad, Dogfish, small Conger Eels, Bass can be taken on float tackle.

MAIN WINTER SPECIES

Whiting, Codling, Pollack, Flounder, Dogfish and small Conger Eels, during the Winter months Dogfish can be a nuisance, taking all kinds of baits.

BAIT & TIPS

Lugworm, Ragworm, Peeler or soft backed Crab, Mackerel strip, live or frozen Sandeel, Peeler or soft backed Crab. Watch the tide run whilst fishing Readymoney as it can come up rather quickly. Most of the fishing to be done from this mark, can be done with float tackle, this account for most of the summer species. Although bottom fishing can be done from most of the rock marks in this area, beware of any under water snags.

GRIBBEN HEAD   O.S. MAP REF. : 095499   SOUTH COAST

This mark is situated approximately 6 miles to the East of St Austell, parking is on a field at the top of a private road that leads to Gribben Head, Pay for parking in the box at the side of the farmhouse. Follow the track down to the sea and then join the coastal footpath out to the red and white beacon on the top of Gribben Head, from here numerous paths lead down to the waters edge . The walk out to this Headland can be very long and quite difficult if rushed. Care must be taken on most of these paths as they are very steep in places.

MAIN SUMMER SPECIES

Wrasse, Bass, Mackerel, Garfish, Pollack, Scad, Dogfish, Plaice, Conger eel and Rockling.

MAIN WINTER SPECIES

Whiting, Codling, Coalfish, Flounder, Dogfish, Pollack, Rockling and Conger Eel. The main winter species caught from this headland are taken from the front, off the rock marks.

BAIT & TIPS: Whole or strip mackerel, live or frozen Sandeels, Squid whole or strip, Ragworm, Lugworm, peeler or soft backed Crab, Smelts, Cocktails of Mackerel and Squid or Squid and Rag or Lugworm. Bottom fishing for Wrasse can produce fish in excess of 4lb. When bottom fishing around this mark, use lead lifts and plain leads as the bottom can be very snaggy. When fishing for flatfish it is best to be on the left hand side of the headland, casting towards Par Docks will produce Plaice, Turbot and Dab during summer and Flounder through the winter months. Float fishing account for most catches of Bass, Wrasse, Mackerel, Scad and Garfish during the summer months. If fishing for Wrasse from this mark, it is best to use a rotten bottom rig as it is better to lose the weight, (old spark plug) than lose the fish. Whilst fishing this venue the angler must keep an eye on the sea and never turn his or her back on it as the swell can be very high around this mark.

POLKERIS O.S.MAP REF. : 092522 SOUTH COAST

This harbour and beach is situated approximately five miles East of St Austell. Parking is about five minutes walk from the beach. Fishing from the harbour wall is mainly done using float tackle, however, ledgering is also possible. To gain access to this mark, follow the A3082 from Par, towards Fowey. About 1.5 miles outside Par turn to the right and follow the sign posts for Polkerris, park in the large car park provided.

MAIN SUMMER SPECIES

Mackerel, Garfish, Scad, Plaice, Pollack, Bass, occasional Turbot and Dab, Dogfish, Small Conger Eels, Mullet and Wrasse to specimen size.

MAIN WINTER SPECIES

Whiting, Codling, Coalfish, Flounder, Pollack Dogfish and small Conger eels, mainly from the area looking towards Par Docks.

BAIT & TIPS

Sandeel live or frozen, Mackerel strip, Lugworm, Ragworm, Peeler or soft backed Crab, bread or Mackerel flesh for Mullet, Smelt, Squid whole or strip, Cocktails of Squid and Rag or Lugworm.

Best fished on evening tides or late afternoon till dusk. Fishing with a float or lure account for large catches of Mackerel, use ledgered Crab or Worm baits for Wrasse. Bass can be taken with live Sandeels either float fished or drifted in the tide. Mullet are mainly caught, using very light tackle, the ideal type being a Carp rod with up to a 2.5lb test curve, a coarse fishing fixed spool or spinning reel, with a main line of between 6 and 8lbs, the hooks used are also coarse type, and about size 8 are used. If and when you catch a Mullet, you must be very careful not to pull the hook through it's lip, as these are very soft, this fish needs to be played until tired, then the fish can be landed with ease.

Fishing from the rocks is possible at this venue and all the species can be taken from here.

CARLYON BAY   O.S. MAP REF. : 05622   SOUTH COAST

This is the main beach in the St Austell bay area and is approximately 1.5 miles long and fairly steep in most places. The sea bed is inundated with sand bars with deep gullies running between them. Parking is on a pay and display car park at the top of the beach. Most fishing is mainly done after 530pm or very early in the mornings during a flooding tide, as the tide rises it is possible to float fish on calm days. Carlyon Bay, with Fishing Point to the far left and Crinnis to the right

MAIN SUMMER SPECIES

Mackerel, Garfish, Scad, Bass, Flounder, Plaice, Pollack and Dogfish. Wrasse are possible from either ends of the beach from the rock marks, mainly on or around low water.

MAIN WINTER SPECIES

Whiting, Coalfish, Pollack, Codling and dogfish, are taken from all along the beach, however the rock towards the right hand side can be very productive during the winter months, if fishing in this area, use heavier line as the bottom can be very snaggy.

BAIT & TIPS

Lugworm, Ragworm, Mackerel, Sandeels live or frozen, Smelts and Squid strip. Ledgered baits between 50 and 80 yards tend to reach the fish, however, Bass will take baits cast almost in to the edge of the water, as Sandeel and Smelt are common on this beach, this is one of the best baits to use. It is possible to float fish from this beach, as it is very deeply shelved.

CHARLESTOWN HARBOUR O.S.MAP REF. : 039518 SOUTH COAST

This harbour is situated 2 miles East of St Austell and is home to many square rigged sailing ships and maritime museum. Parking is on a pay and display car park about two minutes walk from the harbour.

Float fishing is one of the main methods used at this venue, however, ledgered baits work well on a rising tide. Fishing is possible from both inner end outer breakwater. The outside of this harbour can completely dry up on low tides, therefore, fishing is restricted to rise or fall of the tide

MAIN SUMMER SPECIES

Mackerel, Garfish, Pollack, Scad, Mullet, Plaice, Dogfish, Flounder and Bass.

MAIN WINTER SPECIES

Whiting, Occasional Codling and Coalfish, Flounder and Dogfish.

BAIT

Mackerel strip, Lugworm, Ragworm, Sandeel live or frozen, Squid and Peeler or soft backed Crab.

TIPS

The majority of the time there is no water surrounding the harbour at low tide, therefore, it is best fished from half tide up to 2 hours of the ebb tide. Best catches taken early mornings or late evenings. Most of the fishing at this venue is done with float tackle, however, flatfish , Dogfish and Bass are taken on the bottom. This venue can get very crowded during the summer months, therefore it is best to arrive early if fishing this mark.

BLACK HEAD   O.S.MAP REF.: 040480   SOUTH COAST

This venue lies between St Austell and Mevagissy, from the St Austell ring road, turn off towards Penrice Hospital and Porthpean, follow this road through to Lobbs Shop cross roads, here turn left towards Trenarren and park in the car park provided, from here follow the coast path for approximately 3/4 of a mile to Black Head. This venue can be very popular with local anglers and tends to get a bit crowded during the summer months. Most of this mark is surrounded by deep water and a cast of around 30 + yards will find a clean sandy,(in most cases), bottom. To the right hand side of the Headland is a large flat platform of rock, this can only be reached at low water and you must be prepared to stay until after the high tide when the water level recedes enough to get off.

MAIN SUMMER AND WINTER SPECIES

During the summer, Mackerel, Garfish, Bass, Scad, Dogfish, Bull Huss, Pollack, Plaice, Dab, Conger Eel, Ballan and Corkwing Wrasse. During the winter, Cod, Whiting, Pollack, Coalfish, Dogfish and Conger Eels.

BAIT & TIPS

Mackerel whole or strips, Squid whole or strips, Sandeels live or frozen, Peeler or soft backed Crab, Smelt, Rag and Lugworm and Cocktails of Squid and either Mackerel or worm. Float fishing with either a thin strip of Mackerel or a Sandeel live or frozen at about 12 feet deep will catch Mackerel, Garfish, Scad and Pollack, the same method, but changing the bait for Worm or Crab will catch Ballan and Corkwing Wrasse. Main bottom rigs are Pulley, Single or twin Paternoster and Running ledgers.

PENTEWAN SANDS   O.S.MAP REF. : 015473   SOUTH COAST

This long sandy beach is situated between St Austell and Mevagissy, parking is available in Pentewan Village or in the camp site car park. Fishing is possible all along this beach ,however, most anglers prefer to fish this venue later in the evening on a flood tide. The best areas on this beach to fish are at either end from off the beach or on the rocks.

MAIN SUMMER SPECIES

Mackerel, Garfish, Bass, Plaice, Flounder and Dogfish.

MAIN WINTER SPECIES

Whiting, Dogfish and occasional Flounder and Codling.

BAIT & TIPS

Lugworm, Ragworm, Peeler or soft back Crab, Mackerel strip, Sandeels live or frozen, Squid strip.

It is best to ledger Bass baits 50 to 60 yards from the shore in to a rolling surf.

A running ledger is probably the best rig to use at this venue with a 4oz to 5oz grip lead, this rig can be used for Bass or flat fish. Bass are mainly caught when the water is choppy and not calm.

MEVAGISSEY HARBOUR   O.S.MAP REF. : 018448   SOUTH COAST

Situated approximately 5 miles Southwest of St Austell, this is a fully working harbour. Many car parks are situated throughout the village, these are mainly pay and display. The outer wall of the breakwater is very popular with holiday makers, However, fishing from the shorter, left hand breakwater can still be as productive. This can be fished throughout the tide although tackle can be lost at low water.

MAIN SUMMER SPECIES

Mackerel, Garfish, Wrasse, Pollack, Mullet, Plaice, Scad, Dogfish and Conger eel. Occasional Bass are also possible from both the walls

MAIN WINTER SPECIES

Whiting, Pollack, Coalfish, Codling, Rockling, Dogfish and conger Eels. Occasional Flounder are also possible from the mouth of the harbour.

BAIT & TIPS

Sandeel live or frozen, Mackerel, Squid, Lugworm, Ragworm, Peeler or soft back Crab and Mackerel flesh. Float fished baits account for most of the fish caught, however, ledgered worm or crab baits take Plaice and Wrasse some of specimen size. To avoid the main holiday traffic this venue is best fished early morning or late at night.

CHAPEL POINT   O.S. MAP REF.: 029433   SOUTH COAST

This mark is situated between Mevagissy and Gorran haven, to reach this mark follow the road out of Mevagissy towards Portmellon, this is only about 1.5 miles out of Mevagissy. Follow the road through the Village of Portmellon and part way up the hill, now turn to the left on to a narrow road, parking may be possible up this road, however if you cannot park here then you will have to park in the Village, on the pay and display. This mark has a very good reputation for larger than average Ballan Wrasse as well as other species.

MAIN SUMMER SPECIES

Ballan and Corkwing Wrasse, Bass, Dogfish, Mackerel, Scad, Pollack, Pouting, Garfish and Rockling.

MAIN WINTER SPECIES

Cod, Whiting, Pollack, Rockling, Coalfish, Dogfish and small Conger Eels can all be taken during the winter months.

BAIT & TIPS

Peeler or soft backed Crab, Live or frozen Sandeels, Mackerel strip, Squid strip, Ragworm, Lugworm and Cocktails of Squid and mackerel or squid and worm baits. It is best to fish this mark from low water up to high tide if possible, retreat up the rocks as the tide rises. This area is made up from rock gullies, many filled with kelp, use plain leads and pulley type rigs if bottom fishing.

GORRAN HAVEN   O.S.MAP REF. : 01241   SOUTH COAST

This Village and harbour is approximately 7 miles Southwest of St Austell, and is very popular with local anglers, fishing from the rock marks to the right of the harbour during the summer months. A car park is situated within the village and is sign posted. The footpath is well worn and can be located to the side of the chip shop, the walk is approximately ten to fifteen minutes across fields, Although this is a relatively short walk, it can be quite hard on older people as this walk entails going up and down fairly steep hills. The rock marks out to the front of Gorran Haven, towards Vault Beach, fishing over the under water reef, can produce excellent Bass, Mackerel, Pollack and Garfish. Both rock and harbour marks can produce a lot of fish.

MAIN SUMMER SPECIES

Plaice, Ballan Wrasse, Mackerel, Garfish, Turbot, Bass, Pollack, Gurnard (red and tub),Scad to specimen size, Corkwing Wrasse and Dogfish.

MAIN WINTER SPECIES

Whiting, Codling, Rockling, Dogfish, Pollack and occasional Coalfish can all be taken from the rock marks at the front of this venue during the summer months.

BAIT & TIPS

Sandeel live or frozen, Mackerel strip, Squid strip, Lugworm, Ragworm, Peeler or soft backed Crab and Smelts. Best fishing is possible on the flood of the tide and up to 2 hours of the ebb, Although during the summer months Mackerel and Garfish are available from the rocks at all states of the tide. This mark can be very popular with local and visiting anglers, it is best to look from the beach towards the rocks before the walk out to the point. To the left hand side of the beach is a large rock, beyond this is a small cove, this can be very productive for flatfish and bass, best fished at low water. Keep an eye on the rising tide as you can get cut off very easily in this small cove.

VAULT BEACH   O.S. MAP REF.: 012408   SOUTH COAST

This beach is situated to the right hand side of Gorran Haven, This mark can be reached by either following the coast path from Gorran haven or by Turning to the right just before reaching the car park in Gorran and following the road up the hill, this road is very narrow in plaices so care must be taken whilst driving up here, at the top of the hill turn left in to the car park, there is a donation box here, and you are expected to pay for parking. From the car park follow the path and track down to the beach, The best location for fishing at this mark, for surf casting is around the centre of the beach, from the path you can see the clear patches of sand and rocky outcrops. To either end of this beach are large rocky outcrops, the one on the left hand side is an excellent mark for plugging for Bass.

MAIN SUMMER SPECIES

Bass, Wrasse, Pollack, Mackerel, Garfish, Rockling, Scad, Dogfish, Conger eels and occasional Bull Huss.

MAIN WINTER SPECIES

Most of the winter species caught from this area are taken from the rocks to the left hand side of the beach, these are Whiting, Codling, Pollack, Coalfish, Rockling, Dogfish and Conger eels.

BAIT & TIPS: Live or frozen Sandeels, Peeler or soft backed Crab, Mackerel whole or strip, Squid whole or strip, Lugworm, Ragworm, Smelts, Cocktails of Squid and Mackerel or squid and worm baits. If fishing from the beach, use pulley, running ledger or paternoster rigs with a plain lead. Bottom fishing from the rocks can be very hard on end tackle, therefor it is best to use a lead lift. Float fishing from the rocks can produce large Mackerel, Bass and average size Garfish, the float should be set to a depth of about 8 feet. These rocks are an ideal plaice to plug for Bass, numerous fish can be caught in a single session, with the occasional large fish being caught. Bass plugs come in various shapes, colours and sizes, one of the best ones are the J 13.

DODMAN POINT   O.S.MAP REF. : 999403   SOUTH COAST

This superb headland is approximately 7 miles Southwest of St Austell and is part of the National Trust , car parking is on a gravelled area with a donation box.

The walk out to the headland is along a well worn track and fishing spots are easy to find with pathways leading right down to the waters edge , the walk out is fairly easy and has superb coastal views, however the climb down to the waters edge can be difficult, particularly after dark.

MAIN SUMMER SPECIES

Mackerel, Garfish, Pollack, Bass, Scad, Pouting, Gurnard, Ballan Wrasse, Dogfish, Bull Huss and Conger eel.

MAIN WINTER SPECIES

Coalfish, Codling, Whiting, Rockling, Pollack, Dogfish and Conger Eels are the main fish caught during the winter.

BAIT & TIPS

Live or frozen Sandeel, Mackerel, Ragworm, Squid, Peeler or soft backed Crab. Bottom fishing is possible But you will loose end tackle. Spinning with plugs or lures will produce a lot of good fish. Best fished on the flooding tide and in calmer conditions the first 2 hours of the ebb.

Float fishing from the front edge of Dodman Point can produce larger specimens of Mackerel, Garfish, Scad, Pollack and occasional Bass. Fishing for Ballan and Corkwing Wrasse can be an experience at this mark, the best way of doing this is to bait, float tackle with a bunch of harbour Ragworm or Peeler crab and set the bottom at about 17 feet, cast this around 10 to 15 feet from the shore and let it drift round the rocks, when contact is made with the fish, do not let the line get any slack in it, as the fish will find a hole or crevice and lodge it's self in it, if this happens it may result in the lose of end tackle, so do not let this happen. If a fish lodges itself the best thing to do is play the waiting game.

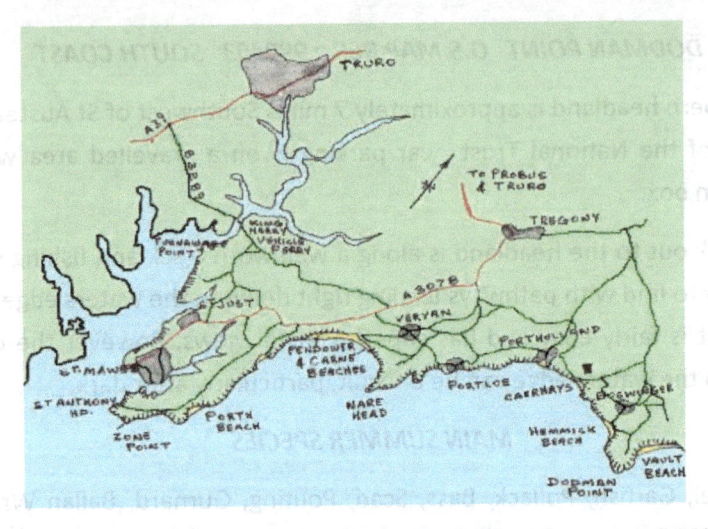

This map covers the ground from Vault Beach to Turnaware Point and takes in the following marks. Although all the marks listed on this page are not described in detail, these all can be fished, and get the same type of results as the marks, nearest to them.

- Vault Beach.   Dodman Point.
- Hemmick Beach.
- Caerhays Beach.
- Portloe.
- Nare Head.
- Carne Beach
- Pendower Beach.
- Porth Beach.
- Zone Point.
- St Anthony's Head.
- St Maws.
- Turnaware Point.

150

CAERHAYS BEACH   O.S. MAP REF. : 974413   SOUTH COAST

Caerhays has a small sandy beach and is approximately ten miles South West of St Austell . To reach this venue follow the A390 out of St Austell towards Probus for approximately 4.5 miles and then turn left down the B3287 towards Tregony for about 2 miles, now turn to the left and follow the signs for Portholland and Caerhays. A castle and gardens behind can be found here, this is privately owned and is not open to the public. The car park is right on the top of the beach where it can be observed whilst fishing this mark. This beach is popular with sun bathers therefore, best fishing can be done in the evenings, on a flooding tide.

MAIN SUMMER SPECIES

Bass, Plaice, Dogfish although Mackerel can be taken here on high spring tides.

MAIN WINTER SPECIES

Whiting, Coalfish, Codling and Dogfish, however these fish are mainly present after a bad winter storm.

BAIT & TIPS: Lugworm, Ragworm, Peeler or soft backed Crab, Sandeel live or frozen. Most fish are caught in twilight, anchor lamps etc. are not recommended at this venue as casting a shadow or light over the water will scare Bass and any other fish away. Best fishing is when there is a small to moderate surf running between one and three feet high. If using Live Sandeels from this mark, larger Bass seem to prefer larger live eels from this beach. Peeler and soft backed Crab can be very productive in this area if the fishing is slow use soft backed Crabs whole with the legs still attached, this looks more natural and will produce better fish. You will need to tie most baits to the hook at this mark, particularly Crab, as this can break up during the cast. The best rigs to use from this beach are running ledger and pulley rigs with a long hook length, use between a size 3/0 and 6/0 Aberdeen type hook, and bait clips. A plain lead works well here as does the dumpy lead.

NARE HEAD   O.S.MAP REF. : 921381   SOUTH COAST

Situated 18 miles from St Austell this is one of the best marks for local anglers . From the car park there are numerous marks to fish , the easiest to reach is Kiberack Cove , fishing from rocks at the waters edge ledgering with worm baits is one preferred method . A walk of about 30 minutes takes you to the front edge , where casting towards the island will produce fish .

MAIN SUMMER SPECIES

Plaice, Turbot, Wrasse, Ray, Pollack, Mackerel, Garfish, Dogfish, Rockling, Gurnard, Conger eel and Bull Huss.

MAIN WINTER SPECIES

Whiting, Codling, Coalfish, Rockling, Pollack, Dogfish and Conger Eels.

BAIT & TIPS

Ragworm, Lugworm, Sandeel live or frozen, Mackerel, Squid, Peeler or soft backed Crab.

These marks are best fished in a West , North or Northeast wind as the lay of the land gives complete shelter. Kiberack Cove is best fished 2 hours after low water until 2 hours after high water. The headland produces fish throughout the tide. Float fishing can account for numerous catches, however fishing on the bottom can produce better and larger fish.

The above map covers the ground from Trefusis Point to Porthoustock and takes in the following marks. Although all the marks mentioned on the map, are not described in great detail, most of these can be fished, however care must be taken.

- Trefusis Point.
- Pendennis Point.
- Swanpool Beach.
- Rosemullion Head.
- Helford River.
- St Antony.
- Nare Point.
- Porthallow.
- Porthoustock.

FALMOUTH ESTUARY   O.S. MAP REF.: 810324   SOUTH COAST

Falmouth Estuary covers a lot of ground so the above reference is given for the town, there are many car parks in this area. The points at Trefusis and pennarrow offer good sport with Rays, Dogfish, Bull huss and occasional Bass, to reach these marks follow the A39 from Truro for approximately 8 miles towards Penryn, and then turn to the left towards Carclew and Mylor, From here follow the signs for Flushing. When reaching Flushing you will need to follow the side of the river up to the end of the road, parking is permitted along here, however these marks can be very popular and the road can be quite full of parked cars. there is not much room to park at these fishing marks . From here follow the coast path through the style, the paths down to the waters edge can be clearly seen. The rock marks at Trefusis and Pennarrow are large areas of almost flat rock. The walk out to these points is quite easy along the coast for about 1.5 miles. The point at Pendennis can be good for Wrasse, Mackerel, Garfish and Scad.

MAIN SUMMER SPECIES

Wrasse, Dogfish, Mackerel, Bull huss, Pollack, Scad, Rockling, Thornbacked Ray, small Conger Eels, Garfish and Bass.

MAIN WINTER SPECIES: Whiting, Cod, Pollack, Rockling, Codling, Coalfish, Dogfish and small Conger.

BAIT & TIPS: Mackerel, Sandeels live or frozen, Peeler or soft backed Crab, Lugworm and Ragworm. It is better to fish the seaward side of Falmouth's Estuary as it is easier to park and not as far to walk, the fishing of Pendennis point should be left to the more experienced angler. The points at Trefusis and pennarrow are easy to fish, however, parking is restricted .Most rigs can be used at these venues, with running ledgers, Pulley and Paternoster rigs being among the favourite. Vary the size of the hook, depending on the species sought, if Ray fishing it is best to use a size 2/0 to 3/0. Plain or grip leads can be used in the Estuary, however plain leads cover more ground.

HELFORD RIVER   O.S.MAP REF. : 760263   SOUTH COAST

Situated about 8 miles Southwest of Falmouth, the Helford River Estuary offers the chance of catching a variety of fish. Parking is in the pay and display car park in Helford or in many of the lanes leading to the river, however, be sure not to block the roads as it must be left open for emergency vehicles or farm traffic. Follow the Southwest coastal path as many fishing marks can be seen and reached from here .

MAIN SUMMER SPECIES

Plaice, Turbot, Flounder, Mackerel, Garfish, Dogfish, Wrasse, Thornback Ray Bull Huss, Conger eels and occasional Bass.

MAIN WINTER SPECIES

Flounder, Pollack, Cod, Coalfish, Dogfish, Conger Eel, Rockling and Whiting. Larger cod may be taken from the mouth of the river after a strong winter storm.

BAIT & TIPS

Mackerel , Peeler or soft back Crab, Ragworm, Lugworm, Sandeels live or frozen .

Use mainly running ledger rigs with up to size 3/0 hooks, if fishing for Rays do not strike on the first knock as Rays tend to sit on the bait, when line starts to be taken from your reel , this is the time to strike. The Helford river covers a large amount of ground that can be fished using different methods, for different species of fish, float fishing can be very productive for Mackerel and garfish with the occasional Bass taking live Sandeels. Fishing for Wrasse with medium tackle can produce a lot of sport, even with the smaller Corkwing, it is best to hold the rod when fishing for any species of Wrasse. Conger fishing can get quite busy as many smaller, and the occasional larger Eel is taken from the shores of the Helford, these tend to take Squid and Mackerel Cocktails fished on the bottom, use large boat type hooks, this will improve the results.

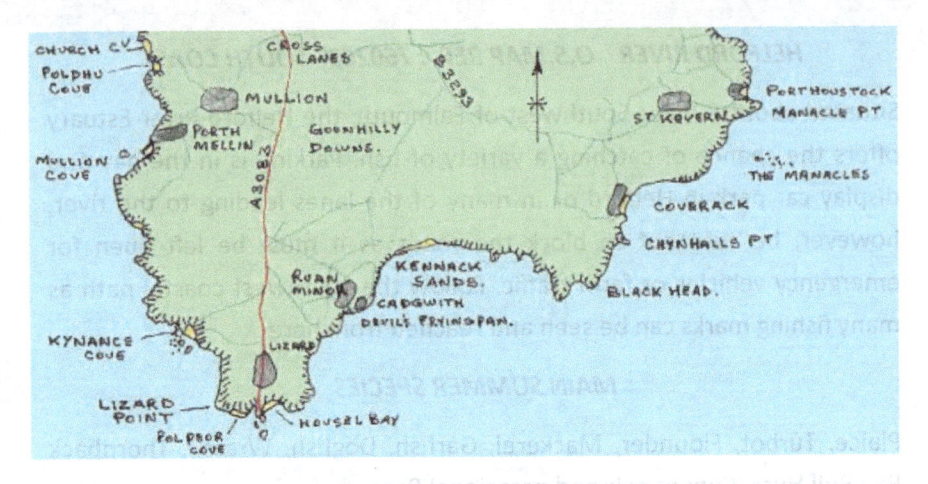

The above map covers the ground from Porthoustock to Church Cove.

- Porthoustock.   Manacle Point.
- Coverack.   Chynhalls Point.
- Black Head (Lizard).
- Kennack Sands.
- Cadgwith.
- Housel Bay.
- Polpeor Cove.
- Lizard Point.
- Kynance Cove.
- Mullion Cove.
- Poldhu Cove.
- Church Cove

The Lizard Peninsula is one of the roughest pieces of coastline throughout Cornwall, even in clear weather this area can be very dangerous. Although some of the marks on this map are sheltered from storms, you must still take care, this area is best avoided during winter storms.

PORTHOUSTOCK   O.S.MAP REF. : 807218   SOUTH COAST

This sand and shale beach is situated about 2.5 miles Northeast of St Keverne off the B3293, parking is on a pay and display car park at the top of the beach. To reach this venue follow the A3083 out of Helston for approximately 2 miles and the turn right and follow the signs for St Keverne for about 8.5 miles, drive through the Village and follow the signs for Porthoustock. Although rock fishing is possible the sea bed can be very snaggy, so rock fishing should be restricted to using float tackle. Casting from the beach can be very productive especially after dark, if rock fishing after dark it will often pay dividends to cast in towards the beach.

MAIN SUMMER SPECIES

Bass, mackerel, Garfish, Pollack, Wrasse, Dogfish, Scad, small Conger eels, Plaice and Turbot are among the main summer species.

MAIN WINTER SPECIES

The main winter species are Whiting, Codling, Rockling, Pollack, Coalfish, Cod, Conger Eels and Dogfish, these are mainly taken from the old wall to the right hand side of the beach.

BAIT & TIPS: Sandeels live or frozen, Mackerel strip or whole, Squid whole or strip, small peeler or soft back Crab, Lugworm and Ragworm, live Smelt if possible, Cocktails of Squid and worm baits or Mackerel fillet and whole small squid. Grip leads may be needed at this mark as the current on the rising tide can get very strong. It is possible to fish from the rocks using worm or crab baits, however, it is best to use rotten bottom rig as tackle lost can be high at this venue. To the right hand side of the beach is an old key, although this is quite high above the water it is possible to fish from here and from the rocks out to the end, the water in this area is fairly deep. The best rigs to use at this venue are Running ledger, Paternoster, Bomber or Pulley rigs, vary the hook size, depending on the species sought, for larger fish use a Pennel hook system, this will help to hook the fish.

KYNANCE COVE   O.S.MAP REF., : 685133   SOUTH COAST

This cove is situated about 2.5 miles Northwest of the village of Lizard, turn right off the A3083 just before the village and park in the cliff top car park ,from here follow the steep path down the cliff to the rock platforms. Fishing in this area is limited to good weather. The sea bed in this area is rough ground made up from kelp and rock, therefore expect tackle losses can be higher than average .

MAIN SUMMER SPECIES

Pollack, Bass, Ballan and Corkwing Wrasse, Dogfish, Conger eel, Mackerel, Garfish and skate.

MAIN WINTER SPECIES

This venue can be very productive for Cod and Whiting after a storm, when the swell has dropped enough to fish from this mark safely. Rockling, Dogfish, Pollack, Coalfish and occasional Conger Eels are also possible.

BAIT & TIPS: Mackerel strip or whole, Squid, Sandeels live or frozen, Peeler or soft backed Crab, Fresh Scad, Ragworm. Spinning with Sandeels ,live or frozen, work well here for Pollack and Bass. Float fish for Wrasse with Crab or worm baits. A number of plugs and lures work very well at this venue. Always keep an eye on the sea when fishing this mark as it can be dangerous if the swell rises, it is recommended that this mark is not fished in bad weather.

MULLION COVE   O.S.MAP REF. : 667178   SOUTH COAST

This small harbour lies on the West coast of the Lizard Peninsula, to get to this mark, turn off the A3083 on to the B3296 and follow the road down to the car park between Mullion and Mullion Cove. From here it is a short walk to the harbour, Please use the car park as the parking anywhere else in Mullion is very restricted.

MAIN SUMMER SPECIES

Mackerel, Garfish, Bass, Pollack, Wrasse, Mullet, Dogfish and Conger eel.

MAIN WINTER SPECIES

This venue, as with most venues around the Lizard Peninsula, can produce large numbers of Cod and Whiting during the winter months, Cod can be up to around 7lbs with larger fish showing occasionally.

BAIT & TIPS

Mackerel strip, Squid, Sandeels live or frozen, Peeler or soft backed Crab. Ground bait for Mullet using bread and Mackerel mashed together and use light tackle with around size 6 hooks. Fish the kelp filled gullies for Wrasse, using running ledgers and Crab baits on size 3/0 hooks.

Float fish for Mackerel, Bass, Garfish and Pollack. Use up to a size 6/0 hook and a long flowing trace for Cod during the winter months.

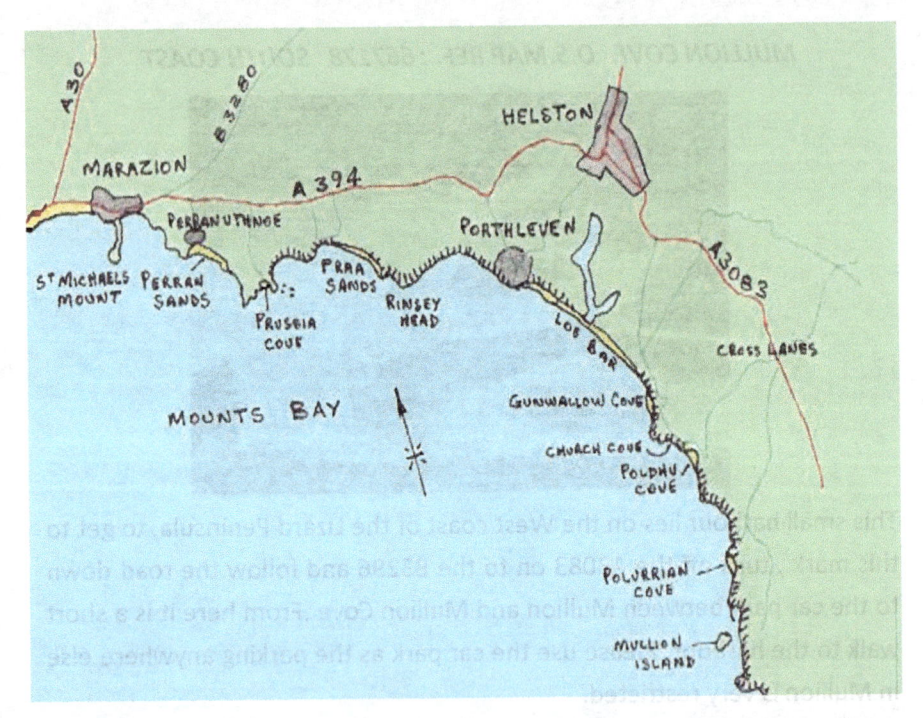

Not all of the marks on this map are described in detail, however these fish similar to the marks nearest to them. Loe Bar is the stretch of sand between Porthleven and Gunwallow this beach can be very productive for many species of fish, however this area can be dangerous in a storm from the Southwest.

- Polurrian Cove.   Poldhu Cove.
- Church Cove.
- Gunwallow Cove.
- Loe Bar.
- Rinsey Head.
- Praa Sands.
- Prussia Cove.
- Perran Sands.

PORTHLEVEN-GUNWALLOW
O.S. MAP REF. : 626254-654221 SOUTH COAST

Follow the A394 to Helston then just out side the town turn left down the B3304 to Porthleven. The small harbour wall at this venue is very good for many species of fish, however, it can be dangerous in bad weather conditions. The beach at Porthleven stretches along to Gunwallow Cove, this beach is better known as Low Bar. The beach is steeply shelved and frequently gets battered by storms so check the weather before planning a trip to this venue.

MAIN SUMMER SPECIES

Mackerel, Garfish, Bass, Small Eyed Rays, Plaice, Blonde Rays, Wrasse at either end of the beach, Pollack, Scad, Dogfish, Conger Eel and Bull huss.

MAIN WINTER SPECIES

Cod, Whiting, Coalfish, Pollack, Dogfish, Rockling and Conger Eels.

BAIT & TIPS

Sandeels live or frozen, Peeler or soft backed Crab, Mackerel, Squid, Lugworm and Ragworm. Most rigs work well here, although, float fishing should be restricted to calm weather. Loe Bar can be dangerous, particularly around the centre of the beach, across from the fresh water lake, so do not fish this venue alone.

PRAA SANDS O.S.MAP REF. : 580280 SOUTH COAST

This mark is situated about 7.5 miles West of Helston, take the A394 from Helston and then turn left at the cross roads at Germoe then follow the road down to Praa Sands. There are car parks at either ends of the beach and one near the centre. This beach is ideal for family members to relax or sun bathe. Fishing is possible all along the beach or from rocks at either end.

MAIN SUMMER SPECIES

Mackerel, Garfish, Bass, Plaice, Turbot, Rays and Dogfish with occasional bull Huss showing.

MAIN WINTER SPECIES

Whiting, and Pollack can be taken from the rocks with Cod showing, however not as common.

BAIT & TIPS

Sandeels live or frozen, Mackerel strip, A Thin Strip of Garfish, Ragworm, Lugworm, Peeler or soft backed Crab.

use a single hooked paternoster or pulley rig at this venue as these work well. Garfish is probably one of the most underrated baits going and without a doubt one of the best for catching Garfish.

Although it is not good practice to fish during a storm or gale , this beach faces to the Southwest, therefor during a Southwest gale of around force 4 to 6 , the surf will be rolling up this beach.

This makes this beach an exception, and a very good Bass beach during the summer months, with larger than average sized fish being taken.

If you are contemplating fishing this mark during these weather conditions, make sure that one, you are dressed for the occasion, and two, that you store all your fishing tackle near to the top of the beach, this should ,hopefully prevent any loss of main tackle items.

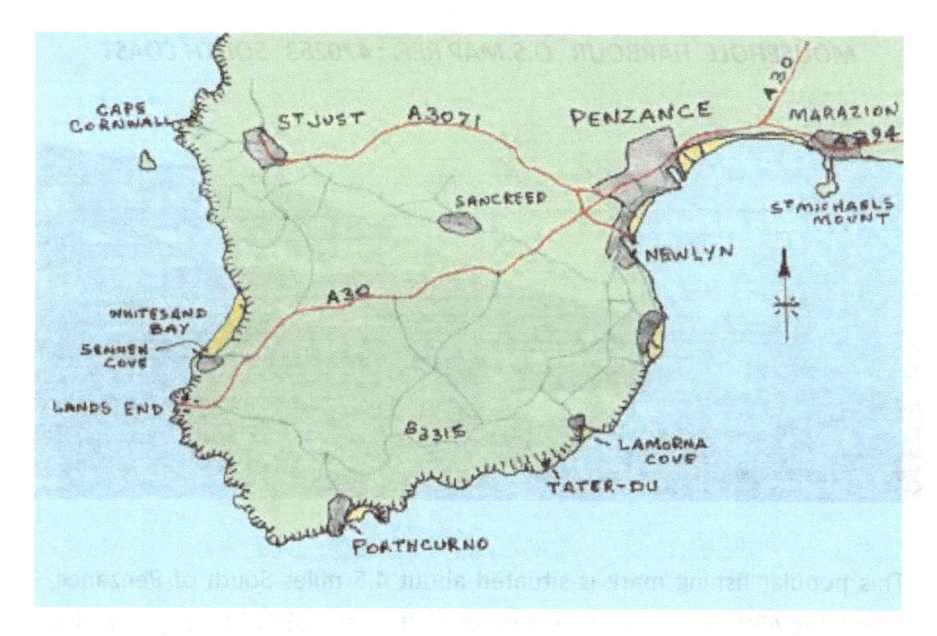

The map above covers the ground from Newlyn harbour to cape Cornwall, and takes in the following marks. Not all of the marks shown on the map are described in detail, however these fish the same as the marks closest to them. Lands End is primarily a tourist attraction and is not recommended to be fished.

- Newlyn.
- Lamorna Cove.
- Tater-Du.
- Porthcurno.
- Lands End.
- Sennen Cove.
- Whitesand Bay.
- Cape Cornwall.

MOUSEHOLE HARBOUR   O.S.MAP REF. : 470263   SOUTH COAST

This popular fishing mark is situated about 4.5 miles South of Penzance, follow the A30 out of Penzance and turn left on the B3315 through Newlyn as far as Trewarveneth, turn left here and follow the lane to Mousehole. There is limited parking in the village, when parked walk down to the harbour and fish from the walls. Fishing is also possible at Newlyn and Penzance harbours, however, it is very restricted.

MAIN SUMMER SPECIES

Garfish, Bass, Mackerel, Scad, Wrasse, Pollack, Conger eels and Dogfish.

MAIN WINTER SPECIES

Whiting, Cod, Coalfish, Pollack, Rockling, Dogfish and conger Eels.

BAIT & TIPS

Lugworm, Ragworm, Sandeel live or frozen, Mackerel strip, fresh Scad, Peeler or soft backed Crab.

Float fishing from this mark can keep the angler very busy and will count for most of the species being caught, however, Bass and Dogfish are mainly caught on the bottom using fish baits on either running ledgers or pulley rigs.

TATA-DU O.S. MAP REF. : 440230 SOUTH COAST

One of West Cornwall's best rock marks, Tater - Du lighthouse is situated to the West of Lamorna Cove, this mark is reached via a narrow road from Lamorna to the lighthouse. From Penzance take the B3315 to Lamorna. This is a rough ground mark with the usual rocky bottom species, fishing can be done from the many rocky platforms round by the lighthouse.

MAIN SUMMER SPECIES

Wrasse, Pollack, Scad, Dogfish, Mackerel, Corkwing Wrasse, Rockling, Conger Eels, Garfish and Grey Mullet.

MAIN WINTER SPECIES

Whiting, Codling, Pollack, Coalfish, Rockling, Dogfish and Conger Eels.

BAIT & TIPS

Live or frozen peeler or soft backed Crab, Live or frozen Sandeels, Fresh Scad, Mackerel, Squid strip, Smelt and Ragworm.

Use ground bait for Mullet and light tackle, use heavy tackle for Wrasse and Dogfish and float fish for Mackerel and Garfish. Mullet fishing is best done on clear, hot, sunny days when the water is calm. Mullet fishing requires the use of extremely light tackle with line of around 4 to 8lbs and a hook size of 6 to 10 (carp type hooks).

PORTHCURNO   O.S.MAP REF. : 388220   SOUTH COAST

This clean sandy beach is made up of crushed sea shells and about half way down shelves off quite steeply. Follow the A30 to Catchall and then turn down to the left on the B3283 and follow the signs for the open air theatre. Parking is on a pay and display car park, from here follow the lane and narrow track for about 300 yards to gain access to the beach. Fishing is possible from rock ledges below the open air theatre and also the beach.

MAIN SUMMER SPECIES

Bass, Wrasse, Mackerel, Scad, Garfish, Pollack, Plaice, Turbot and Dogfish. Rays are possible on neap tides when the weather is warm and calm. Corkwing Wrasse can be found at this mark, by fishing with fairly light tackle, with a small lead, close in to the rocks.

MAIN WINTER SPECIES

Whiting, Pollack, Occasional Coalfish, Rockling, Dogfish and small conger Eels. Codling can be taken from this mark, however these normally show after a rough period of weather.

BAIT & TIPS

Mackerel, Sandeels live or frozen Peeler or soft backed Crab, Squid, fresh Scad and Ragworm. The water at this mark is quite deep therefore float fishing is possible from the rocks and the beach. Use short Paternoster rigs with either one or two hooks and a plain lead a large bunch of Ragworm will attract Wrasse on either the bottom or float tackle. One of the best rigs to use during the winter months from this mark is a pulley rig with a long hook length and a size 3/0 to 6/0 hook.

SENNEN WHITESAND BAY   O.S.MAP REF. : 355265   WEST COAST

This 2.5 mile long beach is situated about 3 miles from Lands End, to find Sennen Cove or Whitesand Bay follow the A30 towards Lands End and turn right following the signs for Sennen Cove. The car park is a pay and display and is situated just above the beach. Whitesand Bay has quite along beach, this is very popular with surfers and sun bathers, therefore, you may have to walk to find quite spot away from surfers. Fishing is possible from both rocks and beach, although care must be taken if fishing from the rocks as the swell can come up very high. At the Northern end of this beach is Aire Point, this is a very good rock mark for all the species in this area.

MAIN SUMMER SPECIES

Mackerel, Garfish, Plaice, Turbot, Dogfish, Pollack, Scad and Bass.

MAIN WINTER SPECIES

Although this is a very popular beach during the summer months, most of the species caught in winter come from the rock marks to the northern end, these are Cod, Whiting, Rockling, Pollack, Coalfish and Dogfish.

BAIT & TIPS: Ragworm, Lugworm, Mackerel, Scad, Peeler or soft backed Crab, Squid strip, Sandeels live or frozen. Mainly use running ledger rigs from the beach and float tackle from the rocks. This mark can be very productive for larger Bass. During the winter months use either a running ledger or a pulley rig, both with a long hook length and a hook size of between 3/0 and 6/0.

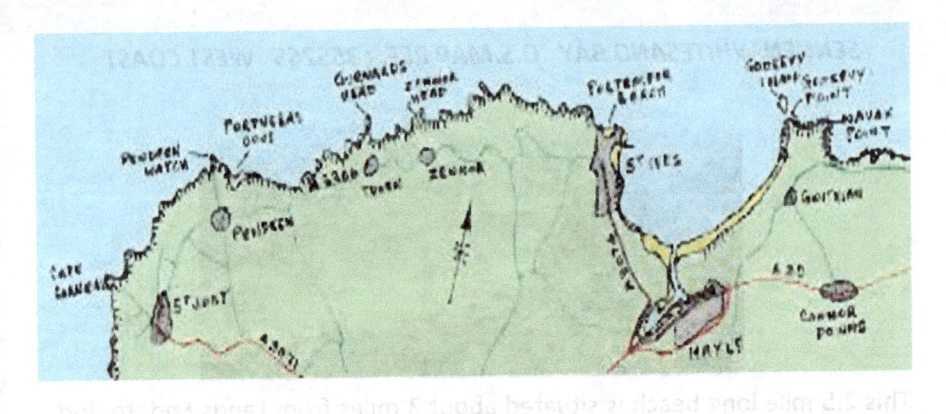

The map on this page covers the ground from Cape Cornwall to Navax Point and takes in the following fishing marks.

Although listed, not all of the marks on this map are described in detail, although these fish similar to the marks closest to them, these marks can be difficult to get to and be hard on legs as well as end tackle.

- Cape Cornwall.
- Pendeen Watch.
- Portheras cove.
- Gurnards Head.
- Zennor Head.
- Porthmeor beach.
- St Ives.
- Gogrevy Point.
- Navax Point.

PORTHERAS COVE (Pendeen)   O.S.MAP REF. : 388358   WEST COAST

This mark is situated approximately 5.5 miles Northeast of St Just off the B3306, turn left at the main cross road at Higher Boscaswell and follow the narrow track down as far as possible, now follow the coast path from the lighthouse to the small sandy cove. This mark is well sheltered from most winds therefore it can be a good spot to fish in bad weather. Fishing is possible from the rocks or the beach.

MAIN SUMMER SPECIES

Mackerel, Garfish, Bass, Scad, Pollack, Dogfish, Rays, Bull huss, Plaice and Turbot.

MAIN WINTER SPECIES

Although this mark can be very productive during bad weather, it is best to keep an eye on the sea as there can be an abnormal swell during periods of bad weather through the winter months. Cod, Whiting, Pollack, Coalfish, Rockling, Dogfish and small Conger Eels are all possible at this mark.

BAIT & TIPS

Ragworm, Lugworm, Sandeels live or frozen, Mackerel strip, small peeler or soft backed Crab, Squid Strip or small whole Squid made up in to a cocktail with worm baits. Rock fishing is done from the Western side of the cove, use single hooked paternoster or pulley rigs for Bass and running ledgers for flat fish, plain leads work well here.

PORTHMEOR BEACH   O.S.MAP REF. : 516410   NORTH COAST

Porthmeor beach is situated at the Northern end of St Ives, parking is on a pay and display car park at the rear end of the town. It is a short walk from here to the beach, this mark is very popular with surfers so great care must be taken when casting (ALWAYS USE A SHOCKLEADER). This venue is a good one to take the family as there are lots of things for children and spouses to do. Fishing can be done from the beach or the rocks at either end.

MAIN SUMMER SPECIES

Bass, Mackerel, Scad, Garfish, Plaice, Wrasse, Pollack, Turbot and Dogfish.

MAIN WINTER SPECIES

Pollack, Whiting, Coalfish, Cod, Rockling, Occasional Flounder, Dogfish and small Conger Eels.

BAIT & TIPS

Ragworm, Lugworm, Sandeels live or frozen, Mackerel strip, fresh Scad, live or frozen small peeler or soft backed Crab, Squid strips and cocktails of Squid and Worm baits.

Some very good flat fish are caught at this mark using running ledger rigs with small worm baited hooks on beaded traces. Bass will take Crab baits , Sandeels, Plugs and Lures at this mark.

This Golden sandy beach faces to the North, therefor it is reasonably sheltered from winds coming from the South, West and East.

Best rigs to use at this venue are Running ledgers, twin paternoster, pulley and bomber rigs, all these can be used successfully with a plain lead, a bait clip or impact shield is a useful item to be built in to these rigs as this will aid casting. If the kneed for a grip lead arises, do not use this on a running ledger, this will only get tangled with the main line and will prevent the rig from working properly.

HAYLE/GODREVY TOWANS BEACH   O.S.MAP REF. : 535388-580430
NORTH COAST

This beach is approximately 6 miles in length and is situated about 2.5 miles North of Hayle. Gogrevy Towans beach, although part of the same beach is approximately 6 miles Northeast of Hayle and is sign posted from the town centre. Across the rear of the beach there are numerous car parks and it is possible, in places to park on the sand, however, check how soft the sand is first as it can be expensive to have a car removed from the beach. Fishing is possible from beach or rocks.

MAIN SUMMER SPECIES

Plaice, Turbot, Rays, Bass, Mackerel, Dogfish and Garfish.

MAIN WINTER SPECIES

Occasional Flounder, Codling, Whiting, Dogfish and Cod.

BAIT & TIPS

Sandeels live or frozen, Mackerel strip, peeler Crab, Squid strip, Ragworm, Lugworm, Smelt .

Use running ledgers or short pulley rigs with size 1/0 - 3/0 hooks, although a plain lead can be used here at low tide it is best to change to a grip breakout lead when the tide starts to rise.

GODREVY POINT   O.S.MAP REF. : 580434   NORTH COAST

Godrevy Point is situated approximately 8 miles Northeast of Hayle and is reached via the A30 and B3301 on the outskirts of Hayle. A very narrow track leads down to a medium sized car park near to the point.

Parking on the track is forbidden and vehicles doing so are liable to be towed away. The sea bed in this area is made up from mainly sand with small rocky outcrops.

MAIN SUMMER SPECIES

Bass, A Variety of Rays, Ballan Wrasse, Dogfish, Small Pollack, Mackerel And Garfish, with Plaice and Turbot occasionally showing.

MAIN WINTER SPECIES

Whiting, Pollack, occasional Coalfish, Cod do show at this mark, but not in large numbers, Dog fish and Rockling.

BAIT & TIPS

Sandeels live or frozen, Mackerel strip, Peeler or soft backed Crab, Squid, Cuttlefish, Lugworm, Ragworm and an assortment of Plugs and Lures.

Bottom fished live or frozen Sandeel will account for most catches. Use a pulley rig or running ledger with a plain 3 - 5oz lead.

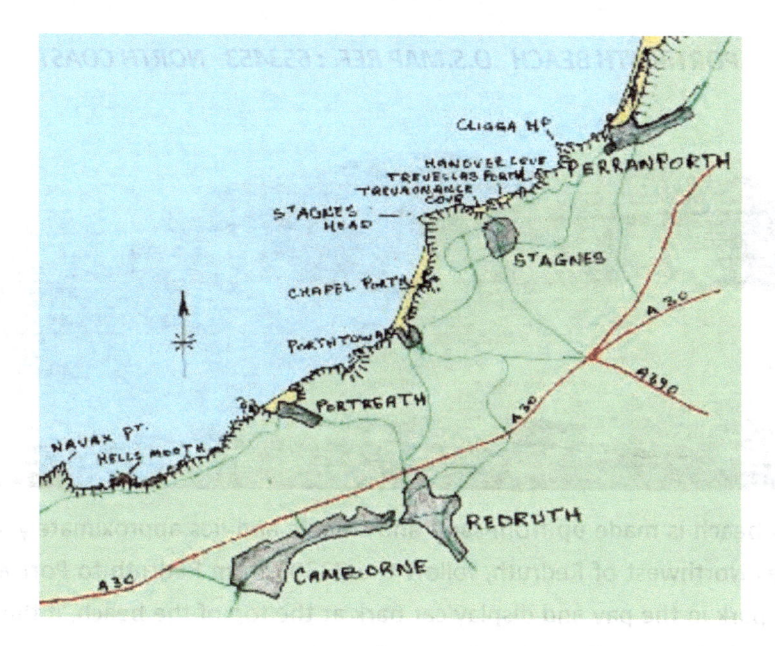

The above map covers the ground from Navax Point to Cligga Head on the north coast, and takes in the following marks. Most of the above marks can be fished ,however Hells Mouth is very dangerous and is not recommended to be fished.

- Navax Point.
- Hells Mouth (no fishing).
- Portreth.
- Porthtowan.
- Chapel Porth.
- St Agnes Head.
- Trevaunce Cove.
- Trevellas Porth.
- Hanover Cove.
- Cligga Head.

PORTREATH BEACH   O.S.MAP REF. : 653453   NORTH COAST

This beach is made up from sand and shingle and lies approximately 4.75 miles Northwest of Redruth, follow the B3300 from Redruth to Portreath and park in the pay and display car park at the top of the beach, if the car park is full there is limited parking in the main street.

This venue has a cafe and amusements for children and is also very popular with surfers. The best area to fish is along the beach as the breakwater is closed and access cannot be gained.

MAIN SUMMER SPECIES

Bass, Plaice, Dab, Mackerel, Garfish and Dogfish.

MAIN WINTER SPECIES

Although this beach can be very productive during the summer months, this venue has very few species show up during the winter, the ones that do are mainly Whiting and small Codling.

BAIT & TIPS

Sandeels live or frozen, Mackerel, Ragworm, Lugworm and Squid strip.

Best time to fish for Bass is when there is a surf running around 2 - 4 feet. Float fishing is only possible when there is very little surf. Plain leads work at this venue.

PORTHTOWAN   O.S.MAP REF. : 490480   NORTH COAST

Situated approximately 7.5 miles Southwest of Perranporth this beach is mainly made up from sand and rocky outcrops. To find this mark head for Chapel Porth but turn left at the cross roads and follow the signs for Porthtowan, alternatively, from the main Truro, Redruth road A30, turn off at the Wheel Rose junction, sign posted, Scorrier and follow the signs for Porthtowan, turn off for the beach after the small bridge and park at the bottom of the lane. This beach being 2.75 miles long at low water is ideal for surf casting , but is also very popular with surfers , therefore , it is best to walk along and find a quite spot before fishing.

MAIN SUMMER SPECIES

Bass, Turbot, Plaice, Mackerel, Garfish and Rays.

MAIN WINTER SPECIES

Beaches along the North coast, although very productive in summer, can be very poor as far species go, with only Whiting and very few Cod showing.

BAIT & TIPS

Mackerel strip, live or frozen Sandeels, Ragworm, Lugworm, Smelt, Squid strip, peeler or soft backed Crab.

Use beaded running ledger rigs with size 1/0 to 2/0 hooks attached to a small flounder type spoon for flat fish. Use a plain lead of 4 - 5oz as this will roll around and cover a larger area. Bass prefer Smelt, Crab or Sandeel baits at this venue.

If using a soft backed crab for Bass fishing, it is best to tie this bait on the hook, whole, without removing the legs. This bait looks more natural than a peeled Crab and tends to have more success when used in a slight surf, approximately 30 to 50 yards from the shore. The best time for Bassing from this beach is either early morning as the sun begins to rise or early evening just before and after sunset.

CHAPEL PORTH   O.S.MAP REF. : 697495   NORTH COAST

This sandy beach is situated approximately 1.5 miles West of St Agnes of the B3277 at the top of the village turn towards Beacon View and follow the road for 1/2 mile, when you reach the junction carry on straight ahead, follow the road down to free car park. There is a cafe at this venue so it is possible to have flasks etc refilled, open 9am to 5pm most days. This venue is mainly sand, however, it is possible to fish from the rocks on the right hand side of the beach.

MAIN SUMMER SPECIES

Bass, Plaice, Turbot, Mackerel, Dogfish, occasional Pollack and Garfish.

MAIN WINTER SPECIES

Whiting, small Codling, occasional Pollack and Dogfish.

BAIT & TIPS

Mackerel strip, Sandeels live or frozen, Ragworm and Lugworm, Peeler or soft backed Crab.

This mark is one for the surf caster and is best fished from low water up. At high tide there is not much room left on the beach. Use a pulley or running ledger rig at this venue.

TREVAUNCE COVE   O.S.MAP REF. : 724518   NORTH COAST

Situated about 3 miles Southeast of Perranporth, this small cove has both shingle beach and rock marks to fish from. Turn off the main Perranporth, St Agnes road at Trevellas and follow the narrow lane to Cross Coombe, on the sharp bend turn down towards the sea front and free car park. This mark has numerous rock pools in which peeler Crab and Prawns are found and used for bait as the tide rises. The rock platforms to the right hand side of the beach are probably the best mark to fish .

MAIN SUMMER SPECIES

Bass, Pollack, Wrasse, Mackerel, Garfish, Scad, Rockling, Corkwing Wrasse and Dogfish.

MAIN WINTER SPECIES

This venue can be very productive during the winter months, if fishing from the rocks to the end of the right hand side, this spot is fairly sheltered from any great swells as there are two small islands of rock, approximately 30 to 50 yards from the shore. main species are Cod, Whiting, Pollack, Coalfish, Rockling, Dogfish and Conger Eels.

BAIT & TIPS: Sandeels live or frozen, Mackerel strip, Squid strip, Smelt, Ragworm, peeler or soft backed Crab. This is a very rocky mark to fish, therefore, tackle losses can be high. It is best to use float tackle when fishing from the rocks .

CLIGGA HEAD   O.S.MAP REF. : 737538   NORTH COAST

This headland is situated approximately 1.5 miles Southwest of Perranporth on the main road to St Agnes, turn into the industrial estate and go past the end of the air field, now follow the dirt track between the two granite blocks down to the old quarry, park here. From here you follow the path down to rock platforms , these are fairly high up and no attempt should be made to reach the waters edge .

MAIN SUMMER SPECIES

Mackerel, Scad, Garfish, Wrasse, Pollack, Bass, Rockling and Dogfish, Conger eels show at this mark, mainly after dark and at low tide up.

MAIN WINTER SPECIES

This venue can be quite exposed to the elements during the winter months, so care must be taken whilst fishing. Main species are Whiting, Cod, Pollack, Rockling, Coalfish, Dogfish and Conger eels.

BAIT & TIPS

Mackerel, fresh Scad, Sandeels live or frozen, Squid, live or frozen peeler or soft backed Crab, Smelt. The sea bed on this area is quite rough so it is best to use short traces and plain leads.

Many of the fish here can be caught on float tackle so use this method or spin with fish baits as this will cut down tackle loss. A fling gaff can be very useful here, as trying to get down to the waters edge can be very dangerous and this is how accidents happen.

If you were to fall from here, this would cause a major emergency and rescue, so keep away from the edge and use a drop net or fling gaff.

DROSKYN POINT   O.S.MAP REF. : 754545   NORTH COAST

This rock mark is just off Perranporth, access can be gained across the beach at low water or by coast path at high water. the car park is situated at the top of the cliff adjacent to the Droskyn apartments and is a pay and display. If gaining access by way of the coastal path, then follow the small road around the rear of the buildings and up to the old lookout post, from here the way down to the waters edge can be plainly seen. The platform from which fishing can be safely done is relatively flat.

MAIN SUMMER SPECIES

Mackerel, Garfish, Plaice and occasional Ray. This is a very popular beach for Bass fishing, with some of the best fish being taken from the right hand side close to the rocks.

MAIN WINTER SPECIES

This venue is best fished during the summer months, however a few species do show in winter, these are Whiting, Flounder, near to the mouth of the small river, Occasional Cod and Coalfish.

BAIT & TIPS

Mackerel, Lugworm, Ragworm, Smelt, Peeler or soft backed Crab, Sandeel live or frozen, Mackerel Feathers and Lures.

Fish 2 hours either side of high water on spring tides for best results, cast around 70 yards with grip leads and 3/0 to 4/0 sized hooks. Watch out for surfers when casting as this can be a popular beach for surfers and bathers alike.

The best type of rigs to use at this mark are, Running ledgers, used with a plain lead, Pulley rigs with a very long hook length, One up and One down rigs, Paternosters and up and over rig types. Use a longer hook length at this mark, as the use of grip leads can be important, and will stop the trace drifting in to the rocks. Longer traces are used to compensate for the lead not rolling around in the surf.

PERRANPORTH BEACH   O.S.MAP REF. : 760560   NORTH COAST

This beach is approximately 2.5 miles long with Perranporth at its western end, a great favourite with surfers it is best fished from about the middle to the eastern end. Car parking is possible in Perranporth, however, best parking is on the Haven camp site at the top of the cliff, follow the path down to the beach, there is no problems parking here as long as you do not block any roads or main entrances, during the main holiday season, however out of season, you will need to find a member of the security staff and let them know where you are parking and fishing, in most cases there is no problem with doing this.

MAIN SUMMER SPECIES

Bass, Plaice, Ray, Garfish and Mackerel are possible on high spring tides.

MAIN WINTER SPECIES

There is a lack of winter species from this beach, however after a storm Cod and Whiting do show up, fishing from the rocks up to and around Droskyn Point will produce fish through the winter months with Flounder being added to the list.

BAIT & TIPS

Lugworm, Ragworm, Mackerel strip, Sandeel live or frozen, Peeler or soft backed Crab. Best fishing mark is at the bottom of the steps from the Haven camp site, use a running ledger cast into the surf between the second and third breaker, with a 3oz to 5oz lead. Use size 3/0 and 4/0 hooks and grip leads on strong tides. During the winter months it is best to use up to s 6oz grip lead on a pulley rig with a long trace and a size 6/0 hook for Cod, a 2/0 to 4/0 hook for Whiting and a size 1/0 to 2/0 flatty hook for Flounder. Always keep an eye on the tide run , as the incoming tide can be very quick.

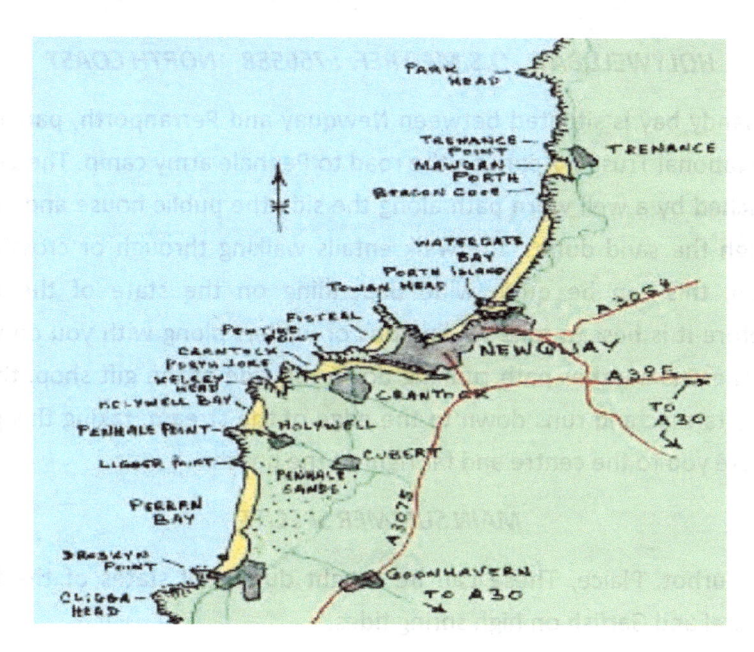

The above map covers the ground from Cligga Head to Park Head and takes in the following marks.

- Cligga Head.   Droskyn Point.
- Perran Bay.   Ligger Point.
- Penhale Point.   Holywell Bay.
- Kelsey Head.   Porth Joke.
- Crantock.   Pentire Point.
- Fistral Bay.   Towan Head.
- Porth Island.   Watergate Bay.
- Beacon Cove.   Mawgan Porth.
- Trenance Point.   Park Head.

HOLYWELL BAY   O.S.MAP REF. : 766588   NORTH COAST

This sandy bay is situated between Newquay and Perranporth, parking is on a National Trust car park on the road to Penhale army camp. The beach is reached by a well worn path along the side the public house and down through the sand dunes, the walk entails walking through or crossing a stream, this can be quite wide depending on the state of the tide, therefore it is best to take wellingtons or waders along with you on your trip. There is another path running down the side of the gift shop, this is mainly tarmac and runs down to the edge of the stream, taking this path will take you to the centre and far right of the beach.

MAIN SUMMER SPECIES

Bass, Turbot, Plaice, These can be caught during all states of the tide, Mackerel and Garfish on high spring tides.

MAIN WINTER SPECIES

Cod and Whiting do show up at this beach, however this is normally after a storm, therefore it is not always worth the walk out .

BAIT & TIPS

Lugworm, Ragworm, Sandeel live or frozen Mackerel, Smelt, Peeler or soft backed Crab. Flat fish mainly caught on running ledgers and Bass fall to pulley type rigs with size 3/0 to 5/0 hooks. Grip leads are necessary if a high surf is running. The best time to fish this beach for Bass is during the evenings or early morning, from low water up to two hours of the ebbing tide. The rocks to the extreme left and right of the beach can be very productive if fished with Crab baits on a running ledger or pulley rig. Do not fish from the rocks, but cast down the side of them, up to ten to fifteen yards from the edge, use plain dumpy leads as these will roll around the bottom and cover more ground. If these areas are already being fished then head for the centre of the beach, whilst here look for the back wash, once found, set up and fish here, the current is a lot stronger here so grip leads may be needed, depending on the state of the tide.

PENTIRE POINT EAST   O.S.MAP REF. : 788615   NORTH COAST

This headland is reached by turning left off the A392 at the roundabout on the outskirts of Newquay, the car park is situated on the headland. There are several rock marks to fish within a 500 yard walk of the car park, these can be seen from the foot path. Fishing here involves scrambling over rocks and should be approached with caution, always keep an eye on the state of the tide and sea conditions. One of the better and safer marks to fish on this headland is Salt Cove, this is situated on the left hand side of the headland, over looking Crantock Beach, Although there is not very much water here at low tide, this mark can produce very good fish, with Bass top of the list.

MAIN SUMMER SPECIES

Bass, Plaice, Turbot, Pollack, Mackerel, Flounder, Garfish and specimen sized Ballan Wrasse, Dogfish and Conger Eel.

MAIN WINTER SPECIES

Anglers must keep an eye on the tide and swell as it can come up very high if the wind is in the wrong direction. Main species are Cod, Whiting, Pollack, Coalfish, Rockling, Flounder, dogfish and Conger eels.

BAIT & TIPS: Mackerel strip, Squid whole or strip, Sandeel live or frozen, Lugworm, Ragworm, Peeler or soft backed Crab. The sea bed is very rocky at this venue so if ledgering be prepared to lose end tackle, float fish for Wrasse with Crab baits. If fishing in the area of Salt Cove, grip leads will be needed whilst the tide is rising and falling, particularly on high spring tides, during neap tides it is possible to fish this venue with plain leads, this is a better time to fish this mark as there is more water around and possibly more fish. The ground out towards the front of the headland is very rocky and filled with kelp filled gullies, unfortunately these are covered most of the time, so fishing this area can result in the lose of end tackle. Many larger sized Wrasse are taken from here.

NEWQUAY AREA

The Newquay area and it's beaches are one of the foremost areas in Europe for surfing, this very statement also indicates that with the presence of a surf environment a large variety of fish species are also present, making this area one of Cornwall's most popular angling venues. Fishing marks in this area are easily accessible from the town, and with good parking facilities for cars in most cases.

Newquay or Towan Head is rated among the top rock fishing areas in the West Country providing a good variety of species through Summer and Winter months.

A cast of around 80 yards or less in some places will reach a sandy bottom, only a few marks are demanding on end tackle uses.

Typical Winter species are Cod, Whiting, Rockling, Dogfish, Flounder, Coalfish and Conger eel whilst Spring and Summer sees the arrival of Mackerel, Mullet, Garfish, Pollack, Pouting, Bass, Scad, Gurnard, Plaice, Turbot and Ballan Wrasse.

During warm Summers of late there has been an increase in catches of more exotic John Dory and Trigger Fish, while the odd shaped Sun Fish can sometimes be seen basking off the shore. When fishing from the rocks the usual precautions should be taken, do not fish down to close to the waters edge, but choose a higher position, particularly if there is a large swell or surf running. Always wear tough non slip footwear and never fish alone particularly at night.

The Fly Cellars mark is a particularly accessible and safe fishing platform, especially for those with mobility problems or young children, The outer breakwater of the harbour is also very accessible, however, it must be remembered that this is a working harbour. On the following page has a sketch map of the Newquay Headland area with all the fishing marks clearly marked with their position, most of which are fully described with details of access, fish species and methods of fishing.

during any angling expedition around Newquay or indeed anywhere around the Cornish Coastline, Please do not leave any litter or old fishing line, hooks e.t.c. on the rocks or beaches, as it can spoil the mark, endanger wildlife and ultimately stop anglers using the same marks in the future. Please take any litter you may have home with you or place it in a rubbish bin. So enjoy fishing one of Cornwall's top venues, tight lines and remember be safe.

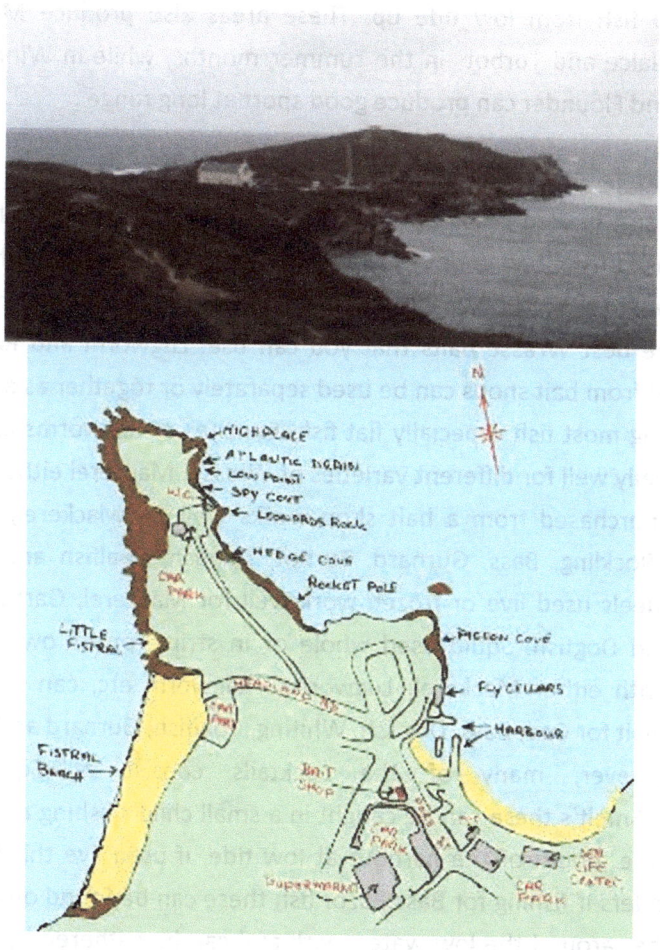

The above map covers the main Headland in the Newquay area, this map also shows the main car parks in and around the Headland and town center.

NEWQUAY'S BEACHES

All of the beaches in and around the Newquay area can be, and are good areas for Bass fishing during the summer season, usually from June to October. The main problem is that all of these venues particularly Fistral, Towan and Great Western are favourites with the surfers, so be patient and try to fish in areas that are not in use. Probably the best fishing is when high tide and sunset or sunrise coincide, however, in these situations it pays to fish from low tide up. These areas also produce Mackerel, Garfish, Plaice and Turbot in the summer months, while in Winter Cod, Whiting and Flounder can produce good sport at long range.

BAITS & TIPS

Peeler or soft backed Crabs can be collected around Newquay at low tide or purchased from bait shops in the town, these can be used both live or frozen, tied to a hook this can be a deadly Bass bait and is most certainly one of the best Wrasse baits that you can use. Lugworm and Ragworm purchased from bait shops can be used separately or together as a cocktail for catching most fish especially flat fish, bunches of Ragworms can work exceptionally well for different varieties of Wrasse. Mackerel either caught fresh or purchased from a bait shop works well for Mackerel, Garfish, Whiting, Rockling, Bass, Gurnard, Turbot, Dogfish, Coalfish and Conger eels. Sandeels used live or frozen work well for Mackerel, Garfish, Bass, Pollack and Dogfish. Squid used whole or in strips, on its own or as a cocktail with either Mackerel, Lugworm , Ragworm etc. can be a very effective bait for Cod, Bass, Dogfish, Whiting, Coalfish, Gurnard and Conger eels, However, many of the cocktails consist of Squid and Mackerel .Smelt's these can be caught in a small child's fishing net in rock pools or the mouth of the harbour at low tide, if used live this bait can work wonders if fishing for Bass.Razor fish these can be found on some of the beaches around the low water mark and can be gathered by pouring table salt into the blow hole and then waiting for the Razor fish to surface from the sand , this can take up to 2 minutes. Remove from shell and tie on to hook, use mainly for flatfish , Bass and Wrasse .

Rigs can be home made or, purchased from most tackle shops, however, it is better to build your own as hook sizes and snood lengths can be customised to suit which ever species of fish being sought, here are a few tips on which fish are taken and on what type of rig used.

Bass

The majority of Bass are caught on running ledger, pulley or a single Paternoster rig with size 3/0 - 6/0 hooks or spinning rigs with artificial Sandeels, Plugs or Lures.

Bream

Both black and red bream can be caught in this area on light line fished on the bottom, use a short hook length, this makes it easier to hook the fish.

Coalfish

Mainly caught on single paternoster , pulley or running ledger rigs, a handy tip is to place a starlight either in the bait or just above the bait as this helps to attract the fish.

Cod

These fish tend to favour a longer hook length than average on either a pulley or running ledger rig with up to size 6/0 hooks, one of the most favoured rigs is the beach Cod rig or up and over, although, Cod prefer long traces many have been taken from headland areas on Whiting rigs and similar types.

Conger eel

These are normally fished for using heavy tackle and a large hook size 7/0 to 10/0 on a running ledger made up from coated wire or up to 200lb breaking strain monofiliment line.

Dogfish

These be caught on almost any bottom rig however, they can be caught on paternoster rigs as well as running ledgers.

Flounder

Most flatfish are caught on free flowing traces such as running ledger rigs or spoons, it is best to place a number of coloured beads just above the hook, this acts as an attractor.

Garfish

This species are normally taken on float or spinning tackle, if using float tackle on a calm clear day then set the bottom between 4 and 12 feet, however Garfish can be caught up to 25 feet deep if spinning.

Gurnard

Mainly taken on running ledgers , single paternosters or one up one down rigs, although with the right bait will fall to any bottom rig.

Mackerel

These fish can be caught on a variety of rigs, the main ones being feathers, float tackle and spinning tackle, this species of fish will also take bottom fished baits on paternoster and running ledger rigs. Some of the best feathers are the silver shrimp and hokkia range.

Plaice

These can be caught on the same type of traces as the Flounder and Turbot.

Pollack

Most of these fish are taken on float or spinning tackle fished over reefs or close in to the edge of the rocks.

Pouting

Caught mainly on paternoster type and whiting rigs.

Rockling

As these fish are found over and in very rocky ground it is best to fish for these using a rotten bottom, this should cut down on tackle loss.

Scad

These can be caught using the same method used for Mackerel, however, it can pay dividends to place a starlight in to or above the bait as these fish are attracted to light.

Turbot

Mainly caught on long flowing traces such as running ledgers and pulley rigs.

Whiting

This species can be caught on most rigs, however, the best one is the Whiting rig which has short hook lengths of around 6 to 9 inches long.

These are short because of the way that the fish attack the bait and with short hook lengths the fish will 9 times out of 10 hook it's self.

Wrasse

There are two or three varieties of Wrasse caught around the Newquay area, although they can all be taken on the same type of rig. Running ledgers and single Paternoster type rigs tend to work better at low water, cast up to 50 yards from the shore with size 3/0 to 4/0 Crab hooks. The best all round rig to use for this species is the rotten bottom rig, using an old spark plug, bolt or nut, using this rig will help to cut down tackle lose as most of the better fish are taken close to the waters edge and that just happens to normally be covered with kelp and other under water snags. Float tackle is also best used fishing from low water up to high water, use a size 3/0 - 4/0 hook and keep changing the depth at which your bait sits. When fishing for Wrasse it is best to tie a short piece of bait elastic to the loop of the hook, this enables you to tie the bait on and aids casting and bait preservation.

Most wrasse are however caught with in the first two to three meters from the waters edge and in most cases casting the bait out more than five meters will result in lose of end tackle or even the fish.

NEWQUAY HEADLAND

This section covers the area from the harbour walls to the near side of little Fistral beach.

NEWQUAY HARBOUR

This has two walls to fish from and is flat and safe as long as you stay away from the very edge, please remember that this is a fully working harbour and it can get very busy during the summer months. Main species caught here during the Spring and Summer are Mackerel, Garfish, Plaice, Bass, Small Pollack, Gurnard and Coalfish, Whiting and Cod during the Winter. The best rigs to use are Mackerel feathers, Paternoster rigs with up to three hooks or running ledgers.

FLY CELLARS

Situated to the left of the outer harbour wall this flat,walled platform is ideal for young children and disabled people to fish from.The main species during Spring and Summer are, Mackerel, Garfish, Pollack, Plaice, Gurnard, Bass, Scad, Dogfish and a variety of Wrasse. During the Winter months Cod, Whiting and Coalfish are the main species caught. The best rigs to use are Float tackle, Running ledgers, Mackerel feathers, paternoster rigs and one up and one down rigs. A useful rig to use at this venue is a spinning type of hook length with a live Sandeel attached on a hook at one end and a swivel and snap link at the other, clip this on to the main line and let the Sandeel swim up and down the line.

PIGEON COVE

This small Cove situated to the left of the Fly Cellars is reached by the coastal path and narrow footpath down the side of the cliff to a long rocky platform, fishing from here is best done on the rising tide from low water up to high water. Main species during Spring and Summer are Mackerel, Garfish, Gurnard, Dogfish, Plaice, Wrasse, Pollack, Rockling and small Conger eels. Winter species are Whiting, Cod, Coalfish, Conger eels and Rockling. Main rigs used at this venue are short pulley rigs, paternoster rigs, rotten bottom type rigs, spinning and float tackle.

ROCKET POLE

This mark is reached by driving or walking towards the Headland and then walking to your right down over the cliff via the well worn path to the rocky platform below, this is about 75 yards long. The sea bed in this area is made up from sand, rock and kelp filled gullies. Main Spring and Summer species are Pollack, Mackerel, Wrasse, Garfish, Scad, Dogfish and small Conger eels. Winter species are Cod Whiting, Rockling, Dogfish, Coalfish and Conger eels. Main rigs used here are rotten bottom rigs, single paternoster rigs, Running ledgers, spinning and float tackle.

HEDGE COVE

To reach this mark, park in the car park on the Headland and walk back up the track about 50 yards and then follow the path down to the waters edge. This mark is similar to the Rocket Pole ,however the sea bed is much cleaner here and not as muck tackle is lost in this area. Main Spring and Summer species are Mackerel, Garfish, Pollack, Wrasse, Scad and Dogfish. Winter species are Cod, Whiting, Coalfish, Dogfish and small Conger eels. Main rigs used here are running ledgers, pulley rigs, paternoster rig types, spinning and float tackle.

OLD SLIPWAY

Situated to the rear right hand side of the Headland car park this small rock mark can be very productive during the spring, summer and winter months, the sea bed in this area is mainly sand with small rocky outcrops. Main Spring and Summer species are Mackerel, Garfish, Scad, Plaice, Dogfish and occasional Turbot. Main Winter species are Whiting, Cod, Coalfish, Flounder and Dogfish. Main rigs used are float and spinning tackle, running ledgers, paternoster type rigs, one up and one down and up and over rig types.

LEONARD'S ROCK

This mark is situated to the right hand side of the toilet block on the Headland, at low tide there are two shelves to fish from, however, in bad weather or sea conditions it is best to fish from the top ledge, as the lower one can get covered by the swell. Fishing out towards Porth Island and round to the light house on Trevose Head, the sea bed is of clean sand. Main species during the Spring and Summer months are Mackerel, Garfish, Scad, Plaice, Turbot, Bass, Pouting, Dogfish and different varieties of Wrasse. Main species during Winter months are Whiting, Cod, Coalfish, Dogfish and small Conger eels. Best rigs to use at this venue are light running ledgers with or without beads Paternoster rig types one up one down type rigs spinning and float tackle.

SPY COVE

This concrete platform is situated to the rear of the toilet block, behind the bus shelter type building, follow the well worn path down to the rock and concrete pad. The sea bed in this area is made up from small rocky outcrops, sand and kelp, however, a cast of around 50 yards straight out to sea will find a clean bottom. Main species during Summer months are Mackerel, Garfish, Scad, Pollack, Dogfish, Rockling and small Conger eels. Main species during Winter months are Cod, Whiting, Dogfish, occasional Coalfish and Conger eels. This venue is best fished three hours either side of high water during the Summer months and from low tide up during the Winter months. Best rigs used at this venue are rotten bottom if fishing close in other wise running ledgers, short pulley rigs, paternosters, spinning rigs or float tackle.

LOW POINT

To reach this mark walk as if going to Spy Cove only follow the coast path to the next point, walk down to the rocks. There is only enough room at this mark for approximately four anglers to fish at any one time, this mark can be very popular with local anglers and visitors alike. A cast of 30 yards and over will find a clean sea bed, however, there is a small reef approximately 125 yards from the shore, this reef is not covered in under water snags and it is quite easy to pull tackle from it.

Main species during Spring and Summer months are, Mackerel, Garfish, Plaice, Turbot, Scad, Wrasse, Rockling, Pollack, Dogfish, Gurnard, occasional Bass and Conger eel. Main species during Winter months are Cod, Whiting, Coalfish, Dogfish, Conger eel and occasional Flounder. Main rigs used at this mark are float and spinning tackle, running ledger types, one up one down type rigs, paternoster type rigs with up to three hooks for Whiting and Mackerel, up and over type rigs and light and heavy bottom rigs.

ATLANTIC DRAIN

Locally known as the sewer outlet , this is situated to the left of and over the hill from Low Point. This venue is well known for many species of fish that are caught on the surface or close to the bottom. Apart from the reef to the left hand side the sea bed in this area is mainly sand. If fishing this venue it is wise not to take food or eat any food whilst at this mark as you are basically fishing in water directly from the local sewer. Main species during Spring and Summer months are, Mullet, Mackerel, Garfish, Wrasse and Scad. Main species during the Winter months are, Whiting and Cod. Main rigs used at this venue are light Mullet floats and tackle, pulley rigs and short paternosters. It is recommended that young children or pregnant ladies do not visit this mark as the way down is fairly steep and from time to time, the remains of sewage gets washed up on the rocks.

HIGH POINT

This mark is found to the front and extreme right of the Headland, this mark can be awkward to get to if you are carrying lots of fishing tackle. High Place covers quite a large area of the right hand side and end corner of the Headland so the seabed in this area can vary tremendously from sand to rock and kelp filled gullies. A cast of around 50 to 80 yards should find clean ground unless fishing out the front end of the Headland in which case it is best to use float or spinning tackle. Main species during the Spring and Summer months are Mackerel, Garfish, Scad, Pollack, Wrasse, Rockling, Pouting, Turbot, Plaice, Dogfish and Conger eels. Main species during the Winter months are Cod, Whiting, Coalfish, Dogfish, Conger eel and occasional Ling. Main rigs used here are pulley, running ledger, paternoster, up and over, float and spinning tackle.

HEADLAND LEFT HAND SIDE

Great care must be taken when fishing this side of the Headland as, not only are you having to clamber over rocks and gullies, but you can also get cut off by the tide very easily, because of this fishing is restricted to the dropping tide and low water and only in calm weather conditions. There are many paths down to the rocks on this side of the Headland, however care must be take when walking down to the waters edge, at low water fishing is possible from all across this side and out the front to the left-hand side. The sea bed in this area is mainly sandy with small rocky outcrops and kelp filled gullies. Main species during the Spring and Summer months are, Mackerel, Garfish, Scad, Pollack, Bass, Plaice, Turbot, Dogfish and Wrasse, with Conger eel and Rockling found closer to the end of the Headland. Main species during the Winter months are, Cod, Whiting, Coalfish, Dogfish, Conger eels and Flounder. It is recommended that fishing from this mark should be restricted to the Summer months as Winter storms can cause the water to cover the rocks.Main rigs used at this mark are, float and spinning tackle, paternoster type rigs, pulley type rigs, up and over type rigs, running ledgers and light bottom type rigs.

PORTH ISLAND   O.S.MAP REF. : 829630   NORTH COAST

Porth Island is situated approximately 2 miles North from Newquay, parking is on a pay and display car park at the bottom of the hill as you come in to Newquay Porth. Walk in a Westerly direction up the hill and through the five bar gate on the left hand side of the road, now follow the well marked path across the bridge to the Island, from here the path splits and you can see numerous fishing marks, the best being on the front and left hand side of the Island, fishing can also be done during the summer months, from Porth Beach on late evening sessions after the surfers have gone home, many larger sized Bass have been taken from this beach in the past.

MAIN SUMMER SPECIES

Bass, Mackerel, Plaice, Turbot, Dogfish, small Conger Eels, early Flounder and Garfish.

MAIN WINTER SPECIES

Whiting, Cod and Codling, Pollack, Coalfish and Rockling from the rocks and Flounder and Dogfish from the side of the island towards the beach.

BAIT & TIPS: Lugworm, Mackerel, Squid, Sandeel live or frozen, Ragworm, Smelt, Peeler or soft backed Crab. Large swells tend to break off this headland so be careful, fish from rock platforms and cast towards Newquay headland. Fish the tide up and about 2 hours of the ebb tide. Float fish for Mackerel and Garfish. If fishing for Turbot, it pays to use a running type ledger rig with a long trace baited with a small piece of Mackerel. After casting the baited rig out to sea, the best thing to do is to leave it where it is for approximately 10 to 20 minuets and then reel it in about 5 to 10 turns of the reel. As Turbot normally ambush the bait, this method gives the fish the impression that the bait is live, and in doing so, the fish will normally bite. You may need to repeat this method a number of times before making contact with the fish. This method enables more ground to be covered with the bait, and increases the chance of tempting a fish.

MAWGAN PORTH AND TRENANCE   O.S.MAP.REF. : 847678
NORTH COAST

Mawgan Porth Beach and Trenance Point are situated approximately 4 miles north from Newquay town, to find these venues follow the B3276 in a northerly direction towards Padstow. When reaching Mawgan Porth, ample parking is available in a pay and display car park to the rear of the garage, from here cross the road to the beach. To find Trenance point follow the road through Mawgan Porth, up the hill keeping to the left, until you find Trenance, this is only about 1 mile up the road. On reaching Trenance turn left at the telephone box and the first right up the private road, follow this to the end where 2 to 4 cars may be parked off the track, do not block any garages or gate ways. From here follow the coast path towards the top of the hill and take the third path down to the waters edge. Mawgan Porth has a clean sandy beach with rocks at either end, a small river runs down through the centre of this. Trenance Point is a series of small rock platforms that stand about 25 feet above the sea.

MAIN SUMMER SPECIES

From the beach, Bass, Plaice, Turbot, Mackerel and Occasional Blond Rays. From the rocks, Blond Ray, Turbot, Bass, Red, Grey and Tub Gurnard, Mackerel, Garfish, Pollack , Dogfish and small Conger Eels.

MAIN WINTER SPECIES

Winter species are not as varied as those during the summer, however the main ones are Cod, Whiting, Pollack, Rockling, Dogfish and small Conger eels. Flounder can be taken from the beach towards the centre.

BAIT & TIPS

Sandeels live or frozen, Soft backed or Peeler crab, Smelts, Mackerel Fillets or Strip, Squid strips, Ragworm, Lugworm and cocktails of Squid and worm.If fishing from the beach, use a pulley rig with up to 6oz grip leads.

If fishing from Trenance use a pulley or running ledger type rig with plain leads, these will move around with the current and cover more ground.

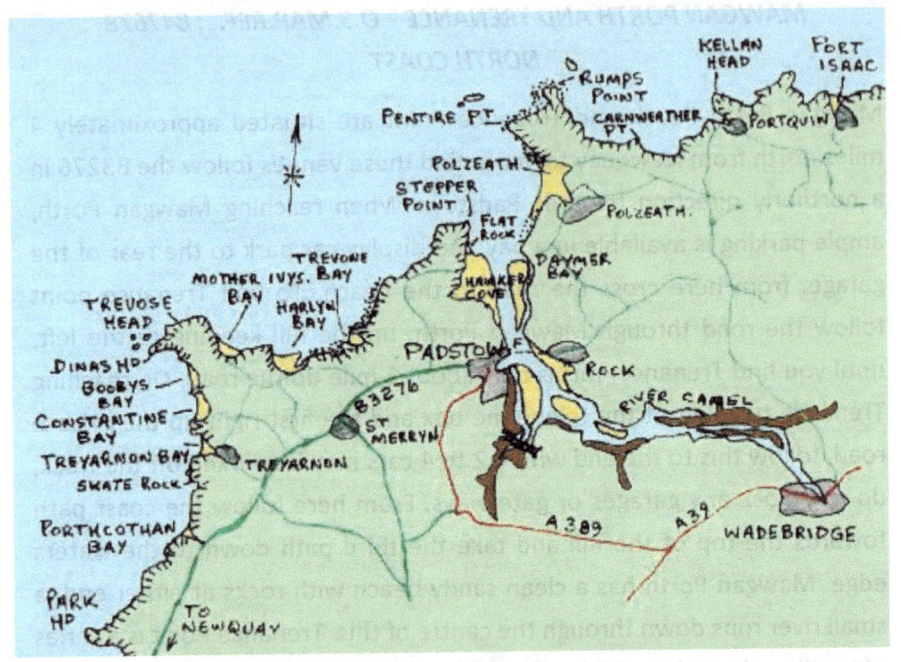

The above map takes in numerous marks from Park Head to Port Isaac, Although not all of these are described in detail, the ones that are not can be fished in a similar way, and with the same methods as the closest marks to them, the fish species will only differ slightly, however this main;y applies to the estuary.

- Porthcothan Bay.   Skate rock.   Treyarnon Bay.
- Constantine Bay.   Booby's Bay.   Dinas head.
- Trevose Head.   Mother Ivy's Bay.   Harlyn Bay.
- Trevone Bay.   Stepper point.   Flat Rock.
- Camel Estuary.   Dammer Bay.   Polzeath.
- Pentire Point.   Rumps Point.   Carnweather Point.
- Kellan Head.   Port Isaac.

PORTHCOTHAN   O.S.MAP REF. : 852722   NORTH COAST

This venue is situated between Mawgan Porth and St Merryn, this small sandy beach offers an opportunity to fish for larger than usual species of fish. Parking is on a pay and display car park at the rear of the houses. To gain access to the mark cross the road and follow the path to the beach, once there cross to the right hand side, go up the steps and follow the coast path for about 200 yards and then fish off the platforms of rock at the point.

MAIN SUMMER SPECIES

Bass, Garfish, Mackerel, Plaice, Dab, Turbot and Dogfish. Rays are possible from the rock point.

MAIN WINTER SPECIES

Winter species are normally taken after a storm, with Cod, Whiting and Coalfish being the main catch.

BAIT & TIPS

Ragworm, Lugworm, Peeler or soft backed Crab, Sandeels live or frozen, Mackerel and Smelts. Best fishing can be done 3 hours before high water and up to 2 hours of the ebb tide. On very high spring tides the path on the beach can be covered.

CONSTANTINE BAY   O.S. MAP REF. : 858745   NORTH COAST

Situated between Mawgan Porth and St Merryn this is a very good Bass beach with larger than average size being taken. On approach to St Merryn take the first left and follow the road for approximately 1.5 miles then follow the sign for the beach, parking is by way of a field, you pay on the gate unless closed then park on side of the road in spaces provided by the toilet block. At either end of the beach there are rocks which can be fished from and are exceptionally good marks at low tide, however, it is not recommend that you fish from these areas when the tide starts to rise, as the tide rises very quickly. To the extreme right of Constantine Bay, beyond the rocks, is a further beach and rock marks, this is called Booby's Bay, the rock marks around this beach are exceptionally good for Bass, Wrasse, Mackerel and Garfish. Whilst fishing this mark, you must always be awhere of the tide as it can rise very quickly and wash over the rocks.

MAIN SUMMER SPECIES

Bass, Plaice, Turbot, Mackerel, Garfish, Dogfish, Ballan and Corkwing Wrasse, Ray and occasional Bull Huss.

MAIN WINTER SPECIES

Both of these beaches and rock marks can produce a large amount of exceptional winter species, these normally show up after a storm, the main fish are Cod, Whiting, Pollack, Coalfish, Rockling and Dogfish.

BAIT & TIPS

Live or frozen Sandeels, Mackerel, Squid, Lugworm, Ragworm, Peeler or soft backed Crab. 5oz grip leads are recommend at this mark, if fishing this venue make sure that your main tackle is well up the beach, due to the fast running tide, the rock marks at either end of Constantine should only be fished at low tide and in calm weather.

Rock marks around Booby's Bay can be fished throughout the tide, however beware of being cut off by the tide.

TREVOSE HEAD   O.S.MAP.REF.:852763   NORTH COAST

This venue is situated between Constantine Bay and Stepper Point, it is reached by following the B3276 until reaching St Merryn, here turn left at the cross roads towards Harlyn and follow the signs to Trevose Head. At the entrance to Trevose Head is a farm with a five bar gate, here is a pay and display machine, you must pay here for parking. The car park at Trevose Head is restricted by time, this closes at 10pm during the summer months, vehicles left after this time are liable to be wheel clamped. If your fishing trip is likely to exceed the permitted time, then the best thing to do is park before the gate and walk, although this walk is fairly easy it is a long way. When you have parked or reached Trevose Head, follow the coast path, fishing spots can be seen from here, with most of the better ones having well worn paths leading down to the waters edge, although this can be around 30 feet above the water in most cases.

MAIN SUMMER SPECIES

Trevose Head offers the angler the chance to catch a number of species that are rearly taken from other venues, many of the following species can be taken on float tackle, Bass, Pollack, Mackerel, Scad, Garfish, Wrasse, Plaice, Bull Huss, Dogfish, Small eyed Ray, Blonde Ray and Small Tope.

MAIN WINTER SPECIES

Although fewer species are caught here during the winter, this venue is still one of the best in Cornwall, however care must be taken whilst fishing here. Main species are Cod, Whiting, Pollack, Coalfish and small Ling.

BAIT & TIPS: Whole or strip Mackerel, Whole or strip Squid, Live or frozen Sandeels, Peeler or soft backed Crab, Ragworm, Lugworm, Smelts and a variety of Lures and Feathers. Safety is very important at this venue, many anglers have been washed off and lost from here. Do not fish this mark alone and always let some one know where you are going. Most rigs work well around this Headland.

STEPPER POINT, FLAT ROCK AND HAWKERS COVE   O.S.MAP.REF. : 905774   NORTH COAST

these three marks can be found at the mouth of the Camel Estuary, on the Padstow side of the River camel. These marks can be reached by following the B3276 from Newquay to Padstow and turning off to the left at the cross roads just after the Village of Treator, from here follow the narrow road until you reach Lillizzick Farm. A field is used as a car park during the summer, to gain access pay at the hut. A short walk down the field will bring you out at Hawkers Cove. to reach Flat Rock follow the private road down to the Village, you must leave your car in the car park, on reaching the Village follow the narrow road until you reach the Southwest Coast path, Flat Rock can be seen and reached from here. If fishing Stepper Point or Flat Rock then the directions above will take you there over a easy but long walk, there is however a shorter way to reach these marks, although this route can be harder to walk. From the car park walk down the road towards the farm, on the left hand side of the road there is a five bar gate and style, from here follow the path to Stepper Point.

MAIN SUMMER SPECIES

The main species for these three marks are practically the same as they are within 1.5 miles of each other. Main species are Mackerel, Bass, Garfish, Plaice, Turbot, Wrasse, Pollack, Dogfish and occasional Rays.

MAIN WINTER SPECIES

These three marks are exceptionally good during the winter months for Flounder, Whiting and Cod.

BAIT & TIPS

Sandeels live or frozen, Lugworm, Ragworm, Squid strip, Mackerel strip, Peeler or soft backed Crab, Smelts and Cocktails of Squid and Worm. It is best to use a running ledger or pulley type rig with a plain lead, grip leads may be needed during high spring tides. At Flat Rock there is a number of bouys, so be careful when casting.

CAMEL ESTUARY   O.S.MAP REF. : 920755   NORTH COAST

The grid reference given above is for the main Padstow harbour. Fishing is possible from the harbour walls but care must be taken as this is a fully working harbour . From the carpark you can join the Camel trail, many good fishing marks can be seen from here , some of the best being, up to and around, the old railway bridge .

MAIN SUMMER SPECIES

Bass, Plaice, Flounder, Pollack and mackerel can be found in the estuary but mainly on very high spring tides .

MAIN WINTER SPECIES

Whiting and Codling travel up the estuary as far as the old railway bridge during the winter months, however Flounder are in abundance during the winter and early spring as are Bass these are the main species to be taken.

BAIT & TIPS

Ragworm, Lugworm, Sandeels live or frozen, Peeler or soft backed Crabs, a variety of spoons work well here also. Best rig is a running ledger although pulley rigs also work well. Plain leads are best, however, a 3 - 5oz grip lead may be needed on larger tides. Most of the estuary fishes well from about 2 hours after low water, right through the tide to almost low water.

ROCK   O.S.MAP REF. : 932767   NORTH COAST

Rock is situated on the Camel Estuary opposite Padstow on the B3314 from Wadebridge, parking is at Daymer Bay. Rock can also be reached via the foot ferry from Padstow.

The sandy beach at Rock offers the angler the chance to cast into the main river channel where currents can vary during different states of the tide. It is best to use baits that can be found in the Estuary.

MAIN SUMMER SPECIES

Bass and a variety of flat fish are always present during the summer months with possible Rays showing occasionally.

MAIN WINTER SPECIES

This is an exceptionally good mark for winter Flounder, with Codling and whiting also being caught.

BAIT & TIPS

Lugworm, Ragworm, live or frozen Sandeels, peeler or soft backed Crab, Smelt and Prawns.

Use a grip lead at this mark as the currents are very strong on rising and falling tides. Pulley rigs work better than a running ledger in these conditions.

Bass will take worm baits, although, larger fish fall to peeler or soft backed Crab.

Use beaded traces for flounder throughout the year with lugworm baits.

POLZEATH   O.S.MAP REF. : 935795   NORTH COAST

Hayle Bay at Polzeath is a prime surfing beach, however, excellent fishing can be done from the rocks at either side of the beach. To find this mark turn left off the B3314 at Higher Rosewin and follow the sign posts to Polzeath, park on the pay and display car park near the caravan site, this is near the top end of the beach. Good fishing is also possible at Broadagogue Cove, to get here follow the coastal footpath, fish from the beach or rocks at either side.

MAIN SUMMER SPECIES

Bass, Plaice, Turbot, Flounder, Mackerel and Garfish can be caught here, but only on very high Spring tides.

MAIN WINTER SPECIES

This is another good mark for Flounder, Codling and whiting during the winter months.

BAIT & TIPS

Sandeels live or frozen, Smelt, Mackerel strip, Lugworm, Ragworm, peeler or soft backed Crab. Fishing in the surf with live Sandeels, plain leads on pulley or running ledger rigs work very well for Bass. Lugworm tipped off with a small white Ragworm work well for flat fish.

RUMPS POINT   O.S.MAP REF. : 934813   NORTH COAST

The Rumps is situated approximately 1.5 miles North of Polzeath, see Carnweather point for parking details. From the car park follow the Southwest footpath North out to Rumps Point, from the top of the headland numerous paths lead down to the waters edge. Very good sport can be had from any of the rock marks around this headland, one of the best being out the very front to the right hand side, casting towards the island.

MAIN SUMMER SPECIES

Wrasse, Rays, Dogfish, Plaice, Turbot, Gurnard, Mackerel, Garfish, Scad, Pollack, Conger eel, Bass.

MAIN WINTER SPECIES

The main species taken during the winter are Cod, Pollack, Whiting, Coalfish, Dogfish, Rockling and occasional Flounder.

BAIT & TIPS

Mackerel strip, Squid strip, Ragworm Lugworm, peeler or soft backed Crab, Sandeels live or frozen or cocktails of most of these baits. Fish a deep float close in for Wrasse or Pollack, try using rubber eels for Pollack, Bass and Mackerel.

CARNWEATHER POINT   O.S.MAP REF. : 950803   NORTH COAST

Carnweather Point is situated approximately 1 mile East of Rumps Point, parking is on a gravel car park owned by the National Trust just past Pentire Farm. To reach this mark follow the B3314 towards St Minver, at the cross roads go straight on, now take the second left towards Porteath, from here follow the road to Pentire farm and the cap park beyond. From the car park follow the coastal path in an Easterly direction for about 650 yards then turn to the left, down a narrow steep path to the waters edge. The sea bed in this area is a mixture of sand with rocky outcrops to either side. Casting out to sea will find an area of sand.

MAIN SUMMER SPECIES

Pollack, Red Gurnard, Bass, Mackerel, Garfish, Tub Gurnard, Plaice, Dab, Turbot, Wrasse, Scad, Dogfish and Grey Gurnard. Occasional Small eyed Rays can be taken from this mark.

MAIN WINTER SPECIES

Although there are not as many species to be caught here during the winter months, Cod, Whiting, Pollack, Coalfish, Dogfish and Rockling can be taken here in large numbers.

BAIT & TIPS

Ragworm, Lugworm, Mackerel strip, Squid strip, Sandeels live or frozen, Peeler or soft backed Crab, Smelt .

Float fishing out to the left or right of this mark, can produce good sized Mackerel, Garfish, Pollack, Wrasse and occasional Bass. Use a running ledger off the front of this mark with a beaded trace and worm baits for flatfish.

The other rigs to use are pulley and paternoster rigs with long traces and up to size 6/0 hooks. Plain leads work very well at this mark, however if the tide is running the best thing to do is replace the plain lead with a gripper.

PORTQUIN   O.S.MAP REF. : 971805   NORTH COAST

To gain access to Portquin follow the signs off the B3314 down a very narrow road for about 1.5 miles, To the rear of the harbour there is a small car park, however, this is only a small car park with parking limited to approximately 20 vehicles.

Fishing is mainly available from the rocks around the harbour, there are numerous rock marks off the coast path, although, these can be dangerous and should only be fished by experienced anglers, and never alone.

MAIN SUMMER SPECIES

Bass, Pollack, Gurnard, Mackerel, Rockling, Garfish, Scad, Dogfish, Wrasse, and Conger eel.

MAIN WINTER SPECIES

The main winter species are Cod, Whiting, Rockling, Pollack, Dogfish, and Conger Eels.

BAIT & TIPS

Mackerel, Squid, Smelt, Lugworm, Ragworm, peeler or soft backed Crab Sandeels live or frozen.

Float fishing works well for most species, however, ledgering will take Gurnard, Dogfish, Conger eel, Rockling and Bass.

Never turn your back on the sea as the North coast Atlantic swell can become very large and freak waves can cover the rocks on this coastline.

This venue is one of the rock marks that you can be fishing about thirty feet above the water, this means that if you manage to catch a larger Conger Eel, you will need to bring it up the cliff, to do this, the best item to use is a flying gaff, this is on a rope and can be lowered down to the fish.

By tugging the rope sharply, you will hook the Eel with the points on the gaff, now you can hand line the fish up the cliff in total safety.

PORT ISAAC   O.S.MAP REF. : 995810   NORTH COAST

Follow the B3267 into Port Isaac and use the pay and display car park in the village, at low water it is possible to park in the harbour on the sand.

The sea bed in this area is mainly rocky outcrops and kelp, the small harbour and bay at Port Isaac are well known for its Mackerel e.t.c. Spinning baits, Plugs and Lures over the rocks can be very productive at this venue, as is night fishing .

MAIN SUMMER SPECIES

Mackerel, Garfish, Pollack, Bass, Wrasse, Scad, Rockling, Dogfish and Conger eels.

MAIN WINTER SPECIES

The north coast of Cornwall, particularly in this area is not renowned for its winter species, however this mark can produce a number of good fish, these are Cod, Whiting, Pollack, Rockling, Dogfish, Conger Eels and the occasional Coalfish is taken.

BAIT & TIPS

Ragworm, Squid strip or whole, Mackerel whole, strip or fillet, Smelts, peeler or soft backed Crab, live or frozen Sandeel, or Cocktails of Mackerel and Squid or Worm baits and Squid.

Use Ragworm in bunches or Crabs on float tackle for Wrasse, plugs and lures spun just below the surface work well for Bass, Pollack and Mackerel, bottom fish for Dogfish and Conger eels .

The best rigs to use at this venue for bottom fishing are, short pulley, single paternoster or a bomber rig, it is best to use a plain lead, bait clip and lead lift , this will aid the retrieval of end tackle. Use wire or heavy monofiliment line for Conger traces.

If fishing for Rockling or Wrasse, a rotten bottom should be used as this will cut down on tackle lose.

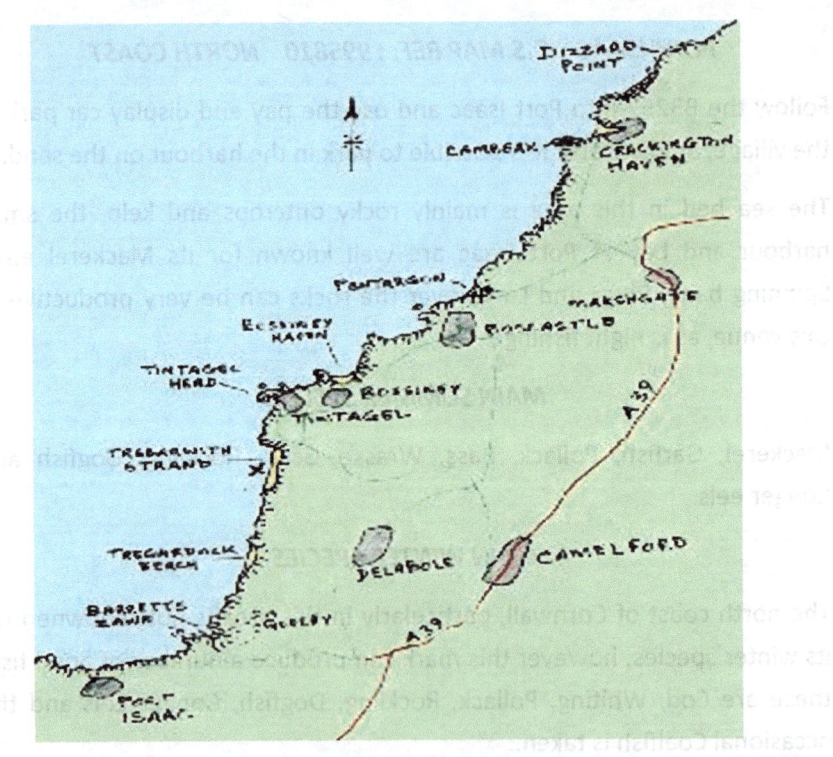

The above map covers the ground from Port Isaac to Dizzard Point, although all the marks mentioned on the map are not described in detail, these tend to fish similar to the nearest mark to them. A list of marks are shown below.

- Barretts Zawn.
- Tregardock Beach.
- Trebarwith strand.
- Tintagel Head.
- Bossiney Havern.
- Pentargon.
- Cambeak.
- Dizzard Point.

BARRETS ZAWN   O.S.MAP REF. : 027818   NORTH COAST

Situated at the Eastern end of Port Isaac Bay, to many anglers this is the home of the legendary Ballan Wrasse. Turn off the B3314 on to the narrow road to Higher Hendra at the cross roads, at China Down.

From here follow the Southwest coast path for approximately 1.5 miles until you reach the disused quarry above Barrets Zawn. Expect to loose some end tackle at this venue, however, the larger than usual Wrasse here are worth the risk.

MAIN SUMMER SPECIES

Wrasse, Bass, Pollack, Mackerel, Garfish, Scad, Small Conger Eels, Dogfish and Rockling.

MAIN WINTER SPECIES

Although this mark is worth fishing during the summer months, this venue can be quite barren during the winter, and with stormy weather blowing the sea up over the rocks, it can be quite dangerous, however the winter species are, Codling , Whiting , Pollack , Rockling , Dogfish and Conger eels.

BAIT & TIPS

Peeler or soft backed Crab, Sandeels live or frozen, Filleted Mackerel whole or strip, Ragworm, Whole or strip Squid, Muscles and limpets, Cocktails of Mackerel and Squid or Ragworm and Squid.

A float rig cast into the gullies works well at this mark, although ledgered rigs catch better fish particularly with Crab baits, Bass and Pollack make good sport on plugs or lures . Rockling fall to fish baits .

The best rigs to use at this mark are pulley or paternoster rigs with short, heavy traces, it is best to use a lead lift here as this will cut down on end tackle loss. It is a very good idea to use a rotten bottom rig for Wrasse in this area, this will also help to cut down on lose of end tackle.

TREGARDOCK BEACH   O.S.MAP REF. : 040840   NORTH COAST

Tregardock is reached from the B3314 at Westdowns follow the coast path from the hamlet. Like Trebarwith Strand this is a Atlantic storm beach, with a strong under tow, the tide advances rapidly up this beach. Make sure that you leave any tackle above the high water mark. This beach is only accessible on the dropping tide and is only uncovered for approximately 4 hours, Make sure that you plan your trip using a tide table as fishing time is restricted.

MAIN SUMMER SPECIES

Bass, Rays, Wrasse and Dogfish, although Mackerel and Garfish do turn up on very high spring tides.

MAIN WINTER SPECIES

Winter species at this mark are very few and far between with Codling, Whiting and Dogfish being the main fish caught here.

BAIT & TIPS

Peeler or soft backed Crab, live or frozen Sandeels, Squid strip and Mackerel strip, Ragworm, Lugworm, and Cocktails of Squid and Worm baits. This mark fishes similarly to Trebarwith Strand, with a strong surf grip leads of 4 - 6oz may be needed. This venue fishes exceptionally well for the amount of time you can spend here. Best fishing is 2 hours either side of low water. The best rigs to use at this mark are, running ledgers, pulley or twin paternosters, use these with a plain lead as this will move around in the surf and cover more ground. If distance casting then it may be better to use a bait clip as this will protect the bait during the cast.

TREBARWITH STRAND   O.S.MAP REF. : 048864   NORTH COAST

This beach is situated approximately 2 miles South of Tintagel, being an Atlantic beach it is much favoured by surfers, however, fishing is possible and can be very productive from the rocks at either end of the beach. Turn off the B3314 just after Westdowns and follow the road through Trebarwith, turn left at the cross roads to the car park, there is a walk of approximately 300 - 400 yds to the beach.

MAIN SUMMER SPECIES

Mackerel, Garfish, Bass, Pollack, Rays, Wrasse, Rockling Plaice and Turbot.

MAIN WINTER SPECIES

Cod, Whiting, Pollack, Coalfish, Dogfish, Rockling and small Conger Eels can all be taken from this mark during the winter.

BAIT & TIPS

Live or frozen Sandeels, Mackerel, Peeler or soft backed Crab, Lugworm, Ragworm and artificial lures. Fish ledgered worm baits for flat fish from the ends of the beach out of the main surf run. When fishing for Bass in the surf it is best to hold your rod as Bass take the bait very sharply and a strike may be missed if the rod is in the rest. Keep an eye on the surf as it comes up this beach quite quickly.

TINTAGEL - BUDE NORTH COAST

This stretch of coast contains many rocky marks and covers a lot of ground, but it is for the most part inaccessible for the average angler. The Atlantic coast swell can also present several problems with anglers either being cut off by the tide or washed off the rocks, so great care is necessary if you decide to fish at any of the marks along this stretch of coast line. Most marks can be reached off the B3263 road, or from off the Southwest coast path.

MAIN SUMMER SPECIES

Bass, Pollack, Wrasse, Mackerel, Garfish, Scad, Plaice, Turbot, Gurnard, Rays, Bull Huss, dogfish and Conger eel.

MAIN WINTER SPECIES

Although this stretch of coast covers a large amount of ground that can be fished during the summer and winter, care must be taken, particularly during the winter as this coast experience numerous storms at this time of year, due to this it can be dangerous to fish this area during winter, however the main species are Cod, Whiting, Rockling, Codling, Pollack, Coalfish, Flounder, Dogfish and Conger Eels.

BAIT & TIPS

Mackerel whole or strip, Sandeel live or frozen, peeler or soft backed Crab, Ragworm, artificial plugs and lures, Lugworm, Smelt, Squid whole or strip, and cocktails of Mackerel and Squid or Worm baits and Squid.

Travel light and have good footwear, excellent sport for Pollack and Bass can be had using light spinning tackle and artificial lures.

Ledgered Crab is good for large Ballan Wrasse and Bass but tackle loses can be high. If plugging in this area it is best to use a short leader as this should help to cut down the loss of plugs and lures. One of the most used methods of fishing in this area is Float fishing, set the depth at between 8 and 12 feet for best results.

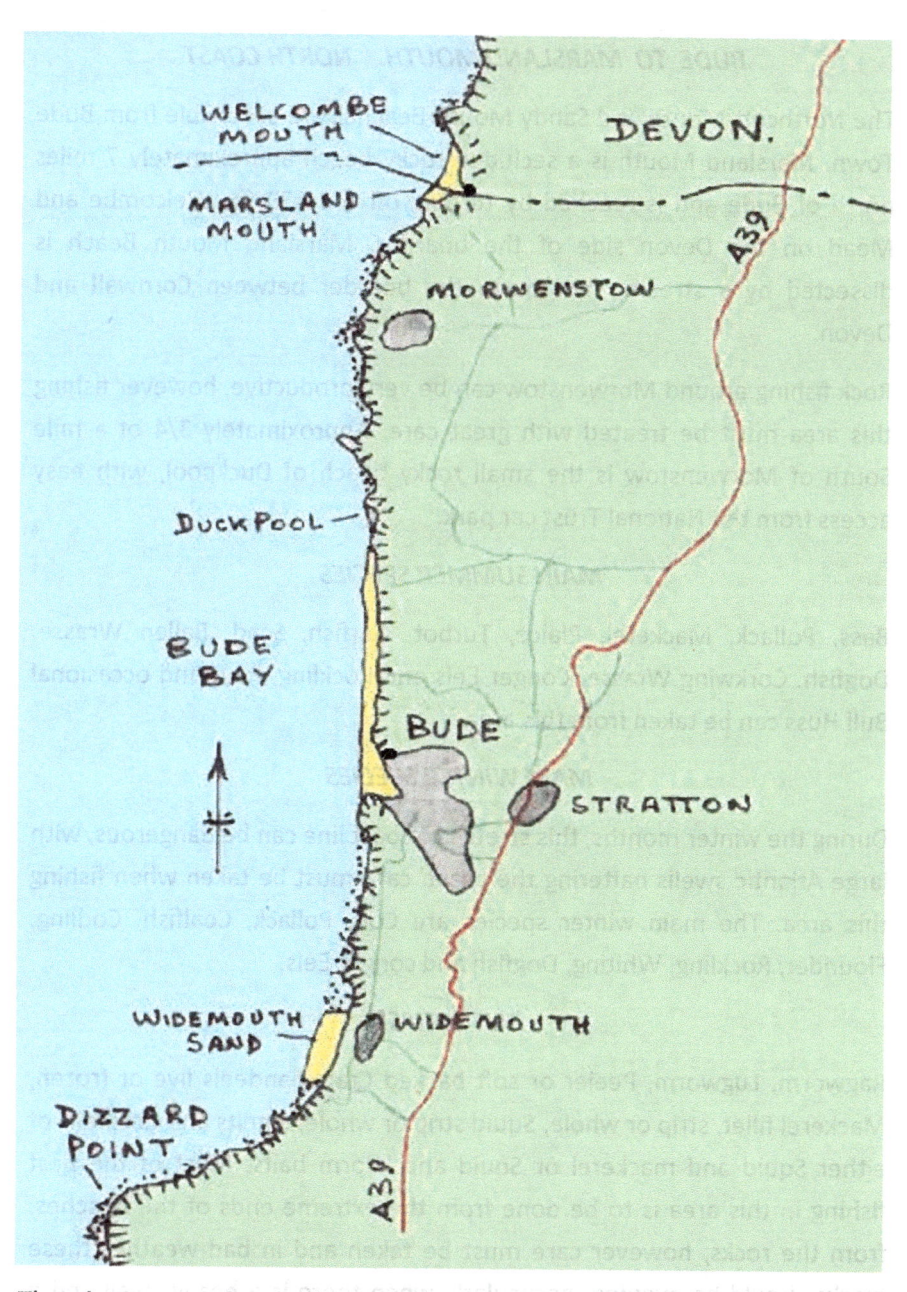

The above map shows the remaining coast line of Cornwall, up to the boarder in Devon, this area will fish in the same way as the marks on the previous page.

BUDE TO MARSLAND MOUTH. NORTH COAST

The Northcott Mouth and Sandy Mouth Beaches are accessible from Bude Town. Marsland Mouth is a secluded rocky beach approximately 7 miles north of Bude and is reached by turning off the A39 for Welcombe and Mead on the Devon side of the boarder. Marsland Mouth Beach is dissected by a stream, this marks the boarder between Cornwall and Devon.

Rock fishing around Morwenstow can be very productive, however fishing this area must be treated with great care. Approximately 3/4 of a mile South of Morwenstow is the small rocky beach of Duckpool, with easy access from the National Trust car park.

MAIN SUMMER SPECIES

Bass, Pollack, Mackerel, Plaice, Turbot, Garfish, Scad, Ballan Wrasse, Dogfish, Corkwing Wrasse, Conger Eels and Rockling, Rays and occasional Bull Huss can be taken from this area.

MAIN WINTER SPECIES

During the winter months, this stretch of coast line can be dangerous, with large Atlantic swells battering the coast, care must be taken when fishing this area. The main winter species are Cod, Pollack, Coalfish, Codling, Flounder, Rockling, Whiting, Dogfish and conger Eels.

BAIT & TIPS

Ragworm, Lugworm, Peeler or soft backed Crab, Sandeels live or frozen, Mackerel fillet, strip or whole, Squid strip or whole, Smelts and Cocktails of either Squid and mackerel or Squid and Worm baits. Most of the best fishing in this area is to be done from the extreme ends of the beaches, from the rocks, however care must be taken and in bad weather these marks should be avoided, particularly when there is a heavy swell and a strong Westerly wind. These areas, however can be very productive after a storm. Best rigs to use are pulley, paternoster and beach Cod rigs.

You are never to young to start Sea Angling, Roseanna age 10 won the Grenville Sea Angling Club, OpenCompetition, 1998, Ladies and Junior section on her first competition outing.

The future of Sea Angling depends on the encouragement and education of youngsters in the pleasures, techniques and responsibilities of our sport, most fishing clubs welcome junior members.

The fish, a Scad weighing in just below the 1lb mark, taken from Gorran Haven on the South Coast.

Roseanna 1998

You are never to young to start Sea Angling. Roseanne age 10 won the Grenville Sea Angling Club Open Competition 1998. Ladies and Junior section on her first competition outing.

The future of Sea Angling depends on the encouragement and education of youngsters in the pleasures, techniques and responsibilities of the sport much fishing clubs welcome junior members.

The first, a Conn weighing in at 9lb 9oz was hit the 21st March, taken from Courtan Haven on the South Coast.

Roseanna 1998

Boat Angling

*Paul Quintrell, Grenville S.A.C.
with a double figure Pollack.*

Nigel Parish with two small Ling taken from one of the many charter boats from Cornish ports

BOAT ANGLING

The main aim of this booklet is to try to help the novice and hardened boat angler to catch more fish.

The main principles of boat angling are :

- To be properly dressed for the occasion.
- To have the right rod and reel for the job ahead.
- Be kited out with the right end tackle and weights.
- To have a supply of properly prepared baits.
- And most of all be safe, comfortable and have fun.

When choosing a charter boat make sure that it is D.T.I registered, this means that you have insurance against any accidents. There are good charter boats around the coast of Cornwall and a variety of ports to choose from, your local tackle dealer should be able to put you on to you on to a good boat if asked. Once a boat has been booked it is essential that you take in to consideration that the weather can change and trips can be cancelled, so always check the radio or television the night before your trip. Many anglers believe that it is essential to have good dry footwear this usually means nonslip Wellingtons, a hat is also a good idea as this will not only keep your head dry but will also keep the sun off.

Always wear or carry waterproof clothing, a floatation suit is best these are 100% waterproof and will keep your body at a steady temperature.

On many charter boats you will have the opportunity to catch bait fish on the way out to the mark that is to be fished these are usually Mackerel or Scad, it is best to ask the skipper of the boat if you will have the opportunity when booking the trip as this could determine the amount of bait you will need to take with you.

RODS AND REELS

Nearly all boat anglers these days carry at least two rods and reels, normally a light class rod (12lb - 15lb) and a heavier class being around (30 - 50) class. Reels used on a light class are normally the size of the ABU 6500, for heavier fishing use a reel in the size range of the Penn 4/0 or ABU 7000. When using a light class rod for example.

- 15lb class rods use 15lb breaking line.
- 20lb class rods use 20lb breaking strain line.

This rule applies all the way up the scale of rods, however it is alright to use 15lb line on a rod upwards of 15lb class. Some boat rods have a rating of 12 - 15lb or 20 - 30lb, 30 - 50lb and 50 - 80lb class if your rod has this type of weight limit on it then you can use line up to the limit. If buying a new boat outfit, always ask the dealer for advice as they will be able to offer a wide variety of rods and the reels to match accordingly. On many of the charter boats you can have the opportunity of uptiding to do this you need a different type of rod as these are around 9 feet upwards and have a casting weight of normally 2 - 8oz and 4 - 10 oz, these are used in a different way to a normal boat rod

ROD LENGTHS

* 12lb class - 7ft - 7.5ft
* 15lb class - 7ft
* 20lb class - 6.5ft - 7ft.
* 40lb class 6.5ft.
* 50lb class - 6ft.
* 50 - 80lb class - 5ft - 6ft.
* The average size for uptiding rod is around 10ft.

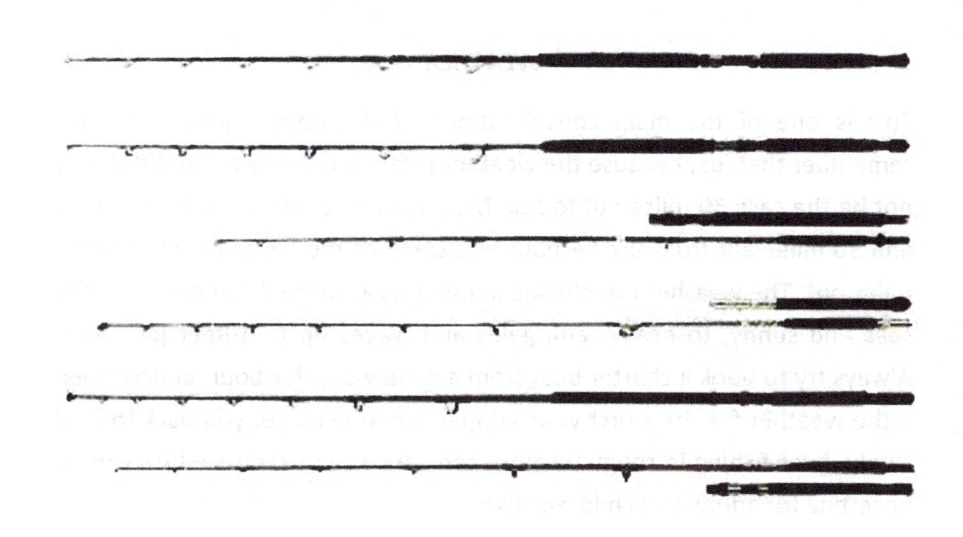

BOAT REELS

These are basically the same as the multiplier's used for shore fishing, however, these tend to be larger in size and hold a greater quantity and strength line. Although these reels can be cast and used from the beach and rocks, they are mainly used by lowering the bait over the side of a boat, this is one of the reasons for the greater line capacity. Many shore anglers use boat reels for conger fishing as these tend to be built out of heavier materials and seem to cope better with a large heavy fish, being retrieved from rough ground or kelp. There are two types of drag used on these reels, as mentioned before, the lever drag is adjusted by pushing the lever towards the front of the reel to increase the drag and pulling it back to decrease it, many of these reels also have the free spool mechanism on the same lever, to operate this pull the lever all the way to the rear of the reel. When casting with one of these reels care must be taken as they tend to suffer with over runs and bird nests more frequently than their smaller counter parts.

WEATHER

This is one of the main considerations of the boat angler, you must remember that just because the weather is fair and sunny on land this may not be the case 30 miles out to sea. Most charter boats travel between 20 and 30 miles out from the harbour and some of the faster boats go as far miles out. The weather can change in minutes at these distances, from flat seas and sunny, to heavy rain, gales and waves up to 10feet plus high. Always try to book a charter boat from a deep water harbour, at least then if the weather for the worst your skipper can at least get you back to land safely, boat fishing in rough weather can cause sea sickness which can be upsetting for adults and children alike.

Weather Chart:

Scale	*Weather Condition*	*Wind Speed*	*Wave Height*
Force 0	Flat calm	Under 1 Knot	Mirror like 0
Force 1	Ripples on water	1 - 3 knots	3 inches max
Force 2	Light Breeze, small waves, glassy look.	4 - 6 knots	6 - 18 inches
Force 3	Gentle breeze, waves start breaking.	7 - 10 knots	about 2ft
Force 4	Moderate breeze, constant white horses on small waves.	11- 16 knots	about 3 - 5ft
Force 5	Brisk wind, white horses breaking with spray.	17- 21 knots	about 6 feet

Anything stronger and it is probably better to stay at home.

Make sure that the boat that you are going on is carrying all the necessary safety equipment on it and has enough life jackets for all the crew and passengers, and a ship to shore radio that is in working order. If in doubt ask the skipper as he or she will be happy to show you. The first thing to do is check the state of the tide on the day of your trip as this will be a guide to the sort of fishing you will be doing, the skipper should be able to tell you what to expect at the time of booking your trip, if you are unsure then contact the skipper a few days before hand.

SPRING TIDES

Spring tides mean that you would be fishing in fast flowing currents, probably drifting over wrecks or reefs with lures or pirks, however, if the chance arises to use Sandeel then do so as this normally will produce decent fish.

NEAP TIDES

On neap tides the boat will probably be anchored above a reef or wreck and you will find that fresh baited hooks will work better that lures or pirks, as the boat could be anchored for long periods of time it will pay to vary the bait as this will attract different species of fish.

The boat will almost certainly be using a fish finder and your skipper should be able to catch Mackerel to use as bait on your way out so, make sure that you are carrying Mackerel feathers with you. Using feathers from a boat is fairly easy as all you have to do is lower them down reel up a few turns and then just raise and lower the rod tip until the fish start to bite.

TIDES

Tides result from the gravitational pull of the sun and moon upon the earth's surface waters. Twice a day the sea level rises and subsides, the period between each high tide is 12 hours, 25 minutes and this does not vary. As the tide interval is not exactly 12 hours, the actual times of high water on the day are about 1 hour later than the preceding day. This means that a beach where the tide is fully in at 9.00am on one day, will experience low water approximately 6 hours 12.5 minutes later at around 3.12pm, and high tide again at 9.25pm, (i.e. 12 hours 25 minutes since the previous high water). Because the moon orbits the earth, and the moon and earth orbit the sun, their alignment will vary throughout the lunar month.

This means that the gravitational pull will also vary, and as a consequence tide height will be affected. Spring tides, where the rise and fall is by a greater amount than the monthly average occur when the sun, earth and moon are in a direct line with each other at periods of full and new moon, when the greatest gravitational influence is exerted. Neap tides which are produced during the moons first and last quarter, have a rise and fall

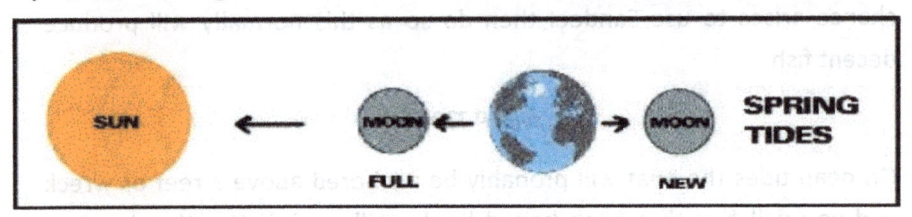

[Diagram: SUN ← MOON ← EARTH → MOON — SPRING TIDES (FULL / NEW)]

which are below the monthly average, due to the moon exerting a gravitational influence lateral to the sun's.

The moon and suns pull on the earth are not the only things to effect the

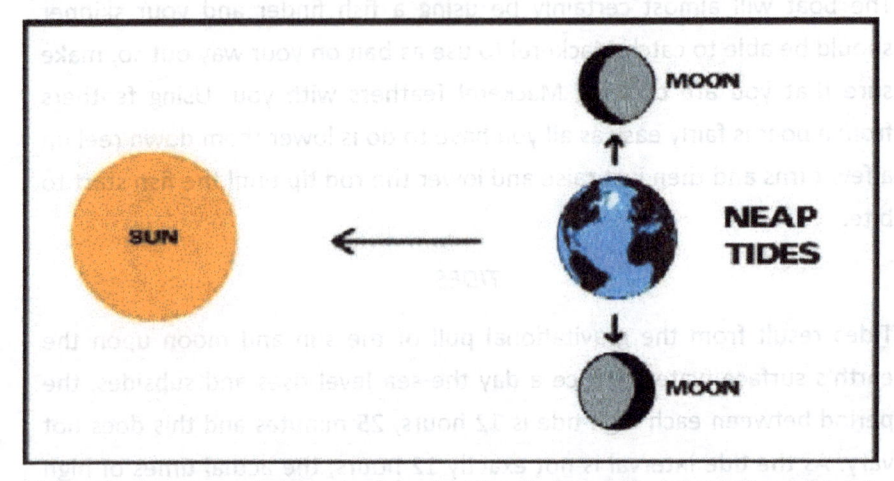

[Diagram: SUN ← EARTH with MOON above and below — NEAP TIDES]

tides, for instance the gravitational pull will determine the tide coming in and out and to a certain degree it will determine the height but throw a gale force six wind on shore and the tide will significantly grow becoming at least 33% higher, turn the wind around and make it an offshore gale and the tide will be lower, although the waves will get backed up and become bigger, so always take in to account what the wind is doing when organising your fishing trip.

SHOPPING LIST

This shopping list has been put together to enable the boat angler to sort through existing end tackle and possibly add to it if necessary, the following items can be purchased quite cheaply from local tackle dealers. Although many boat anglers use large hooks when fishing, many specimen fish are caught each year on smaller baited shore fishing hooks.

- *monofiliment or braided line breaking strain to rod class.*
- *An assortment of crane swivels, and 3 way swivels*
- *Assorted beads.*
- *An assortment of hook types and sizes.*
- *Wire trace material, Assorted crimps and pliers.*
- *An assortment of booms (wire and plastic).*
- *Rubber eels (assorted colours, Red gill, Eddystone Delta)*
- *Assorted Plugs and Pirks.*
- *An assortment of different size and type weights.*

Unless uptiding, there is no need for a shockleader as you do not have to cast your weight out from the boat, just let the weight go over the side of the boat and sink to the bottom. If you are fishing over clean ground you can leave it there, however, if the area has rough ground, it pays to raise the lead about seven turns on the reel to bring the weight clear of any snags.

LINES

There are now only two main types of lines used from the boat, these are monofiliment and braided line. monofiliment line is quite thick and is best used when not fishing in a current, whilst braided lines being a lot thinner have less drag in the water and are therefore better in all conditions. Although braided line is more costly, the difference in diameter drag makes it worth while most braided lines are less than half the diameter of the same breaking strain monofiliment line.

TRACES

These are made from various breaking strains of line from a light trace of 10lbs for the smaller species to traces made from 250lb line used for heavy fishing over rough ground for Conger eels. Nylon coated wire can be used however it has to be crimped at either and as it is not worth trying to tie knots in this material. Wire traces are best used for fishing over wrecks and a breaking strain of around 100lbs is recommended.

BOOMS

Booms are an essential item in boat fishing, these can vary in size and shape depending on what type of fishing is being done. Booms are best used when fishing in deeper water as these stand the trace away from the main line and prevents tangling of main and trace lines. French booms of around 8 - 10 inches should be used when drift fishing over wrecks and reefs, a more solid boom such as the boat boom, sea boom or Eddystone boom should be used when bottom fishing as these stand up to the wear and tear. Zip slider booms should be used when fishing with a running ledger, this puts less strain on the main lines, compared with just using a swivel. Two other types of booms are the uptide and down tide booms, these work in very much the same way as the ones above, however, these are used for a different type of fishing altogether.

WEIGHTS

The amount of weight used depends on the type of fishing and states of the tide. it is best to carry a selection of weights with you on the boat, ranging from 4oz to 1.5lbs for use in strong currents. During high water the weight used can be 8oz plus to hold your position, however, on slack water you will find that, out of the current you will only need a weight of 6oz and possibly less. Drifting weights should be of the torpedo type as these cut through the water and do not spin, bottom weights should be of the bopedo type as these lie flat on the bottom. The other types of lead are the uptide and down tide breakaway lead, these have four stainless steel legs which hold in the bottom until a fish bites or the angler strikes at which time the legs turn back on themselves and release the lead.

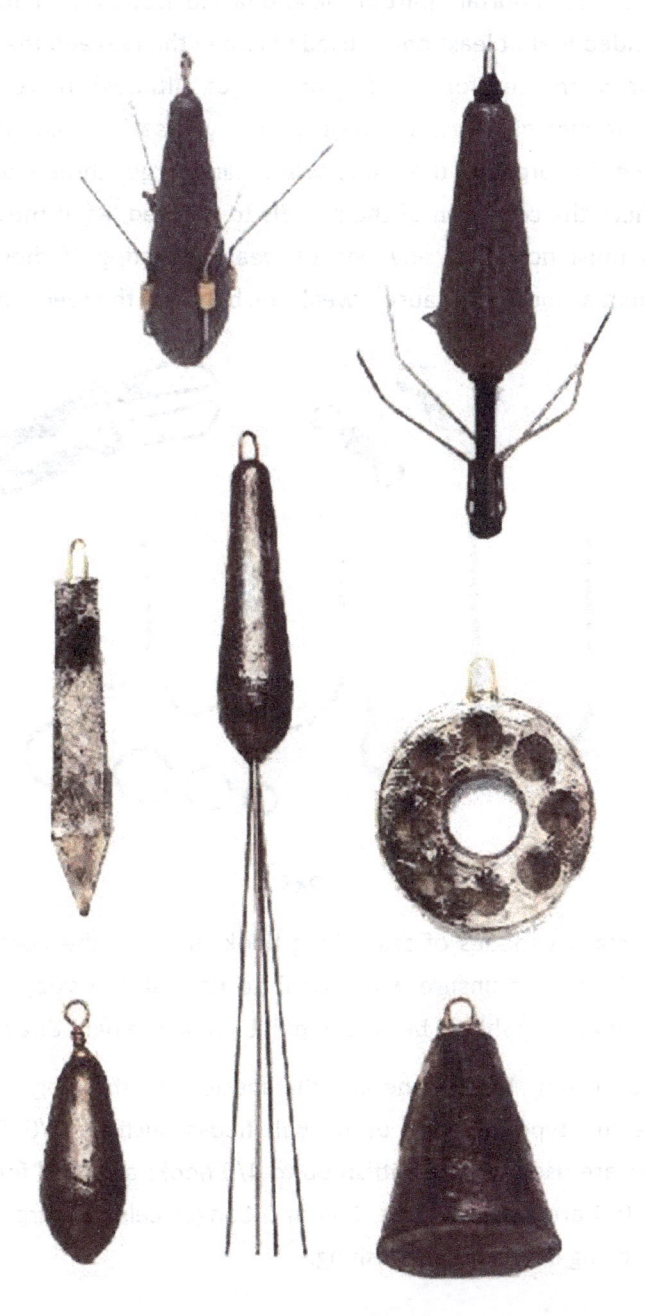

SWIVELS

These are a very important part of the end tackle used by boat anglers, it is recommended that at least one is used between the reel and the hook and up to four when used for Sharking or Conger. Although there are many different varieties of swivel it is best to limit yourself to using two types, these being the larger of the crane swivels and larger three way swivels. Always check the condition of the swivels to be used, as, if these are not new they must not show any sign of wear or rusting, if they do then discard them as these can cause a weak link between the reel and hook.

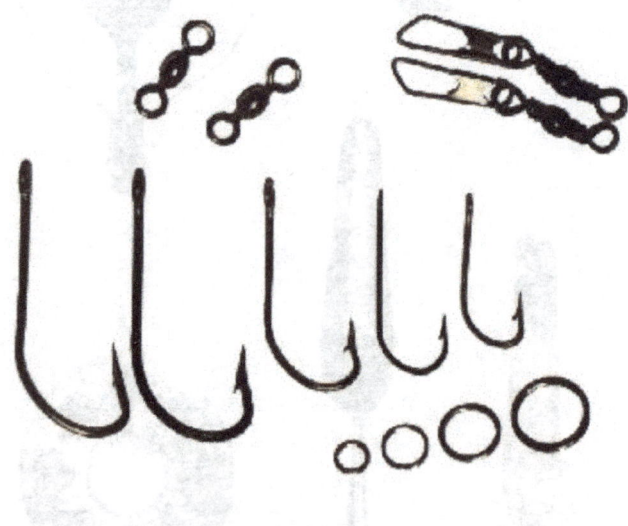

HOOKS

There are many varieties of sea fishing hooks used on the boats around the coast, if you are unsure which hook to use ask the skipper or local tackle dealer as they should be able to point you in the right direction.

The type of angling being done and the species of fish being sought will determine the type of hook used, small hooks such as 1/0 BLNs and Aberdeen's are used for the flatfish up to 4/0 hooks are used for Whiting and 6/0 - 0/0 are used for Ling, Cod and Conger eels. The largest of the hook sizes being used for Shark fishing.

ESSENTIAL ITEMS

When doing any boat or shore angling there are a few items that you should carry with you these are:

- *A very sharp knife.*
- *A T-bar forceps or pliers.*
- *Polarised sun glasses.*
- *A nylon bag for taking fish home.*

BUT PADS ETC

These are recommended to help protect the boat angler from any unnecessary strain whilst playing a heavy fish, fighting a large Conger Eel or Ling from the deep can cause damage to the groin area. To carry all of the tackle you have including spare reels, flasks, food, lures, pirks, swivels, hooks and beads etc: it is best to acquire a seat box as this is not only used for storage but can also be used to sit on whilst the boat is getting out to the marks that you will be fishing.

BAITS AND LURES

The main bait by far for boat anglers is fresh Mackerel, these are usually caught on the day. Live Sandeels are the best bait for fish, such as Pollack, Bass, Coalfish, and Whiting, whilst frozen eels large Launce, Ling and Pouting.

Squid is a primary bait fished whole for Ling although large Pollack and Coalfish will also take the bait. Ragworm or Lugworm is best for species such as Plaice, Flounder, Wrasse and Bream.

PIRKS

Pirks are common tackle for wrecking. These are solid metal bars with large treble hooks which can be baited and used for Cod, Pollack and Coalfish. Ling can be caught if baited with fresh Squid. Sizes vary from 8oz - 2lbs.

LURES AND FEATHERS

Ready made feathered traces such as Silver Shrimps, Gold Shrimps or Hokkai lure are ideal for catching fresh Mackerel, but baited with Mackerel or Squid will catch Whiting, Ling, Pouting and occasionally Pollack, Coalfish or Cod.

ARTIFICIAL EELS, LURES

The most popular of lures is the redgill rubber eel, although, Eddystone and Delta eels work as well, these come in a multitude of colours and four different sizes, 115mm rascal, 178mm raver being the most popular among anglers. these come in a multitude of colours and four different sizes, 115mm rascal, 178mm raver being the most popular among anglers. For some unknown reasons different coloured eels needed for different areas being fished, these can be trolled or cast and retrieved at different speeds to attract fish.

Mainly used for drifting for Pollack, Coalfish, although, can be very useful for Cod and Ling. Small single black, red, silver-grey or orange eels trolled from the side of the boat can be a deadly method for catching Mackerel and the Garfish or Scad, a small piece of fish bait on a small eel will attract Pouting and possible Dogfish in most areas.

FLIERS

This is a term used for a rubber eel placed at the top of the trace. This gives the impression that the larger rubber eel at the bottom of the trace is following or chasing the one at the top.

For best results with this method use two eels the same colour either black or red, as these seem to work best, especially in deeper water.

A flier can also be used with fresh fish baits or live eel baits, for Cod and Ling. When using a flying eel it often pays to use a longer trace as this lets the larger eel move more freely in the water, not recommended whilst wreck fishing.

WRECK FISHING

Wreck fishing is the best and possibly the most productive way of boat angling giving the angler consistent changes of specimen fish. The best wrecks to fish possibly are outside the 20 mile band as these are not fished as often.

The secret in catching good fish is all down to the skippers positioning and anchored in the right place according to wind and tide. The most dominant species found on wrecks are Conger eel, Ling, Pollack, Coalfish and Black/Red Bream, although Cod and Whiting can be present at different times of the year.

Conger eel and Ling are mainly taken on heavy tackle using ledgered Mackerel or Squid baits, Pollack and Coalfish will fall to medium tackle used with artificial eels. The most productive zone being the bottom 10 - 15 fathoms.

Black and Red Bream is best fished for using light tackle and small hooks baited with Lugworm or Crab and dropped right into the middle of the wreckage, note, this is only possible when the boat is anchored and not drifting.

Other species to be found around wreckage and on the sand bars are various types of Ray i.e. Blond Ray etc:, Turbot, Whiting, Pouting, Mackerel, Scad, Dogfish and occasional Cod and Garfish. On inshore wrecks it is possible to pick up most of the above species of fish and possibly on or around more shallow wrecks, Bass, Wrasse, Plaice and Rockling.

REEF FISHING

Most reef fishing is done by drifting or trolling artificial eels and lures or hooks baited with strips of Mackerel or Squid, baited feathers such as Silver Shrimp work well in this environment. Most species of fish caught over the reef are usually Pollack, Pouting and Coalfish, Mackerel are usually present and are taken on Silver Shrimp or feathers, Pouting fall to feathers baited with Mackerel strip. The most successful end tackle used in this environment is a long boom with up to a 10oz lead and 15 foot trace, with a 178mm black or red artificial eel attached, fliers also work well over this type of ground. Bass are also caught with this method, but the most successful way is to drift slowly over the reef using a lighter lead, 10foot trace and live Sandeels. One of the best known reefs is situated in Cornwall and is called the Eddystone Reef. This reef is made up from a large variety of various sized rocks and corals, which give many different species of fish numerous habitats and hiding places. The Eddystone Reef has a great reputation for specimen sized Bass and various other species of fish caught each year. When anchored over a deep water reef during a neap tide it is possible to catch medium sized Ling of approximately 15lbs in weight and Conger eels can give the angler some fantastic sport when weighing in at around 14lbs average.

Shallow water reefs are normally the home to the Rockling, Pouting, Bass, Mackerel, Scad, Garfish and different varieties of Wrasse, these are best fished for on light tackle of around 12lb - 15lb class rod and small multiplier, using fresh bait such as Ragworm for Wrasse and fish bait like Mackerel or live Sandeels for Pollack etc.

It is surprising just how many inshore reefs can be found around the United Kingdom, many of these even come right up to or within casting distance of well known rock marks, however these if fished from the shore should be done using a float system, however this is a boat angling section. To fish these inshore reefs you will, for safety reasons need a fish finder or depth gauge, fish finders come with this feature as standard, always make sure that even in calm waters you have at least eight feet clearance between the boats hull and the rocks below.

These reefs are fished in much the same way as deep water ones, however you will notice the difference fishing shallower water and will also stand a good chance of catching different species compared to deep water marks.

Trolling

To use this method you really do need fixed rod rests on the sides or rear of your boat, these can be purchased from some angling stores and many boat shops at a very reasonable price. Very few boat anglers use this method, which is a pity as this technique can be absolutely devastating, catching large numbers of Mackerel, Garfish, Pollack and of coarse Bass.

Although I have used this method with a carp rod I wouldn't recommend it as the boat will be moving and putting a great strain on it a heavier rod is required for this technique and in most cases a six to eight foot twelve pound class boat rod is ideal.

You can troll using either feathers, spinners, lures and even bait, it's not what you use but more the method of moving the feathers/lures around the water that counts, this method works very well in estuaries, inshore and offshore, but care must be taken in estuaries as there are always boat moorings etc. to manoeuvre around.

If you are using feathers for trolling then apart from the weight you need no other end tackle, however should you want to use either a spinner/lure or bait it is best to use a French boom, this is basically a wire boom that comes is different sizes, you would require the small or medium for this purpose. To use the French boom simply tie it to the end of your line using a half hitch blood or clinch not, attach a six ounce plus lead weight to the other side of the triangular frame and a long hook length to the extended arm, the hook length can be of any length but between four and six feet is best, now tie the spinner/lure or hook if using bait on the end, you are now ready to use the boom.

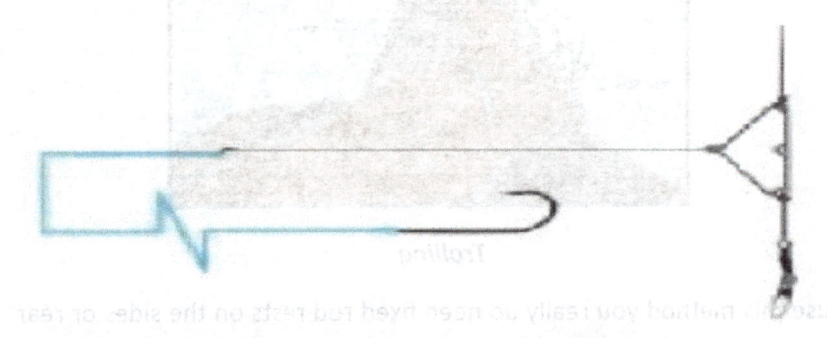

With the boat stationary or slowly drifting lower your rig or feathers over the back of the boat, when the lead hits the bottom reel it back up about ten turns of the reel, this should move your feathers, spinner/lure or bait away from the bottom sufficiently enough to clear most snags and as the weight will rise as the boat starts to move this should be an adequate depth to fish at, as your boat moves over deeper water you can let line from the reel to compensate for any depth change. Now put the rod or rods in the rod rests and start to move the boat, you do not want to be moving around the surface like a bat out of hell four to five knots should be fast enough to start with, as the boat starts to move forwards the lead will start to lift until your line is roughly at a 45 degree angle to the boat, if it doesn't reach this angle speed up slightly, or above that angle slow the boat down. Mackerel tend to feed in the mid to surface water, however skimming the surface with feathers, spinners/lures or bait will not catch anything so get the speed right and you will be in the fish, get it wrong and you could be loosing your end tackle. When a fish does take the bait so to speak, you should take hold of the rod from the rest and reel in any slack line, again this method normally hook the fish for you so there really is no need to strike and in doing so could lose you the fish, continue reeling in until you have the fish safely on the boat, remove your feathers, spinner/lure or hook from the fishes mouth check all the knots and put it back out and start all over again. As stated Mackerel tend to feed in the top third of the water, this is because they chase sandeels towards the surface before ambushing them, the same applies to bass, however they are not always chasing the sandeels, the fact of the matter is that they chase mackerel to the surface, when this happens the surface of the water looks as if it is boiling, pollack feed in all layers of water, from top to bottom, these facts should be taken in to account when trolling.

Only dig where permitted

Cleaning And Filleting Fish

Before you start to clean or fillet fish, there are a few essential tools that are required, these are a sharp filleting knife, a sharp pair of kitchen scissors and a chopping board or work surface.

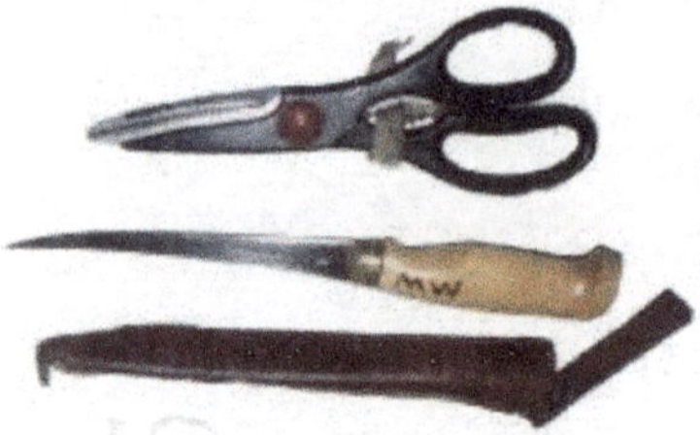

The following method of Cleaning and Filleting fish can be used for the preparation of fish to be cooked or for bait fish. With most fish for cooking, the need to remove the scales is very important. To do this, First wash the fish and plaice it on a flat surface, now, using the back edge of a knife, run the blade, almost flat, from the tail to the head of the fish, going against the run of the scales. Once this has been done wash the fish again to remove any remaining scales. Now the fish is ready to be Gutted and Filleted.

REMOVING THE HEAD

Most fish can be cooked with the head still attached, however with most recipes it is best to remove this. If preparing the fish for bait do not follow this step. With a sharp knife, plaice the edge of the blade just behind the gill cover and with a small amount of pressure cut through the skin and bone.

With larger fish, the use of a cleaver may be required to cut through the spinal cord.

REMOVING THE GUTS

With the head removed, cut the under side of the fish, between the ventral fins and all the way down to the tail.

Once this has been done, remove all of the internal parts of the fish, plaice this in a bag or bin. Now wash the inside of the fish to remove any blood etc left behind.

REMOVING THE BONES

With the internals of the fish removed, cut down each side of the back bone, try not to go through the skin.

Now turn the fish over and with the palm of your hand apply pressure to the back of the fish, start at the end where the head was and work down to the tail end.

Turn the fish back over and locate the end of the back bone, using the filleting knife, cut across the end of the bone and with your finger and thumb hold the bone, place your other hand at the head end of the fish, to hold it in position.

Now pull up the bone, this should come away from the meat of the fish, place the bone in a bag , bin or keep for fish stock.

Your fish should now look like this. Once again rinse the fish to remove any pieces of bone still remaining, The fish is now ready for the last step.

REMOVAL OF FINS

This can be done at the very beginning of the section on cleaning and filleting fish, however doing this as the last part means that the fish does not get holes cut in the back and side, if the back bone has already been removed, this part is easier to do .

With a sharp pair of kitchen scissors, cut through the fins at the base. Now your fish is ready to be cooked.

Although a Mackerel is used to show the filleting, this method can be used on most species, i.e. Bass, Cod, Pollack, Ling, Garfish, Coalfish etc. However this is not the way to fillet a flatfish, this is done by firstly removing the guts by cutting the fish from the rear of the anal fin to just below the gill cover, remove the guts and then wash and lay the fish on a flat surface.

With a sharp knife cut the skin on the upper side of the fish just below the dorsal fin, do not go through the bones, these act as a guide, now with the knife laid on it's side using the bones as a guide cut into the fish until you reach the lateral line. This is a small row of bones, once reached, turn the fish around and once again cut down to the bone of the anal fin and use it as a guide to go to the middle of the fish, cut around the back of the head and then gently pull the side fillet from the lateral line bones. Once done repeat the operation on the underside of the fish. If you do this right you will have two bone free flatfish fillets.

Fish
Recipe's

There are several reasons for people to go fishing.

People who go fishing for a living, this is hard work but the fishermen enjoy their job, and most of all they have a love of the sea.

People who go fishing just for the sheer fun of it, and sometimes, these people are not very selective in what they catch, and how they catch it.

People who go fishing as a sport these people are more selective and usually make sure that the fish are the correct size or larger than the size specified by the M.A.F.F.

There are people that go fishing because they want to fish to eat, these people are the ones who only fish when it is necessary.

The recipes that are in this book have been carefully thought out for people who have been fishing to eat their catch which is the desirable thing to do.

Should you go fishing and have the fish that you require to eat, please put the other fish back carefully into the sea for another day, or for someone who may at some future date want to eat fish.

Patricia. M. Weaver

1938 - 2002

COD (STUFFED)

Preparation time 35 minutes.

Oven temperature 180c: 350f: Gas mark 4.

Cooking time 45 minutes approximately.

Ingredients.

Tail end piece of Cod 2 - 2.5lb.

1/2 Lemon (juice and rind.)

4oz Breadcrumbs. 1.1/2 Melted Butter.

Salt and Pepper to taste.

1 teaspoon of chopped fresh tyme.

1oz of fresh Chopped Parsley.

1 Egg. Olive oil for cooking.

METHOD.

Take the bone from the fish and lay flat on a board, to place stuffing into the fish. Then pour the lemon juice onto the fish, add seasoning to taste.

Place breadcrumbs into a bowl with the melted butter with the fresh tyme and parsley, lemon rind and beaten egg add extra breadcrumbs if required.

Spread the stuffing on the one side and cover with the other side of the fish.

Oil the baking tin and place the fish onto the tin. Cover with a piece of greaseproof paper, place in the centre of the oven and cook for approximately 45 minutes, or until the fish is tender. Serve with green salad or mashed potatoes and peas. Another alternative is saffron rice which can be a very pleasant change.

Serves four persons.

BASS

This fish is one of the most versatile fish, it is the fish with the mostest. Baked, grilled, fried, in butter served with a hint of lemon and Tartare Sauce. Poached Bass is a lovely delicate dish for some one feeling under the weather. and there are many other sauces that can be served with Bass.

BASS WITH PIQUANT SAUCE.

Preparation time, 30 minutes. Cooking time: 25minutes.

180c: 350f: Gas mark 4.

Ingredients.

2lb Bass. 1oz Butter (melted)

Seasoning to taste. 2 Olives (chopped)

1 tablespoon of capers . 1 Onion (chopped)

4 oz Mushrooms (chopped) 1 Green Pepper (chopped)

1 oz Seasoned flour. 4 Tomatoes

5 fluid ozs fish stock or water .Olive oil

1 teaspoon paprika.

METHOD.

Place the Bass in a baking dish, brush with melted butter and sprinkle with seasoning. Pour in the fish stock or water, cover with greaseproof paper and bake in the centre of the oven for approximately 15 minutes. Remove from the oven and retain the stock for the sauce. Heat the Olive oil and brown the onions, mushrooms and green pepper. Add the flour, tomatoes seasoning, paprika, olives, capers and stock. Bring to the boil and cook for about 5 minutes. Pour over the fish and serve with Salad and Duchess potatoes.

Serves 4 persons.

MACKEREL (SOUSED)

Preparation time 20 minutes.

Oven temperature 180c: 350f: Gas mark 4:

Cooking time in a preheated oven 20 minutes or until the fish is tender to the touch.

Ingredients.

1 Mackerel per person.

Enough vinegar and water to cover the fish.

Seasoning to taste. 1 Ovenproof dish.

Place dish with fish in the middle of the oven and cook for 20 minutes.

Serve hot with vegetables or cold with salad.

GURNARD

Served as a starter this fish is good.

Once filleted.

Lightly fry in olive oil.

Serve with Caper sauce

and Green Salad.

BALLAN WRASSE.

This fish once cleaned and descaled, can be stuffed with mushrooms, ham and cooked rice. Then wrapped in foil and baked for 20 - 30 minutes at 180c: 350f: Gas mark 4: Serve piping hot with salad.

It is said that Ballan Wrasse is very bony and is used in France alot more than it is used in England. Never the less the Ballan Wrasse has a lovely delicate flavour and should be taken into account much more than it is.

WHITING STUFFED.

Preparation time 30 minutes. Cooking time 45 minutes.

Oven temperature 180c: 350f: Gas mark 5:

This recipe is for 4 persons, for 1 person just divide the ingredients by 4.

Ingredients.

4 Whiting. 4oz Rice.

2oz Ham (cut into small pieces)

2oz Small button Mushrooms. (chopped up small)

Seasoning to taste.

2 oz Butter.

Cooking Foil.

METHOD

Clean fish and remove fins top and bottom. Put to one side.

Place Rice on to cook in salted boiling water. When the rice is cooked leave to cool for a few minutes and cut ham and mushrooms up.

Take a small amount of butter and place into a frying pan and put rice, ham and mushrooms together in pan, on a gentle heat for a few minutes until butter has infused with mixture. Place on one side to cool.

take fish and put rice mixture inside the cavity from where the fish gut has been removed. Grease foil and place each fish on a individual piece of foil and wrap. Place into a preheated oven.

Cook for 25 - 30 minutes or until fish is tender to the touch.

Remove from oven and stand for a few minutes being very careful when uncovering fish as there is alot of heated steam inside which can cause a nasty burn. Serve this dish with Salad or Duchess Potatoes and Peas.

DOGFISH CAKES.

Preparation time : 1 hour. Cooking time: 45 minutes for fish to cook, 20 minutes for potatoes , 10 minutes for fish cakes to fry.

Ingredients.

1 - 2 lb Dogfish (skinned and boiled)

1 lb   Potatoes. (mashed with butter)

1 Tablespoon of Parsley (fresh and chopped.)

A Bay leaf and seasoning to taste. Oil for frying

Fresh baked breadcrumbs. 1 egg. 1oz of flour.

METHOD

The skin on a dogfish may prove difficult to remove, so ask the fisherman /lady how it is done and I am sure they will advise or indeed do it for you. Once skinned and cleaned the fish is easily dealt with. Place the fish in a deep saucepan cover with water and put in a Bay leaf. bring to the boil and then simmer. Peel the potatoes and put in salted water to cook. When the fish is cooked, take the cartilage out and flake the fish,

put to one side and once the potatoes are cooked mash them and add egg and flour and mix well. Add fish and chopped Parsley .

Allow to stand for 5 minutes.

Shape into rounds and place in fridge until ready to use. Fry in oil on moderate ring , for approximately 5 minutes per side.

These fish cakes can be served with various things such as Salad, Chips, Duchess Potatoes, Croquettes, or Savoury Waffles children enjoy them with Kentucky Fries.
Note/The stock from the boiled fish can be placed to one side and used in fish sauces with some other fish dish.

FISH SOUP:

Preparation time. 30 minutes. Cooking time . 1 15 minutes.

Cook on the Hob. Ingredients.

2lb of any white fish cut into strips.

3 medium Onions(sliced) 2 Carrots (sliced)

8oz Potatoes. (sliced and cubed) Knob of Butter.

A teaspoon of Cayenne pepper or Paprika if preferred.

Bouquet Garni, Seasoning to taste.

A tablespoon of Olive oil. 5 oz white Wine.

1 1/2 oz Plain Flour. 1 1/2 pints of fish stock.

METHOD.

Heat Butter in Oil in deep pan - until butter has melted,
turn down heat and put onions, carrots and potatoes in and allow them to simmer on low heat for about 10 minutes add the cayenne or paprika and stir for a few minutes.

Pour in white wine, fish and stock.Cook for a further 40 minutes

Allow to stand for 5 minutes before serving.

If you prefer a creamy thick soup,

place all through a sieve and then blend after which pour all the liquid into the blender and blend for a further minute

add a good spoonful of cream as an option should you want a really creamy soup and then reheat and serve.

This is a good recipe for persons feeling under the weather or an elderly person who does not eat very well .

Serves four persons.

HADDOCK IN CREAMY CHEESE AND MUSTARD SAUCE.

Preparation time   45 minutes. Cooking time   40 minutes.

Oven setting. 180c: 350f: Gas mark 5.

Ingredients :

2lb of White Haddock (cut into 4 equal pieces)

8oz Low fat Cream Cheese. 1 Tablespoon of Dijon Mustard.

2 Tablespoons of Whole Grain Mustard. 2 Packets of Savoury White Sauce,

(or make a pint of Savoury White sauce.) Seasoning to taste.

METHOD.

Grease oven dish well and then place fish in oven dish and cover.

Put in preheated oven and cook for 20 minutes.

Take out of oven and put to one side for a few minutes

whilst making the creamy cheese and mustard sauce.

Make the white savoury sauce first and then continue as follows:

Turn down heat under sauce and once sauce has cooked out

add cheese to sauce continue stirring all the time,

gradually add mustard,a teaspoonful at a time until all mustard is infused.

Leave on low heat for a few minutes still stirring,

until sauce is cooked out . Then pour over fish and cover.

Cook in hot oven for 5 or 6 minutes take cover off

and cook for a further 5 minutes. Serve piping hot with potatoes and peas,

or savoury rice on the side.

Serves four persons.

FISH CASSEROLE

Preparation time 30 minutes.

Cooking time. 30 - 40 minutes.

Oven temperature. 180c: 350f: Gas mark 4.

Ingredients.

1lb of white filleted fish. 2oz Butter.

2 large tomatoes. 2 large Onions.

1 oz Plain Flour. A tablespoon of chopped Parsley.

Seasoning to taste. 5 fluid ounces of Fish Stock
(This can be bought in stock cube form, or you can make your own)

1 Oven proof Casserole Dish.

METHOD.

Grease the dish with a knob of the butter from the ingredients, season.

Peel and cut tomatoes and onions into small pieces. Mix in Parsley.

Place half the mixture on the bottom of the dish. Put the fish on the top of mixture and place the rest of the mixture on the top.

Pour in stock. Cover and put into preheated oven and cook for 30 minutes or until tender to the touch.

Drain off liquid and make into a sauce by melting the remainder of the butter in a deep pan and then slowly add the flour stirring all the time.

When sauce is made you will find that it is quite thick season and add back to the casserole dish with the other ingredients and reheat for about 10 minutes. If its a special occasion add some cream and garnish with a small sprig of Fennel or Dill.

Serves four persons.

SALMON KEDGEREE

Preparation time 25 minutes. Cooking time. 30 minutes.

Ingredients.

1lb Salmon

(cooked and flaked)

2 oz Butter. 8oz Rice . (cooked)

2 Eggs (hard boiled) Seasoning to taste.

A tablespoon of fresh Parsley.

1 teaspoon of English Mustard.

METHOD.

Melt Butter in pan.

Flake Salmon carefully removing all bones and skin.

Add the butter, and one chopped hard boiled egg,

seasoning and rice,

place the mixture in pan over hot ring ,

until all the mixture is very hot. Pile on a large plate.

Garnish with chopped parsley .

Take the other hard boiled egg and using the yolk only,

flake and place over the top of the kedgeree,

with a small sprig of parsley.

Serve with salad, or on its own,

either way its a pleasing dish to serve.

Serves six persons.

FLOUNDER WITH SPINACH

Preparation time 20 minutes. Cooking time 15 minutes.

(If fish is cooked whole it will take longer to cook).

Cooked on the hob.

Ingredients.

Fillet Flounder or cook whole which ever is preferred.

8oz of fresh young Spinach.(per serving)

1 Egg per Flounder serving. Season to taste.

Knob of butter (per serving)

METHOD.

Place knob of butter in pan and melt.

Add flounder and cook gently.

Place salted water into deep pan

and bring to boil and add Spinach ,

cook for about 3 - 5 minutes.

Put Spinach on the centre of large plate

and flatten slightly. Then place Flounder on the top.

Lightly fry an egg ,

put on the top of fish.

Garnish with a sprinkling of Paprika.

This makes a lovely supper dish,

not at all heavy on the stomach.

Use one larger fish for two persons.

DAB WITH CHILLIES.

Preparation time 30 minutes. Cooking time 45 minutes.

Cooked on the hob.

Ingredients.

4 Dabs (Filleted) Bones from fish to make stock.

2 Teaspoons Thai Fish Sauce.

Thickening. Butter. Seasoning to taste.

2 Red Chillies (chopped finely and seeds removed).

1/4 lb Small button Mushrooms (thinly sliced)

4 fluid oz of Dry White Wine.

METHOD.

Put knob butter in shallow pan .

Melt on a low heat.

Add Thai fish sauce and allow to cook gently for a few minutes.

Place fish in pan,

skin side to the top and after two minutes turn fish over skin side down add more butter if required.

Remove fish and add a little White wine to the residue in the pan then add red chillies and mushrooms,

when cooked add a little thickening if required or leave sauce as it is which ever is preferred.

Either way the dish is tasty.

Serve hot straight from pan with Rice or noodles.

Serves four persons.

CORNISH COD.

Preparation time 15 minutes. Cooking time 45 minutes.

Cook on hob.

Ingredients.

4 Cod Cutlets. 2 oz Butter. Parsley.

4 medium Tomatoes.

5 fluid ozs Dry Cider.

Seasoning to Taste.

Cayenne Pepper.

1 Clove Garlic.

METHOD.

Melt butter in shallow pan.

Add crushed Garlic and Chopped Parsley.

Cook Gently for a few minutes until the aroma is strong enough to fill the air.

Place Cod cutlets on the top and cover with the tomatoes sliced thinly.

Cook gently for 5 minutes and then add Cider and other seasonings.

Using a good pinch of Cayenne (optional)

simmer until the fish is tender to the tough,

remember that Cod is a very white fish,

when cooked so it is reasonably easy to tell when its cooked enough.

Take the fish out of the pan carefully.
Place on a dish. Serve with Salad.
Serves four persons.

SALMON CUTLETS WITH PRAWNS.

Preparation time. 35 minutes. Cooking time 30 minutes:

Oven setting: 180c: 350f: Gas mark 4:

Ingredients:

1 Medium sized cutlet per person.

1 Lemon   (juice only). 2 oz Prawns per person.

A small sprig of Fennel per person.

A piece of greaseproof paper 8 inches x 8 inches to wrap cutlets in for cooking.

Seasoning to taste. A knob of butter for each cutlet.

METHOD.

Trim cutlets. Squeeze juice from lemon.

Rub lemon juice into Salmon cutlets.

Place each one on its piece of greaseproof paper.

Pile the prawns onto the top of Salmon ready to cook and put a knob of butter on the top of the Prawns. Bring paper up either side of Salmon, and put a fold into the top before making a parcel. Place into the centre of the preheated oven and cook. When cooked take out of oven and carefully open the top of each parcel, leaving the paper around the Salmon and serve with out removing the paper. This is a very attractive way to serve a Salmon cutlet. Side Salad can be served with it or Croquettes and Green beans.

This is a fish that must be purchased unless of course the person catching Salmon,has a licence to catch Salmon .

A N.R.A licence can be bought from the local Post Office.

CONGER EEL PIE.

Preparation time. 35 minutes. Cooking time. 55 minutes.

Oven Setting. 200c:450f: Gas mark 8.

at first and reduce heat to 180c: 350f: Gas mark 4.

Ingredients.

2 lb Piece of Conger eel. 1 medium Onion (finely chopped)

1 Carrot (chopped into small cubes.)

1 Teaspoon of Fresh chopped Parsley.

Bouquet Garni. Seasoning to taste.

Enough fish stock to cover the fish and vegetables.

(home made fish stock can be used).

1 Tablespoon Vinegar. 8 oz Puff Pastry.

(This can be purchased from the shop frozen, or you can make your own)

METHOD.

Wash, dry fish thoroughly, removing all skin and bones.

Cut fish into small cubes. Put into oven dish, in layers seasoning each layer as you go then place on each layer pieces of onion and carrot.

Add fish stock enough to cover fish and vegetables.

Roll out puff pastry and cover oven dish cutting a small hole in the middle

to

allow the steam to come out. Serve hot with boiled potatoes or mashed potatoes and peas. Serve cold with new potatoes and salad.

Serves 6 - 8 persons.

FRIED FLOUNDER.

Preparation time (if cleaning the fish yourself)

2 hours 30 minutes. Cooking time 10 - 15 minutes.

Cook on hob.

Ingredients.

1 Flounder per person.

(1 . 1/2 lbs. per fish before boning and cleaning.)

Seasoning to taste. Egg. Breadcrumbs.

Olive oil for cooking. Chopped fresh Parsley (for Garnish.)

METHOD.

It is said that to improve the taste of Flounder,

it is best to clean the fish,

a good 2 hours before it is needed.

At the same time rub seasoning all over the fish to make them firm.

Leave them for the 2 hours, and then wash and dry them thoroughly.

Place the pan on the hob and put the oil in to the pan.

Holding the fish by the tail end,

cover with beaten egg and then dust well with breadcrumbs,

on both sides. Cook each side for roughly 5 minutes,

then remove from pan and place onto kitchen roll,

to remove any excess oil.

Put on large plate and garnish with chopped parsley.

Serve with chips and peas.

GARFISH. GRILLED WITH FENNEL.

Preparation time 25 minutes. Cooking time. 15 minutes.

Cook under the grill.

Ingredients.

1 Garfish per person. Butter.(for grilling)

Fennel (chopped) Thai fish sauce. Cream.

A small quantity of Fish stock.

METHOD.

Clean the fish remove head and spines.

Spread some butter over the fish and place under the grill.

Add some chopped fennel and baste several times as the fish cooks.

When the fish is cooked remove fish from grill pan .

Place to one side and keep warm.

Add a little fish stock to the juices in the pan

and some Thai fish sauce, Finally add a large spoonful of cream

and stir quickly to stop curdling.

Place fish on a large plate and serve hot,

pour the sauce over the fish just before you serve.

Ratatouille as a side dish can be a change

and with the sauce over the fish

will be a different experience.

Remember the bones of the Garfish,

are green in colour.

PLAICE STUFFED AND BAKED

Preparation time. 20 minutes. Cooking time. 20 - 35 minutes.

Oven Setting 180c: 350f: Gas mark 4.

Ingredients.

1 Medium Plaice. 2 oz Shrimps (cooked)

2 Large spoons of Breadcrumbs.(white)

2 oz Butter. 1 large spoonful chopped fresh Parsley.

Bouquet Garni. A pinch of Paprika. Seasoning.

1 Egg. Some Brown breadcrumbs. A little milk.

METHOD.

Mix the white breadcrumbs, Parsley,Seasoning, Paprika,and half the egg (beaten)and enough milk to moisten the stuffing.

Add a few cooked shrimps. Next, make a cut down the centre of the top of the Plaice as if you are going to fillet. Place the knife flat and slide it underneath the flesh and along the bone towards the outside of the fish.

Repeat the same thing with the other half of the top of the fish.

When this is done put the stuffing inside make sure there is enough to come up over the bone in the centre of the fish

and flatten where the stuffing has gone inside gently with a spatula.

Brush the rest of the egg over the fish, place into a ovenproof dish and put a few small knobs of butter on the top of the fish.

Bake in the oven for 20 - 30 minutes or until the fish is tender to the touch. Serve piping hot with Savoury Rice.

Serves two persons.

FISH PIE WITH A DIFFERENCE.

Preparation time 25 minutes. Cooking time 35 minutes.

Oven Setting 180c: 350f: Gas mark 4.

Ingredients.

2 Rashers of streaky bacon.(Cut into small pieces.)

2 onions.(chopped finely) .2 large Tomatoes (chopped)

1 oz Plain Flour. 20 fluid ounces (1 pint) Fish stock.

2lbs Cooked flaked Haddock.

Seasoning to taste. 2lb Potatoes cooked and creamed.

METHOD.

Fry chopped rashers of bacon with the chopped onions.

Skin the tomatoes and chop. Add tomatoes to the bacon and onions simmer,

for a few minutes and then gradually add the flour,

stirring all the time cook gently for 5 minutes, and continue to stir.

Add stock blending slowly so that the sauce does not go lumpy.

Bring to the boil and stir until mixture thickens.

Add the flaked Haddock carefully, season to taste.

Place the mixture into a ovenproof dish .

Pipe creamed potato onto the top ,

cook in oven ,

until golden brown on the top.

Serve with Green beans or Sweet Corn.

Serves four or five persons.

Other Titles available from M.P.Dawn Publications

Sea Angling A Beginners Guide

Sea Angling Bass Fishing Made Easy

Sea Angling Cod Fishing Made Easy

Sea Angling Mackerel & Garfish Fishing Made Easy

Sea Angling Wrasse Fishing Made Easy

Sea Angling Flatfish Fishing Made Easy

Sea Angling Pocket Fish Identification book

Sea Angling Pocket Rig Book

Sea Angling Pocket Bait Book

Sea Angling Around Devon South Coast

Sea Angling Mediterranean Sea Fish Identification

Sea Angling Shore, Float, Spin & Plug Book

Sea angling Pocket Boat Book

Fresh Water Pocket Fish Identification Book

These and More Books Available From

M.P.Dawn Publications through

Amazon Kindle & eBay